W9-ABB-937

EFFECTIVE HUMAN RESOURCE DEVELOPMENT: A CHALLENGE FOR DEVELOPING COUNTRIES

Effective Human Resource Development: A Challenge for Developing Countries

Edited by
FARHAD ANALOUI
Development and Project Planning Centre
University of Bradford

Ashgate

Aldershot • Brookfield USA • Singapore • Sydney

© Farhad Analoui 1999

Published by
Ashgate Publishing Ltd
Gower House
Croft Road
Aldershot
Hants GU11 3HR
England

Ashgate Publishing Company
Old Post Road
Brookfield
Vermont 05036
USA

British Library Cataloguing in Publication Data
Effective human resource development: a challenge for
    developing countries
    1. Personnel management - Developing countries
    I. Analoui, Farhad
    658.3'0091724

Library of Congress Catalog Card Number: 98-73750

ISBN 1 84014 854 3

Printed in Great Britain

Contents

List of contributors

Editor

Dr Farhad Analoui Senior Lecturer, Director of Professional Development and Training Programmes, Development Project Planning Centre, University of Bradford, UK.

Contributors

Dr Ali R Analouei is currently with InfoPro as a Group Manager and has previously held key managerial positions including, Associate Professor of Research, Georgetown University, U.S.A.; Vice-President, International Healthcare Development, Inc. U.S.A.; Director of Research and Development. Mass Lab, Inc. U.K.

Cleofa Assey Economist at the President Office, Planning Commission, Dar es Salaam, Tanzania.

Nancy Bell-Edwards PhD Research Student, Development and Project Planning Centre, University of Bradford.

John Cusworth Senior Lecturer, Head of the Department, Development and Project Planning Centre, University of Bradford.

Professor David Edwards Professor of Economic Development, Former Head of the Development and Project Planning Centre, University of Bradford.

Suzanne Fogg Graduate from Development and Project Planning Centre, University of Bradford. Project Evaluator, Co-operation for Development, UK.

Dr Mark Hiley is a Lecturer at the Development and Project Planning Centre, University of Bradford.

Professor Andrew Kakabadse is Professor of International Management Development and he is currently the Deputy Director of the School of Management at Cranfield University.

Abdullah Kisuju Senior Planning Officer, Ministry of the Community Development, Dar es Salaam, Tanzania.

Dr Hassan Labbaf Senior Lecturer, Human Resource Development, University of the Isfahan, Iran

Dr Farhad Noorbakhsh Senior Lecturer, Centre for Development Studies, University of Glasgow, UK.

Dr Rajalaxmi Rath Research Scientist, Sinha Institute of Social Studies, Patna, Bihar (India).

Dr R I Sarkar Professor of Agriculture, Former Dean of the Faculty of Agricultural Engineering and Technology, Bangladesh Agricultural University.

Preface

Nowadays, human resources constitute the most important component of the modern organisations. Naturally, attention ought to be paid to their long term advancement and development.

The misguided view that, HRD is becoming a concern for organisations and enterprises only in the Western World is a folly. The need for HRD's contribition to development has not only become accepted but also it has been widely promoted by the national and international funding and aid agencies in field. Today, after experiencing a string of failed development programmes and projects within Less Developed Countries (LDCs), it has been recognised that the sustainability of such planned interventions can only be assured by emphasising on the development of the organisational human resource involved.

While the economic contribution still plays a significant role in bringing about change, the long lasting results of the intervention and development process can only be guaranteed by having effective and developed people in charge of such programmes and projects. Such is the importance and significance which is attached to the development and management of human resources.

Dealing with complex and interrelated issues of HRD however, has posed a challenge for the academics and scholars who assume the role of providers of know-how for the practitioners in the development field. At the Development and Project Planning Centre (DPPC), University of Bradford, this need and necessity has long been realised. The formation of a research cluster in Human Resource Management and Development in 1993 was a response to this need. The international seminar held in March 1996 and subsequent International Conference which was held at the Centre in 1997 allowed a greater participation and involvement of both scholars and practitioners to explore HRD issues and share their understandings and experiences of human development.

What is presented here, therefore is a selection of contributions which deal with relevant aspects of developing human resources in organisations, mainly within LDCs, though it is envisaged that it would be even more realistic to deal with HRD and its related issues in the wider context of developing organisations regardless of their physical locations.

Professor Andrew Kakabadse
Professor of International Management
Deputy Director, Cranfield University School of Management

Acknowledgements

The editor wishes to acknowledge the contributions made by so many who have been either directly or indirectly involved in the preparation of the present volume. In particular, I would like to thank Pauline Fell who organised the HRD conference which provided the basis for the present collection of papers. Also, thanks are due to to Jean Hill for the production of many drafts of the manuscript, Sue Mackrill for assisting with the print of the final camera - ready copy of the work and finally, my wife Janet Analoui for reading through the text and her constructive and detailed comments and suggestions.

I am grateful to the authors for their contributions to this volume and for accepting to make their work available to other students, scholars and practitioners so that a better understanding of the subject can be gained. Of, course the reader ought to bear in mind that what is presented in each chapter, forms the views of the authors and the authors alone and does not in any way represent the views of a particular organisation, institute or agency with which they are associated.

Finally, I would like to thank Professor Brenda Costall, Pro vice chancellor for her support and encouragement and to acknowledge the efforts of the members of the Human Resource Management Development Research Cluster at the DPPC, University of Bradford for their support and contribution.

1 Motivating managers in developing countries and economies

Dr Farhad Analoui

Introduction

Motivation originates from the word 'move' and therefore can be seen as an internal drive necessary to guide people's actions and behaviours toward achievement of some goals. It is often orientated towards the satisfaction of some needs and expectations. Of course, the strength and intensity of the drive determines the amount of effort, time and talent people invest in their work.

Motivation can also be described as a process which may lead to job satisfaction. Mitchel (1982) defines, motivation as 'the degree to which an individual wants and chooses to engage in certain specified behaviour' (p.80). According to Kakabadse et. al. 'an individual's motivation is the result of the interaction of needs, incentives and perception' (1987, p.119). This is a subjective process which is also influenced by the element of communication. These factors together provide the basis for understanding the cognitive processes involved. Basically, there are two different approaches which explain work motivation: content and process theories.

The content theories of motivation attempt to explain what actually motivates people at work. These theories have identified needs, incentives and the work itself as the most important causes of job satisfaction (Maslow, 1943; McClelland, 1951; Herzberg, 1959; Alderfer, 1972). One underlying assumption for these theories is that, there is a direct relationship between job satisfaction and improved job performance. In contrast, the process theories try to describe how behaviour is initiated, directed and sustained. These theories are more concerned with the dynamic interaction

1

between the variables involved and how they influence behaviours (Adams, 1963; Vroom, 1964; Porter and Lawler, 1968; Locke, 1968).

In order to gain a better understanding of the senior managers' motivation for improved performance and their effectiveness at work, first the content and process theories of motivation will be briefly reviewed. In light of this review an attempt will be made to provide an overview of the empirical research on the subject. In this section the results of the latest study which has recently been carried out in the Romanian Public Sector, which specifically deals with the motivating factors for increased effectivness of senior managers, will be dealt with in some detail.

Content theories of motivation

Maslow suggested that there exists a hierarchy of needs which determines the motivation of people to work. It explains how five categories of needs manifest themselves in a sequential order and tend to dominate people's behaviour. At the lowest level, the needs are physiological, followed by safety, social, self-esteem and finally self-actualisation needs which are at the highest level. According to Maslow (1943), needs are strong motivators when they are not satisfied. It is proposed that higher needs begin to dominate behaviour only if the lower level needs are sufficiently satisfied. Although this view has been challenged by many writers it has provided a basis for the development of the subsequent theories and still is a popular explanation for people's behaviour at work.

The McClelland theory of motivation suggests the presence of a set of socially acquired needs which are also assumed to be culturally specific. These needs are labelled as achievement, power and affiliative needs. Although the extent of the motivations varies from one individual to another, according to McClelland (1962), managers tend to show a higher level of need for achievement than, for example, the need for affiliation. Based on his extensive research, McClelland maintains that effective managers should possess a high need for power. However, a distinction is drawn between two kind of powers, 'socialised' and 'personalised' power. The former is used for organisational and group concerns, while the latter is exercising dominance over other people. McClelland's research suggests that providing systematic feedback to the staff with essential information about what goes on around them in their organisation of events and matters that concern and influence their daily activities and career, acts as a powerful motivating factor.

Alderfer's three factor theory of needs; Existence, Relatedness and Growth (ERG), a simplified version of Maslow's hierarchy of needs theory, distinguishes between three categories of needs which are assumed to progress at three different levels: the need for existence, the need to relate to others and the need for personal growth. Unlike Maslow, Aldefer (1972) suggests that these needs constitute a continuum and do not necessarily emerge in a sequential order independant of each other. More importantly, a need assumes greater importance if it is not satisfied. Therefore, more effort and energy is likely to be directed towards its satisfaction.

Herzberg's two-factor theory is essentially concerned with job satisfaction. The two-factor theory suggests that the nature of the job and the content of the work itself affects the degree of job satisfaction experienced. According to Herzberg (1966), the motivators are actually associated with the content of the job. They are called motivators which include achievement, advancement, recognition, responsibility and the work itself. It was also argued that factors that are derived from organisational settings, environmental in nature, can only help to prevent dissatisfaction. These factors usually prevent people from getting hurt but they are not motivational in nature. These are referred to as hygiene or maintenance factors which include company policy, supervision, salary, interpersonal relations and physical working conditions.

Herzberg (1966) argued that a lack of maintenance factors may cause dissatisfaction, while their presence may not necessarily increase job satisfaction. People are only motivated when hygiene factors and motivators can both be experienced in the job. A summary list of hygiene factors and motivators are presented below.

Hygiene factors

1. Pay, or salary increase
2. Technical supervision, or having a competent supervisor
3. The human relations quality of supervision
4. Company policy and administration
5. Working conditions or physical surrounding
6. Job security

Motivators

1. Achievement, or successful task completion
2. Recognition, or being singled out for praise
3. Responsibility for ones' own or others' work
4. Advancement and growth or changing status through promotion

It is evident that there are similarities between Maslow's, Alderfer's and Herzberg's theories.

Scott Myers (1964) has carried out an interesting repetition of Herzberg's study based on which he has identified two groups of workers - motivation seekers and maintenance seekers. According to Myers, motivation seekers are motivated primarily by the nature of the job itself, whereas, maintenance seekers are interested in the factors which are of an environmental nature. People are highly motivated when they derive satisfaction from the work they do. Essentially, the results of the study support Herzberg's finding and the conclusions are mainly the same which include the following.

- A challenging job is a powerful source of motivation to work. It provides a feeling of achievement, responsibility, growth, advancement, enjoyment of work itself and earned recognition.
- Maintenance factors which are peripheral to the job usually cause dissatisfaction amongst employees. These factors include supervision, work relations, job titles, job security, seniority, salary, fringe benefits and working conditions.
- Lack of opportunity for meaningful achievement, advancement and growth causes dissatisfaction, people then become sensitised to their environment and begin to find fault.

Job enrichment

Based on his theory, Herzberg introduced the concept of job enrichment and believed that it would serve as an alternative approach to job design. The notion was that the nature and the content of the job affect work motivation and job satisfaction. Through the process of job enrichment, the jobs' contents are restructured in a way that they become more appealing and challenging to the workers. Based on this premise, Hackman and Oldham (1980) have also developed a model of job enrichment which identifies five job dimensions - skill variety, task identity, task significance, autonomy and feedback. They argue that these dimensions, if incorporated into a job, will have the potential to increase job satisfaction and will allow the job holder to experience three psychological states. These are;

1. Experiencing the meaningfulness of the work,
2. Feeling responsible for the outcome of the work, and
3. Having knowledge of the result of the work.

It is also claimed that people with enriched jobs tend to experience high internal work motivation and job satisfaction which could in turn result in improved performance.

Process theories of motivation

Process theories of motivation recognise the complex nature of work motivation and attempt to explain the relationships involved. The core argument is that people's perception of the expected results of their actions also influences their motivation and their increased satisfaction. Porter and Lawler's expectancy model (1968) suggests that job satisfaction is more dependent upon performance than performance is upon job satisfaction.

Motivating factors and improved performance

The nature of the managers' work, their behaviour and performance is essentially complex. The quality of job performance is affected by a wide range of variables. These relate to the individuals themselves, and organisational and environmental factors. The performance of a manager is also jointly influenced by their ability and motivation. With reference to the work of Porter and Lawler (1968), Campbell et. al. (1970), state that,

> task performance is a resultant of effort and choice behaviour as they are moderated by situational factors and the ability of the individual. No matter what choices are made or how much effort is expanded, motivated behaviour may not lead to change in performance if the work situation does not permit it or the individual does not have the abilities necessary for turning effort into result (p.359).

The underlying assumption is that performance is generally a function of not only the individual's will, but also a function of abilities and situational factors. The work of Porter and Lawler (1968), can therefore be considered a hierarchical list of influential factors important to the performance and effectiveness of senior managers.

Self-efficacy

The effect of self-referent thoughts in psychological functioning of people is very substantial. As Bandura (1986) notes, perhaps no other aspect of self-knowledge is more important to people's motivation and behaviour than the conceptions of self-efficacy. According to Bandura (1986), self-efficacy is central to the functioning of human beings. It operates as a generative capability which involves cognitive, social and behavioural subskills organised into integrated courses of action. The way people judge their capabilities therefore, largely determines their level of performance. As Bandura states,

Perceived self-efficacy is defined as people's judgements of their capabilities to organise and execute the course of action required to attain designated types of performance. It is concerned not with the skills one has but with judgements of what one can do with whatever skills one possesses. Knowledge, transformational operations and constituent skills are necessary but insufficient for accomplished performance. Competent functioning requires both skills and self-beliefs of efficacy to use them effectively (1986, p.391).

According to Bandura (1986), self-belief determines the quality of performance and has diverse effects on people's choice of behaviour. Accurate appraisal of one's own capabilities is, therefore, an important issue for personal development which may eventually lead to improved performance.

Job satisfaction

As explained earlier, one assumption underlying the content theories of motivation is that satisfaction of motivational needs has a direct effect on performance. According to Campbell et. al. (1970), job satisfaction can be defined as 'a positive or negative aspect of an individual's attitude or feeling toward (their) job or some specific feature of his job' (p.378). Focusing only on the positive aspect, Locke (1976), defines job satisfaction as 'a pleasurable or positive emotional state resulting from the appraisal of one's job experiences', (p.130). As Campbell et. al. (1970), notes, a great deal of research on work motivation has not dealt with job satisfaction as a job behaviour. Job satisfaction is not the same as motivation. Job satisfaction is more of an attitude, an internal state, whereas motivation is a process which may lead to job satisfaction.

There are many dimensions to job satisfaction. The level of job satisfaction thus, varies considerably with respect to different individuals, social, cultural, organisational and environmental factors (Mullins, 1993). Individual factors consist of a number of personal attributes and characteristics such as personality, education and skills. Social factors are present in different forms of interactions involved in an individual's work situation. Cultural factors are the individual's beliefs, values and attitudes. Organisational factors are associated with different aspects of the work organisation such as organisation structure, policies, leadership and working conditions. Environmental factors are beyond either organisational or individual control and may have a substantial influence on job satisfaction. Economic, social, political and technological factors are the major environmental influences.

Although the satisfaction of motivational needs may well lead to improved performance at work, as emphasised above, the willingness to work is only one determinant of good performance. One important variable in Porter and Lawler's model of motivation (1968) is satisfaction. Accordingly, they argue that job satisfaction is more dependent upon performance than performance is upon job satisfaction. It is stressed that other personal and situational factors must also be taken into consideration.

Empirical research on motivation

Existing research on managerial work motivation may be divided in three different groups depending on the methodologies employed by the researchers involved.

First, there are the studies which set out to measure the importance of a number of motives or needs by rating the importance of these needs via a questionnaire (Porter, 1961, 1963), test instruments (McClelland, 1965), or semi-structured interviews (Pellegrin and Coates, 1957).

The second group are organised around the question of what managers tend to prefer in terms of rewards or incentives. Furthermore, the second group were interested to see which rewards were actually linked to different motives and which rewards were instrumental in satisfying specific needs in managerial personnel (Andrews and Henry, 1964; Mahoney, 1964).

Unlike the first and second group, the third group of studies have been organised around a more fundamental question of how various incentives and rewards actually affect job performance and behaviour (Vroom, 1964).

Overall, the evidence suggests that in terms of motives, managers are more concerned with factors such as achievement, power, status, income and advancement (Campbell et. al., 1970). For example, Morse and Weiss (1955) found that from amongst several different occupational groups, non viewed achievement and accomplishment as more important to their motivation than the management group. Although there is evidence that achievement need may be different with respect to cultural differences

7

(McClelland, 1961), basically the similarities in the motivational needs of managers across various countries are considerable (Haire et. al., 1966).

A study of senior managers in Romanian public sector

Recently, (1995-96) following a PHARE funded project, a study was carried out in Romania which was concerned with senior managers/officials who work for private and public organisations. The study was concerned with practitioners who were, in one way or another, either related to or indeed were in charge of one or a cluster of projects. These projects, developmental in nature, are designed to facilitate the process of 'economic transition' from the old central planning system to that of an open market and competitive one. It must be said, that the majority of senior managers held sensitive posts and therefore their effectiveness was surely a major concern for those in charge of the European Integration Unit who have assumed the role of change agents in Romania.

Although the process of change had begun with their independence in 1989, still a 'lot needs to be done' as was asserted by one senior executive. Still there seems to be resistance to change, especially on the part of 'core bureaucrats'. Experiencing frustration and difficulties with the adoption of new ideas and values is not uncommon even amongst the implementators of change.

However, one of the main reasons for selecting Romania for this study was mainly based on the fact that most managers whom were, at first casually observed, showed a willingness to change and concern for 'improvement', though often those concerns proved to be unrealistic, but generally those involved in managerial responsibilities spoke of 'effectiveness', 'efficiency' and their roles as senior managers 'towards the attainment of the goals which reflected their concerns for themselves, their organisations and the country as the whole.

The study formally began in October, 1995 and involved a survey consisting of questionnaire and subsequently the use of semi-structured interviews. It included several visits to various organisations and a number of hours collecting relevant data. The final stage of the fieldwork was completed in April, 1996 and the respondents were informed of the results shortly after. It may be interesting to note that although the government of Romania has already in place a network organisation, the International Foundation for Management, with the aim of providing managerial excellence in Romania, this study constitutes the first to be carried out amongst the managers and officials who are involved in the process of change and transformation of the economy in this Eastern European country.

Scope of the study

The study targeted more than 70 senior managers, in a total of 23 organisations. These organisations ranged from Telecom, Ministry of Agriculture, the Restructuring Agency, to FIMAN, Railways and the Ministry of Education and Finance. Access to such a wide range of organisations insured against contamination of data primarily caused by the strong influence of 'organisational culture' in one or two sites. In this way, an overview of the perception of the senior managers, their needs and their effectiveness at work was achieved, together with the advantage of having a fairly varied and maybe comprehensive selection of constraints, demands and difficulties which senior managers thought were impeding their progress and effectiveness at work.

After close examination of the data collected, it was felt that the spread of the respondents and the data collected may provide a few clusters which in turn could affect the validity and reliability of the results. In addition, close examination also pointed to some incomplete sections in the returned questionnaires. Thus, it was decided in order to ensure the quality of the data and its usefulness, only 41 responses should be selected, as complete, for the first stage of analysis. As for the interviews, 13 organisations were selected within which more than 60 percent of the senior respondents worked.

This strategy was employed to ensure the reliability of the data already collected as well as attempting to generate data and qualitative information which otherwise would have been missed or neglected (Ackroyd and Hughes, 1982). It must be noted that the methods which were employed, were not chosen for their statistical elegance (Ravetz, 1970), nor were they used to overwhelm the reader with statements based on an abundance of data as a result of the application of procedures which although seemingly scientific and sound would have been seen as meaningless to the senior managers. Thus the results would have very little effect in terms of enabling them to change their behaviour and/or attitudes for their increased effectiveness. The study was confined to 23 major organisations, in the hope that the results would provide a better understanding of the elusive, difficult to measure concept of senior managers' effectiveness (Analoui, 1995).

9

The lowest number of respondents from any one organisation was one and there were eleven such organisations, whilst the highest number in a single cluster was seven. There were two groups from private ownership funds and the Ministry of Labour had four respondents from each of its two sites. Two other organisations provided three respondents each and the remaining organisations each provided two senior managers. The majority of the respondents came from public service organisations (96 percent). Only two respondents were from private organisations and these were already familiar with the ethos of working in public sector enterprises.

Respondents age, education and years of service

In contrast with the previous studies which were carried out in Asia and Africa, a large proportion of the senior respondents (45 percent) were female. This was reported to be due to the availability of education during the 'old times'. As a whole, organisations seemed to show a preference for female employees and many female senior managers/officials were found to be competing with their male counterparts. While most managers in these organisations did not show a particular preference, on the whole, it was felt that female managers were thought of highly and were perceived as being more 'reliable' in so far as their effectiveness at work was considered. The concept of 'career development', not surprisingly was felt as strongly amongst female senior managers as it was amongst their male counterparts.

The age range of the respondents varied with the youngest at 27 and the oldest at 60 years old. Most respondents were in their 30's (25 percent). A large proportion were in their 40's (13 percent) and a few were below 30 or above 50. What is intriguing however, is that although still seniority seemed to constitute a major criteria for determining the significance and importance of the individual managers in the operational outfit, in most organisations senior managers showed an appreciation of the professionalism and acknowledged the improved work performance of their junior staff or colleagues.

The respondents in the age category 28-40 regarded those who were older as 'maybe reluctant' to change. It was a general perception that, the process of transition necessitates dealing with change and the older senior managers and executives may still carry with them the beliefs and value system of the past. In all, effectivness in some organisations was still judged by seniority in terms of age and maybe experience, but in all cases it was observed that the question of gender did not seem to have added weight when the issue of effectiveness was considered.

All senior managers were educated with at least a first degree and a few with masters and higher degrees such as Ph.D. On the whole, the majority seemed to believe that earning a first degree from a university provided the foundation for operating as a senior manager and clearly had an effect on the effectiveness of the managers involved. Most senior managers reported, 'we took our first degree because we carried on and we have limited choice. It is good to have it and we went for it'. To those who were not familiar with Eastern European countries and the centralised economic background, it may come as a surprise to see so many managers with an engineering background. Indeed, 53 percent of the senior participants in the study had graduate degrees in engineering with emphasis on mechanical engineering. A few possessed a first degree in electronics, or systems and computing. 31 percent of the senior managers reported that they were economists and had a different perception of themselves and their likelihood of increased effectiveness. As one explained,

> Prior to independence like many other states, the emphasis was on engineering and very little on other social fields. People were not supposed to know or ask questions. Engineers were safe and would work in factories. Industrialisation was the aim and the government did not want to educate people to become critics.

Others explained that choice was not available and most people were encouraged to learn hands on skills. Intriguingly, however, it was observed that unlike western countries where a high proportion of graduates in engineering are male, a large proportion of Romanian engineering graduates are female and did not see this as a disadvantage to their career development. What, however did seem to preoccupy the graduates was that they were aware that in order to achieve a high level of effectiveness, they were deemed to require advance training in management or that they ought to possess academic and professional qualifications in social sciences. The economists, it seemed, were clearly in an advantageous position. The process of transition made sense to them, but most felt that they should not leave the certainty of central planning and control altogether, 'most people do not understand. It gets worse before it gets better... but the public are not patient and want immediate change'.

When senior participants were asked if they thought having a first degree in engineering was advantageous to their managerial effectiveness, almost all responded positively by claiming that, 'management is a scientific process', 'people have to be organised and controlled to get the job done'. But increased effectiveness was seen as requiring access to 'new

11

knowledge' one which is taught in the western countries. None of the senior participants were graduates in administration or business studies, though they occupied high positions in their organisation.

When the same participants were asked if they would consider taking an MBA or similar advance management programmes as a mean for improving their performance and effectiveness at work, their responses differed according to their age and seniority in the organisation. The senior participants in the age range of 30-35 reported that they would consider this providing they were offered a grant and it was evident that they showed suspicion about similar courses when they were offered locally. The senior participants with long term experience saw more benefit in short sharp management development and business training. Almost all senior managers said that with hindsight they should have taken their education in social science. If they had had a choice.

The recent economic changes in Romania has meant that more opportunities have been made available to those who wish to pursue managerial and administrative career or interests, but still the opportunities are few and far between. One major intervention has been the establishment of the International Foundation for Management, a non governmental organisation with a mandate for promoting managerial excellence throughout the country. Such organisations are actively encouraging the establishment of new managerial values systems which would facilitate and accelerate the process of economic transition on the whole. Senior managers were aware of the inadequacy of their educational background and that they had the need for more experience, preferably through management training, for their increased effectiveness. This again supported the thesis that senior managers indeed are aware of factors which can contribute to their improved performance.

Senior managers work experience, of course, varied from less than five years to twenty years and over. This was due to the differences in age rather than any other organisational factors. As a rule, graduates in Romania begin their career almost immediately after the completion of their university study. This suggests that almost all the senior managers involved in the survey secured employment immediately after completion of their graduate education. They changed employment thereafter every few years.

There also seemed to be a correlation between the participants' age and the years of accumulated work experience. On the whole, 25 percent of the senior managers had between 1-10 years of work experience. The managers and officials in this category showed the most enthusiasm for change in career and a willingness to meet the challenges of the new changing environment. The most intriguing issue raised was that of the senior managers' awareness of their own effectiveness at work and that they felt the degree of effectiveness in their work was partly determined by motivation to work and partly their competence and knowledge and skills. Often, it was reported that hygiene factors such as salary, supervision and working conditions were not perceived as the sole contributing factors for a decision to change job but the need to be effective and to do the right thing became increasingly important to them.

More than 40 percent of the senior respondents had between 10-20 years of work related experience. The managers in this category, in terms of seniority, ranged from senior managers to executives and were not as keen to change career as the managers in the first category. However, they placed much emphasis on work experience and management training as the main factors towards improving their effectiveness at work. As the work experience of the respondents increased, there seems to be present a tendency amongst the senior participants towards seeing effectiveness not solely in terms of improved performance and attainment of goals, but rather as a part of the overall picture of the organisation's capability to 'get things done' and more importantly in relation to others, colleagues, peers and the like.

> In my job my effectiveness is determined by others. I can not say how effective I am because I have to rely on my colleagues to see a project through. It is frustrating at times.

Seven senior managers had between 20-30 years experience and 3 executives had more than 30 years work experience. The respondents in the last 2 work experience categories, like most of their senior management colleagues in the previous category had experience of working under the previous regime with different economic ideals and working practices. For them the change to a new market economy was a good thing and they thought that managerial effectivness could be improved given the right training and priorities at work. However, the impression given was that managerial effectiveness could also be maintained by adhering to a 'rational and logical order of things'. As one explained,

> I have doubts about these new practices, some of the younger managers do not know the basics but they achieve a lot. I need to be convinced.

It was interesting to observe that they all welcomed participation in management training and development, but for a different reason. 'You got to go along, if you don't try they label you as old-guards. There are of course benefits in these activities, but the principle remains the same'. The senior participants in the survey and executives with relatively more than average years of experience (mean =14.2 years) described themselves as role occupiers such as directors (n=5), deputy and general managers (n=4). Those with less than 14.2 years of work experience saw themselves as experts (n=11) and managers (n=11). The older the senior managers the more likely they were to describe their role in terms of administration and management, whereas the younger managers and executives described their role in more personal terms such as 'managers', 'experts' and 'advisers'.

On the whole, all managers showed awareness of their effectiveness at work with the difference that the younger senior mangers perceived the situation as being largely determined by their increased knowledge, skills and expertise, whereas the older executives often blamed the organisation and others for their inability to improve their performance at work.

On the other hand, it becomes evident that the respondents with more experience had a better understanding of their organisation in relation to others and the market economy as a whole.

Senior manager in the Romanian public sector

Scope of the study

The methodology employed in Romania for exploring the motivating factors behind increased effectiveness was somewhat different from that which was adopted in India. The senior manager respondents were first provided with a series of open and less structured statements and were asked to place a value and make comments on them. They were asked what, in their opinion, and in order of priority to them, were the motivating factors for their increased effectiveness.

The responses provided were allocated relative values of 0.6, 0.4, 0.2 according to whether they came first, second or third respectively. They were then categorised and tabulated in order to establish the nature of the response, as well as to determine the value which had been allocated and the frequency which shows the degree of importance of a particular item.

On the whole, 35 categories of responses were identified. Then, the cumulative values allocated to each item indicated that the responses provided two groups of motivaters. The nine items (see Table 1.1) proved to be indicators and motives groups which were viewed as most important in terms of motivating senior managers towards increased effectiveness.

As shown (see Table 1.1), two items namely; recognition and appreciation (psychological factors), and money and salary (financial incentives) seem to take the first place in the order of priority. The discussions in the interviews with senior managers, by and large, evolved around the subject of remuneration and receiving feedback from their superiors. The senior participants believed that such feedback provides the basis for recognition of work done well by the individual manager involved.

Table 1.1
Main motivating factors towards increased effectiveness

Items	Description	Cumulated Value	Order
1	Recognition and appreciation	12	1st
2	Money and salary	12	1st
3	Improving task performance	7.8	2nd
4	Increased knowledge/managerial styles	7.4	3rd
5	Promotional status	6.8	4th
6	Team work involved	6.0	5th
7	Job satisfaction	5.8	6th
8	Self development and discipline	5.4	7th
9	Ability and confidence	4.6	8th

Significantly, other factors such as increased knowledge and skills (7.4), involvement in team work (6.0), job satisfaction (5.8), self development (5.4) and improved competence (4.6), all pointed to the presence of three major underlying factors, namely; the managers themselves, the nature of the job and the contextual nature of the work related issues concerned.

Interviews

Having analysed the quantifiable data, sample interviews were then carried out and senior managers were specifically asked to make comments on the factors which constitute the main motivation for them and what they perceived as the contributing factors to their motivation of others, colleagues, peers or even their superiors. The rationale for this was not only to validate the results which had been obtained through the survey questionnaire, but also to gain a measure of objectivity by comparing the perceived factors with those of the actual ones. Of course, it is almost impossible to ascertain 'actual' in so far as the subjective views of the senior managers involved. However, as argued elsewhere, senior managers' awareness of their need for effectiveness ultimately leads to them identifying their needs in order to achieve increased effectiveness, a point which is often not taken seriously.

In relation to the motivation of senior managers for increased effectiveness, the most rated factors with cumulative values of 12 each (Items 1 and 2) not only revealed the most significant difficulty (financial rewards) which is faced by all public sector organisations, they also indicated the motivating factors whose absence constitutes a source of dissatisfaction and discontent. It was revealing to discover that those who saw themselves as being the spearhead, forerunners and to some extent the implementors and guardians of the transition process, felt deep dissatisfaction with the ways 'things are managed at government level'.

Some senior managers felt alienated and saw no rapid solution to the problem of motivation in the public sector. Others maintained that while they did not wish to return to the situation as it was prior to 1989, still they were unhappy with the present situation.

Motivating factors

Salaries and dissatisfaction

It was interesting to observe that while senior managers are not expected to be overtly and excessively concerned with remuneration and economic incentives, in reality against the background of change, increased competition and ever increasing inflation they found themselves preoccupied with the satisfaction of basic needs. The importance of 'hygiene factors' such as accommodation and maintenance of a very modest standard of living (Maslow, 1948; Hertzberg, 1968; Kakabadse et. al., 1987), had almost forced some to question 'why increased effectiveness?' Almost all the respondents who were interviewed showed dissatisfaction with the 'budgetary system' of salaries in the public sector;

> For me working here... is a career not just a job. Salaries are very low in the public sector as the whole in comparison with the private sector. I worked as ... for a number of years and gained a lot of knowledge and skills. It is important for me to use these skills so I have to stay. I suppose I feel responsible, but I am not happy with what I earn. At the moment there is a big gap between the private and public sector. Salaries in the private sector are as much as 5 - 6 times higher. You need to have a

16

great professional motivation (intrinsic) to carry on doing what you are able to do effectively.

Many senior managers felt uneasy about bringing up the subject of remuneration and even felt embarrassed to convert their salaries to foreign currencies. One even referred to it as;

> It is organised crime. The system has changed, well apparently... but the promises are still the same. Years ago before the revolution, there was talk of a Golden Age which never arrived. An idea which is like a dream. Transition is the same. We find it difficult to believe that one day everything will be OK. So far no one from the socialist societies has the benefit of the transition. So we can't say or even compare ourselves with others. It is a matter of faith.

Comparison with the private sector seemed inevitable. All senior managers showed an awareness of the fact that increased prices and ever increasing inflation was continuously biting into their static salaries;

> A good pair of shoes costs around 150,000 Lie, my monthly salary is 300,000. For how long do you think I can maintain the present situation? Something needs to be done.

What the senior managers found even more disturbing and to a large extent 'demotivating' is the presence of a dual system of 'payment' even within the public sector. Apparently, some managers who work in 'Project Management Units' (PMUs) which are directly funded from Brussels and the European Union, are paid in US Dollars instead of Romanian Lie. Thus, they tend to earn as much as 4-8 times more than their senior colleagues within the same ministry. However, one manager pointed out, that there are those who although they work for offices such as 'Phare Programmes', which are funded by Brussels, they are still paid in Lie simply because they are located in a ministry;

> It is gross and unfair, we do the same work. Some of us get paid 6 times higher and have access to fringe benefits such as travelling to other European and western countries and make good killing of their subsistence.

The low salaries in the public sector leads to high staff turnover and consequently a 'vicious circle' of institutional inefficiency. In one government organisation, in its bi-annual report, showed that their staff turnover in 1993 was 1000. It was reported that most managers leave to work in the private sector and inevitably their vacant positions are filled with 'inexperienced' graduates who lack training.

> They come to us, young, inexperienced and only stay till they get some work experience and a better CV, then they leave.... Last year I lost my entire team who assisted me in implementing the project. The staff I have now are not good enough. I have no resources to train them and even if I do, I know they will leave as soon as a better choice emerges. The budgeting system is to blame. Our top government officials either cannot understand or they do but do not acknowledge it.

Appreciation and concern

All managers showed their discontent with the managerial style and traditional attitudes of their top management who took things for granted. Good work and high quality performance is not often recognised. The old style and culture of passive interaction still persists especially in ministries and other government organisations. Some top management were referred to as 'old guards' who have not really changed.

> They have to show that they are for transition but in reality they found it difficult to change. Change of attitude is not as easy as a change of words. They are the ones who need training and a lot of it.

Lack of recognition is not always a direct consequence of the presence of old values and traditional managerial styles. Often, the organisational set-up in its bureaucratic form, prohibits the presence of and promotion of different cultural values, thus effective communication is often frustrated as a result. Insufficient interpersonal skills on the part of top team management leaves the senior managers feeling left out in the cold.

Observation showed that the need for recognition of good work and appreciation of 'hardwork' seems to become exaggerated because it acts as a substitute and replacement for a lack of purchasing power.

The compensatory nature of motivating factors such as 'improved skill', 'promotion', 'teamwork' and 'involvement' all pointed to the increased expectation of the senior managers from their superiors.

It boils down to change of management style at high levels, we need to be managed differently, especially when our basic needs are not met...the dissatisfaction is growing.

Nature of the work

Senior managers were asked why are they still around and more importantly why are they so much concerned with their increased effectiveness? The response shed some light on the complex phenomenon of motivation in the Romanian public sector. Three factors emerged.

Nature of the job Most senior managers stayed in their post despite financial problems, simply because they 'liked their job'. As one put it, 'If you like what you do you stay the motivation is here, to do the job'. Most senior managers were in charge of projects of one form or another which provided the challenge and direct feedback on their efforts. This seems to be a major source of satisfaction for them.

Increased knowledge, skills, competence and self development The second main reason for staying in public sector employment was reported to be the opportunity to maximise learning, acquisition of skills and improvement of self as a whole. It was interesting to see that in comparison with other senior managers, the Romanians, maybe because of the transition, showed a greater awareness for their self-development. There seemed to be a sense of urgency amongst the managers for self improvement and development. As one succinctly put it, 'there is still a hope and feeling that once the transition is successfully completed, we ought to be ready for new life opportunities'.

Pride and status Senior managers reported that the most obvious alternative for them was private companies and private enterprises. This, however, meant that in order to 'escape the monster' they had to accept the lower position, middle management. Whilst this satisfied their lower order of needs, based on their proposed hierarchy of needs, it tended to dent their ego and the pride associated with their professional self image.

The second reason put forward by more senior managers was that by changing their jobs, they had to work in the capacity of a consultant who would then be sent to the public sector to work with ex-colleagues and peers but not in the same managerial capacity. As one confirmed;

I am in charge of the projects funded by European Community Programme, consultants are coming from the private sector here and we have no time for them. I don't want to come back here and wait in the corridor for someone like me to see me.

Most other factors with a cumulative value of 1-4 referred to the compensatory nature of motivating factors in the absence of superior recognition, inadequate pay and increasing self and career development as a result. The least motivating factor such as learning the English language or being able to deal with foreign consultants still supports the view that apart from the most important factor which was identified above, all others refer to the presence of an awareness on the part of the manager concerning their level of effectiveness and the need for self development through the acquisition of knowledge and skills to achieve this.

Conclusion

On the whole, the senior managers in the Romanian public sector all reported facing difficulties such as low pay, inferior working conditions, long hours, too much responsibility without power or authority and an awareness of their worth (hygiene factors) when compared with their counterparts in the private sector organisations. Motivators such as responsibility, nature of the job, appreciation, recognition and the need for achievement (psychological) seemed to be the main driving forces behind senior managers attitudes towards increased effectiveness.

References

Adams, J. S. (1963), 'Toward an understanding of inequity', *Journal of Abnormal and Social Psychology*, Vol. 67, pp.422-436.

Alderfer, C. P. (1972), *Existence, Relatedness and Growth*, Collier Macmillan.

Andrews, I. R., and Henry, M. M. (1964), 'Management attitudes toward pay', *Industrial Relations*, No. 3, pp.29-39.

Atkinson, J. W. (1958), (ed.), *Motives in fantasy, action and society*, Princeton, N. J.: Van Nostrand.

Bandura, A. (1986), *Social Foundations of Thought and Action: A Social Cognitive Theory*, Prentice Hall, Inc., Englewood Cliffs, New Jersey.

Campbell, J.P., Dunnette, M.D., Lawler, E.E. III, and Weick, K.E. Jr, (1970), *Managerial Behavior, Performance, and Effectiveness*, McGraw-Hill, New York.

Edwards, W. (1954), 'The theory of decision making', *Psychological Bulletin*, No. 51, pp. 380-417.

Hackman, J. R. and Oldham, G. R. (1980), *Work Redesign*, Addison-Wesley.

Haire, M., Ghiselli, E. E., and Porter, L. W. (1966), *Managerial thinking: An international study*, Wiley, New York.

Herzberg, F. W., Mausner, B. and Snyderman, B. B. (1959), *The Motivation to Work*, Second edition, Chapman and Hall.

Herzberg, F. (1966), *Work and the nature of man*, World Publishing, Cleveland.

Kakabadse, A. Ludlow, R. and Vinnicombe, S. (1987), *Working In Organisations*, Gower, England.

Locke, E. A. (1976), 'The nature and causes of job satisfaction', in M. D. Dunnette (ed.), *Handbook of industrial and organisational psychology*, Rand-McNally, Chicago.

Locke, E. A. (1968), 'Towards a theory of task motivation and incentives, *Organisational Behavior and Human Performance*, Vol. 3, pp.157-189.

Luthans, F. (1989), *Organisational behaviour*, Fifth ed., MacGraw-Hill.

Mahoney, T. (1964), 'Compensation preferences of managers', *Industrial Relations*, No. 3, pp.135-144.

Maslow, A. H. (1943), 'A Theory of Human Motivation', *Psychological Review*, Vol. 50, No. 4, July, pp.370-96.

McClelland, D. C. (1962), 'Business Drive and National Achievement', *Harvard Business Review*, Vol. 40, July-August, pp.99-112.

McClelland, D. C. (1988), *Human Motivation*, Cambridge University Press.

McClelland, D. C., Atkinson, J. W., Clark, R. A. and Lowell, E. L. (1953), *The achievement motive*, Appleton-Century-Crofts, New York.

Mitchell, T. R. (1982), 'Motivation: New Directions for Theory, Research, and Practice', *Academy of Management Review*, Vol. 7, No. 1, (January) pp.80-88.

Morse, N. C., and Weiss, R. S. (1955), 'The function and the meaning of the work and job', *American Sociological Review*, No. 20, pp.191-198.

Mullins, L.J. (1993), *Management and Organisational Behaviour*, Third edition, Pitman, London.

Myers, M. S. (1964), 'Who are Your Motivated Workers?' *Harvard Business Review*, Vol. 42, January-February, pp.73-88.

Pellegrin, R. J., and Coates, C. H. (1957), 'Executives and supervisor: Contrasting definitions of career success', *Administrative Science Quarterly*, No. 1, pp.506-517.

Peters, T. J. and Waterman Jr. R. H. (1982), *In Search of Excellence: Lessons from America's Best-Run Companies*, Harper and Row, New York.

Pettigrew, A. M. (1979), 'On Studying Organisational Culture', *Administrative Sciences Quarterly*, Vol. 24, December, pp.570-81.

Porter, L. W. (1961), 'A study of perceived need satisfactions in bottom and middle management job', *Journal of Applied Psychology*, No.45, pp.1-10.

Porter, L. W. (1963), 'Job attitudes in management, II. Perceived importance of needs as function of job level', *Journal of Applied Psychology*, No. 47, pp.141-148.

Porter, L. W. and Lawler, E. E. (1968), *Managerial Attitudes and Performance*, Homewood, Dorsey-Irwin, Ill.

Porter, L. W., Lawler, E. E. and Hackman, J. R. (1975), *Behaviour in Organisations*, McGraw-Hill, New York.

Vroom, V. H. (1964), *Work and motivation*, Wiley, New York.

Vroom, V. H. (1965), *Motivation in management, American Foundation for Management Research*, New York.

2 Globalisation, competitiveness and need for change. The case of development records and training institutions in European countries

Professor David Edwards

Introduction

The post-Second World War period saw the establishment of training programmes at the tertiary educational level in both the First and Second Worlds, for nationals from Developing Countries.

These programmes were affected drastically in the Eastern Bloc countries by the breakdown of the bloc and its opening up to the rest of the world in the 1990s. Starting earlier and more gradually there was increasing and continuing competition in West European countries for resources to fund such training programmes.

After looking briefly at the patterns of training provided by the First and Second World countries and at the impact of changes on the provision of training in Eastern Europe, the chapter will concentrate on the effect of increasing competition on Development Training and Research Institutes in one of the major providers of training, the United Kingdom. Attention will be focused in turn on, the UK institutions and their training programme, the evolving context in which they operated, and the response of a small number of institutes to the opportunities provided by the recent changes in the East. Finally some conclusions will be drawn.

The patterns of training provided before 1990 in 'first world' and 'second world' countries, for 'third world' nationals

The Universities and other Higher Education institutions in Europe received students in the post Second World War era from outside their own borders, including students from Third World countries. Numbers of foreign students increased as the capacity of the institutions grew. The catchment areas for the institutions in each case were mainly restricted to countries from within the same ideological bloc, either Western capitalist or Eastern socialist.

Students from the Third World were registered for degree courses in Eastern bloc institutions lasting some years, which included language training because the language of instruction was not common to the students. Ideological instruction was included as it was for national students.

The pattern in the Western countries was more varied. Language training was not needed for nationals from many countries because they shared a common language with the host country. There has also been a trend towards teaching in English even where it is not the national language (as in Holland) in order to facilitate foreign students. In some of the Western countries short courses - of weeks or months - were established where lengthy language training was not generally required. Longer postgraduate programmes were also widely available.

The motives of the Governments which supplied funding for training Third World nationals were concerned not only with increasing the capacities of the students to assist their countries' development but also to strengthen the relationship between the host and recipient countries.

The impact of the changes in Eastern Europe on the provision of training for nationals from developing countries

The breakdown of the former regimes in Eastern Europe affected their provision for students from Developing Countries in three broad respects.

(a) The priority given to training such students disappeared with the weakening of the dominant ideology.
(b) Resources for the training of nationals from Developing Countries were rapidly reduced.
(c) The administrative system and society were disrupted in ways which discouraged students from Developing Countries.

In more particular terms, the presence of students was discouraged by: the falling value of scholarships in real terms caused by high rates of inflation; the less attractive living conditions and in some cases hostility from the local community.

Fewer scholarships were granted and they were not generally adequate. The higher educational institutions were increasingly short of resources for all purposes and especially for foreign students, while the academic staff were distracted by low salaries and difficult conditions of life. In short neither the institution, staff nor students had the same incentives as previously to participate in the programmes.

Development research and training institutes: the case of the UK

The country focused on here is the United Kingdom. The set of Development Research and Training Institutes which came into existence in that country is strong in number and diversity. The Institutes have shared a period of strong growth and support, followed by an era of declining support and increased competition, which will be described in the following sections of the chapter. Thus, attention will be focused on the origin and nature of the Institutes.

It should be noted that prior to the emergence of these Institutes, the British Government had - in the immediate Postwar period - established universities, many with institutes of social and economic research in colonies in Africa, Asia, the Pacific and the Caribbean. The (social science based) Development Institutes in the UK were established in various ways. The leading institute, the Institute of Development Studies (IDS) was set up at the University of Sussex, in 1966, by the Overseas Development Ministry (ODM), with the former Director General of Economic Affairs at ODM (Dudley Seers) as the Director, and with a substantial budget and official support.

There had been a small number of training initiatives set up earlier, during the later colonial era, in social work, and in administration, for example. But most of the initiatives came into existence after the establishment of IDS, as offshoots from UK-oriented university departments, but focusing their attention on perceived Third World needs or (in other cases) as new institutes. These initiatives were often quite specialised in their programmes: such as administration of local government, urban planning, and project planning, for example. In their early years they provided training for Third World nationals exclusively in the United Kingdom. (One of these institutes, which concentrated on training in short courses, has trained over 4,000 persons in the UK up to the present time.)

Although the institutes or programmes were within universities many of them were unusually free of regulation and even control by their universities. The courses taught were more policy and operationally oriented than the conventional university degree courses. They were relatively free to respond more quickly and flexibly to changing needs and opportunities. In some cases they were able to appoint to academic positions individuals (mainly men) with considerable practical overseas experience who could not have been appointed to posts in normal academic departments.

The evolving context in which the UK institutes cooperated: the parent universities and the official support for training

The capacity of the university sector was substantially increased in the 1960s by enlarging established universities, by transforming existing tertiary level institutions into universities, and by creating new universities. The universities were funded primarily from Central Government revenue, with the relatively low student fees being provided from Local Government funding.

The buoyancy of the sector facilitated the introduction and growth of development institutes and departments. The encouraging institutional setting provided by the universities was reversed in 1982 when Government funding was substantially reduced in aggregate: the variation in the reduction of central funding ranged from very small up to one third funding.

The number of students has continued to increase, from 0.87 million in 1983/85 to 1.55 million in 1993/94. The universities' own costs are 13 per cent higher in real terms than in 1985/86. The universities in 1996 received less than three-quarters of the resources per student they received in 1989/90. Academic salaries have declined by 30 percent (since 1983), relative to other professions including teachers, despite increasing work loads.

Book purchases for libraries have fallen, by 30 percent per student, since 1984/85. Building and equipment provision and maintenance have been neglected to an estimated £3 billion to meet sensible standards. The 1995 Budget made further cuts of 7 percent for the academic year 1996/97. Unless the situation is reversed academic staff will have to be made redundant and some universities may have to close.

Development institutes have been adversely affected in various ways by the worsening financial status of the universities.

(a) Tuition fees for overseas students have been raised from low, highly subsidised 'home student' levels to the much higher 'overseas student' 'full cost' rates. The fee increase has reduced the number of students from Developing Countries, especially poorer students.

(b) Universities have substantially increased the charges to Development Institutes for the use of premises, facilities and services.

(c) University departments which are largely financed as part of the central university system have increasingly moved into training and consultancy for Developing Countries in competition with the Development Institutes which are largely responsible for earning income to cover their costs.

The increasingly difficult financial situation of the universities has been paralleled by the decline in official support for training and other activities in the Developing World. The predominant official source of support for the British Institutes was the Overseas Development Ministry (or Administration) ODM/ODA, assisted by the British Council which administered the training awards and many of the overseas projects.

Key institutes earlier received guaranteed annual incomes to cover training programmes for Developing Country trainees in the UK, subject to trainee numbers and quality of courses being maintained. This guarantee was removed but replaced by preferential allocation of trainees to institutes which were of proven capacity. While numbers of training awards were buoyant these arrangements proved satisfactory to the institutes involved, but when the earlier increase in number of awards was followed by a fall in numbers the institutes found themselves under considerable pressure as competition from within Britain and abroad strengthened.

Two trends in the location and process for deciding training priorities also adversely affected the position of the institutes. The first was the emphasis given to 'in-country' and to 'Third in-country' training programmes. The emphasis given to these overseas based programmes made additional demands on the institutes and produced much lower incomes for a given investment of staff time than in home based training programmes.

The move of Department of International Development (DFID), the Overseas Development Administration (ODA) to project-related training, on a competitive basis, led to greatly increased uncertainties in the recruitment of nationals from Developing Countries on ODA funded awards.

The institutes responded to the increasingly difficult situation by seeking support from a wider range of agencies - bilateral, multilateral, and NGO - in consultancy and research as well as for training. They also looked to the prospects which were opening up in Eastern Europe.

Response of the UK institutes in the 1990s to the opportunities following the changes in Eastern Europe

The fundamental changes in the Second World which gathered momentum during the late 1980s and early 1990s, opened up needs for transformation of social, political and economic systems. Opportunities emerged for the Development Institutes - which were suffering from a declining level of activities relating to the Developing Countries - for new programmes of training and consultancy to satisfy the needs of Eastern Europe.

Table 2.1
Trends in the number of students on training awards at UK institutes 1990/91-1995/96

Year	Technical cooperation training (TCT)	Know how fund (KHF)
1990/91	12,500	306
1991/92	11,919	1,096
1992/93	11,378	6,028
1993/94	8,305	6,765
1994/95	5,080	9,540
1995/96	5,409	n.a.

TCT = Mainly Programmes for support of Developing Country nationals for Training in UK.
KBF = Main Programme for support of nationals from the East for Training
Source: The British Council

The leading national institute (IDS) under Dudley Seers' leadership had been engaged for some years in discussion and cooperation with individuals and institutions in Eastern Europe and was well placed to extend these activities. In the event, IDS did not become heavily engaged in Eastern Europe, in comparison with its programmes with Developing Countries. Other Development Institutes which had focused its work on (non Socialist) Developing Countries were not geared to bilateral activities with individual East European Countries. Their Mission Statements would have specified Developing Countries and would not have mentioned the East. These Development Institutes had directed their programmes to the situation and perceived needs of Developing Countries and were staffed by individuals with expertise of, and experience in, Developing Countries. In some institutes there was only general knowledge of UK institutions and processes which were of great interest to trainees from Eastern Europe, such as those relating to privatisation.

In 1993 Helen O'Neill reported at the EADI General Conference that the main focus of West European institutes remained fixed on the Third World. She saw the change in emphasis as one of additionally and diversification. The current situation in many of the leading Development Institutes in the UK is essentially unchanged but in a small number work on Eastern activities has replaced work on Developing Countries to a considerable extent. In two such institutes, about one-half of the revenue earned from training and consultancy comes from activities conducted for the East. The institutes which have become most involved appear to be those involving planning, management and administration, and particularly with privatisation, instruments and procedures: that is with institutional and individual change. Many of the programmes are designed to meet ODNs aims of 'encouraging... sound, development policies, efficient markets and good government - and of enhancing... productive capacity and to conserve the environment'.

The responses of these Development Institutes have required a major refocusing of their programmes with consequences for many aspects of their activities. One institute which had had no direct contact with the East now runs contracted training courses in the East as well as in the UK, with a course annually delivered in Russian. Staff members have been seconded to countries in the East for two and more years. What conclusions can be drawn about the Development Institutes which have been changing their focus and pattern of activities during the 1990s?

Some conclusions

There can be no doubt that globalisation, involving the profound changes in the East has through increased competition affected the need and opportunities for Development Institutes in the UK to redirect their programmes from work with Developing Countries to a substantial involvement with countries in the East. This redirection of effort was not part of a voluntary change in their purposes and policies which had been focused on Developing Countries, but came about by force of circumstances.

Extensive changes have been made within a few years to meet needs for which the institutes had not been initially prepared. While it is too early to make a definitive evaluation of the effects on the changes on the institutes certain consequences are apparent.

1. The financial viability of the institutes has been maintained by a greatly increased effort and at the cost of reduced concentration on working with Developing Counties.
2. The expansion of Development Institutes came to a halt in the 1980s.
3. The institutes have been involved in a demanding learning process in redirecting their programmes.
4. All the institutes have been forced to recognise the indivisibility of the process of development and to see their particular preoccupations as part of this larger global process.
5. Focusing attention on the needs for change in the East has involved much closer attention to the capitalist system in which the institutes are located. Previous experience in, and continued work with Developing Countries has naturally led to a comparison of the situation of the countries in the East, the South and the West.
6. Even institutes which had concentrated on techniques in a particular social science frame of reference would have been forced to place these techniques in a broader socio-political system when looking at the transfer of the use of techniques from the West (or South) to the East.

To conclude, just as these Developing Institutes are assisting the East to transform its situation, the institutes are themselves being changed by their own involvement in the process.

References

de Kadt, Emmanuel (1990), 'Introduction: State and Development in South and North: Some Lessons From Development Studies', in *Development Research*, Vol. 2, No. 2, December.

Iredale, Roger (1992), 'A Review of Training: Needs and Criteria', in *The Power of Change*, Overseas Development Administration, London. November.

Killick, Tony (1994), 'What Can We Learn For Long-Term Development From Experiences with Restructuring', in *Development Research*, Vol. 6, No. 1. June, Frank Cass, London.

Klugkist, C.W. (1994), 'Training in Europe for the Third World: Trends of the Nineties', in Training Circular of the *Working Group cooperation in Training*, NUFFIC/EADI, The Hague, No. 8. April.

O.D.A. (1996), *Baroness Chalker Announces New Aims and Priorities for the British Aid Programme*, ODA News Release 96/3, ODA, London, 14 February.

O'Neill, Helen (1994) 'Development Studies in Europe in 1993: Plus needs a cedilla Change?' in *Development Research*, Vol. 6, No. 1, June. Frank-Cass, London.

Roberts, Sir Derek (1996), *Excellence in Higher, Education The Need for Action, Now* A statement from the Provost, University College London, April.

Seers, Dudley (1980), 'European Conscience and European Social Science', in *Europe's Role in World Development Milan*, FINAFRICA/CARIPLO.

Squires, R. (ed.) (1995), *Development Studies in Britain: A Select Courses Guide*, Conference of Directors of Special Courses, April.

Williams, Peter (1993), *Changes in Train: Wither British Technical Assistance Training*, A paper delivered at the Symposium on the 'Power of Change', Bradford, March.

3 Senior manager's effectiveness and their required categories of managerial skills: the case of the steel industry in Iran

Dr Hassan Labbaf, Dr Farhad Noorbakhsh, John Cusworth and Dr Farhad Analoui

Introduction

In the recent past, scholars, educators and practitioners of management have shown much concern for learning and acquisition of the managerial knowledge as apart from the development of management skills (Cameron and Whetten, 1983; Hayes, 1983; Livingston, 1971; Mintzberg, 1974; Mumford, 1984, 1986; Peters and Waterman, 1982; Waters, 1980). Nowadays, the attention is turned to the improvement of managerial skills as the most appropriate means for achieving management training and development objectives (Bigelow, 1991; Boyatzis, 1982; Drucker, 1974; Katz, 1955; Livingston, 1971; Mintzberg, 1973). The effectiveness of managerial behaviour is thus, considered to be both a function of knowledge and of skills. In addition to analytical skills, it is argued that managers, in particular senior managers, require skills for managing themselves, other people and task (Kakabadse, Ludlow and Vinnicombe, 1987). For example, Katz (1955) developed a management development model which incorporated the above basic categories of skills: technical, human and conceptual.

Since Katz's original concept, however, a host of theorists and writers on management have contributed to the development of this on going debate. Recent attempts (Analoui 1991, 1993, 1995) in the Zimbabwean Public Sector and Indian Railways not only confirm Katz's categories of managerial skills, they go further and suggest that there appears to be a hierarchy of skills for senior managers and the more senior the position in which the manager performs, the more his/her needs are for 'people-related' and 'analytical-self development' as opposed to 'task-related' skills.

The discussions in this chapter are concerned with the major findings of the authors' research programme drawn from the analysis of the data generated by the means of survey questionnaires and sample interviews. It attempts to examine the validity of Analoui's findings and their relevance for the management development needs of the senior managers in the Steel Industry in Iran (SII). The main concern is to assess the importance of managerial knowledge and skills as perceived by senior managers for their own effectiveness. Moreover, the question posed is, do senior managers have different training and development needs because of their position of seniority in the organisation? The implication of this for increased effectiveness of senior managers is then discussed and relevant conclusions are reached.

Theoretical background and hypotheses

Managerial skills and hierarchy

Katz's commentary on his original article written some twenty years earlier contends, 'I now realise more fully that managers at all levels require some competence in each of the three skills. A clear idea of these skills and of ways to measure a manager's competence in each category still appears to me to be a most effective tool for top management, not only in understanding executive behaviour, but also in the selection, training and promotion of managers at all levels' (1974, p.102). His work, provides some support for the argument that the hierarchical level in which managers function tends to influence their need for the three broad categories of technical, human and conceptual skills. He further contends that in practice these skills are so closely interrelated that it is difficult to determine where one ends and another begins. Moreover, although all three sets of skills are important they vary in relative importance at different managerial positions. Technical skill is said to be seen as more important by those who function at lower levels of the managerial hierarchy, whereas human skills are thought to be essential at all levels. For top management however conceptual skills become increasingly important.

Katz's model however, did not address a set of very important skills, 'analytical and self development', which are now believed to be highly influential in terms of achieving managerial effectiveness (Analoui, 1990a; Drucker, 1974; Kakabadse, 1985; Margerison, 1984a, 1985). Thus, little

34

seems to have been established about the importance of managerial skills and knowledge and their exact contribution to the effectiveness of senior managers.

Aspects of management

Managerial tasks and responsibilities may be divided into three primary areas: managing self, managing work and managing others. This we refer to as 'aspects of management'. Rosemary Stewart (1963), explains clearly the nature of the manager's job based on some commonly known features drawn from both theories and practice. She makes a distinction in the manager's functions between deciding what to do and arranging for it to be done. She favours a simple and practical definition and broadly defines the manager's job as, 'deciding what should be done and then getting other people to do it' (p.65). She explains in detail how these two tasks, which are actually overlapping in practice, demand different sets of capabilities from managers. The first task demands that the manager should be capable of setting objectives, planning, decision-making and organising the work in the organisation. The second task requires the ability to motivate, communicate, measure and control as well as develop other people. Clearly the emphasis here is placed both on 'managing the work' and on 'managing the people'.

The importance of self-management has only recently been brought to attention as a major part of managerial behaviour (Jones and Woodcock, 1985; Luthans and Davis 1979; Manz and Sims 1980; Margerison, 1984a). As Luthans and Davis (1979) have observed, the aspect of self-management, is perhaps the most overlooked areas in the field of management. Locke (1976), has also recognised this gap and states that 'one of the most unresearched subjects in the area of job attitudes is the individual's view of himself and the way in which this view affects what he seeks for pleasure on the job and how various job conditions and experiences affect him' (p.1325).

According to Brief and Aldag (1980), the formulation of social cognitive theory by Bandura (1974, 1986) provided the theoretical basis for recognition of self-management as the most important determinant of effective managerial behaviour. Based on this theory, self-referent thoughts mediate the relationship between knowledge and action and affect people's motivation and behaviour (Bandura, 1986). Furthermore, the 'cognitive self' plays an important mediatory role in job satisfaction and organisational behaviour. Looking from the perspective of social learning theory, Luthans and Davis (1979) view self-management as a basic prerequisite for increased managerial effectiveness. They claim that 'behavioural self-management may be the important missing link - the first step in the inductive chain - for increased managerial effectiveness' (1979, p.43). Based on the premise that behavioural self-management is the missing link for improved managerial performance, Luthans and Davis (1979) have put forward an argument that supports our views. They assert that;

> observational studies of managerial work suggest that individual managers in highly 'reactive' jobs need some techniques and skills that will allow them to exercise more control over their own behaviour. The ability of managers to manage other individuals or organisational units effectively when their own behaviour is continually in turmoil is highly suspect. Observational studies indicate that managers do not spend their time in 'other-centred' activities, such as planning, organising, controlling, motivating or leading. Instead, they spend their time worrying about their own situation and taking care of their own immediate demands. Behavioural self-management is closely related to what managers actually do when effective managerial action is absolutely necessary (p.47).

In their concluding remarks and based on their research on successful use of behavioural self-management with a wide variety of managers in advertising, retailing, manufacturing and public service settings in both line and staff positions, Luthans and Davis feel that this new approach has much to offer for increasing managerial effectiveness.

In an effort to present a holistic picture of what really constitutes effective managerial behaviour Jones and Woodcock (1985) contend that managing self is the core of managerial effectiveness. Accordingly, they assert that self management sets a ceiling for managerial effectiveness;

> Managers who look after themselves have more energy available for directing the work of others. On the other hand, managers who feel stressed, who do not direct their own career development and create situations for their own advancement, waste a lot of time and energy that might otherwise be available for organisational tasks (p.43).

To be effective, therefore, implies that managers must first ensure their self-development as a continuous process through personal and professional growth and then the acquisition of sufficient related managerial skills required for managing tasks and people. Each aspect of management therefore, we argue, demands a different set of demonstrable skills from effective managers at all levels. It is for this reason that managerial skills are classified into three basic, albeit overlapping major categories; analytical and self-related, people-related and task-related skills which all need to be incorporated in a model of management training and development. A model originally developed by Analoui (1989, 1993) is based on the above theoretical premises.

Our classification of various managerial skills into three categories is mainly valid by definition. It has been noted that these skills are overlapping in many instances (Katz, 1974). Other writers have paid attention to the importance of the complementary nature of managerial skills. For example, Whetten and Cameron (1991) conclude that critical management skills are interrelated and support one another. Kakabadse et. al. (1987) assert that senior managers require a combination of skills for managing themselves, other people and tasks. Mintzberg (1975) goes as far as suggesting that the required managerial skills form an integrated whole. The focal point of the above debates is the question of interrelationships between these skills. In the light of this we decided to investigate the possible existence of common patterns amongst the selected skills. Many interesting questions may be raised. Would the perception of senior managers in SII support the grouping of skills as suggested in the literature? More importantly, how are such skills linked? The interrelationships between various skills may therefore result in the emergence of some common patterns which may be highly significant in terms of their implications.

Hypothesis

According to Analoui (1993), task-related skills are those which enable managers to effectively manage the work in hand by determining objectives, forecasting, planning and organising the tasks involved. These may include a range of managerial skills and knowledge which are specific to the nature of the task performed by them. In addition to this there may be a set of other managerial skills and knowledge which are common in nature such as managing the financial aspects of the organisation and a knowledge of working with computers. The category of people-related skills argued to be essential for managing people at work may include communication, handling conflict, motivating, leading, appraising and developing people. Although conceptual in nature, the analytical and self-related category of Analoui's model however, takes into account a set of important skills which are essential for self-management. These include the development of one's own potentials as well as abilities to make decisions and solve problems creatively, all of which are proved to be vital for the effective performance of senior managers (Analoui 1993, 1995).

The study of the senior managers within the SII has established empirical grounds for the examination of Analoui's model (1991, 1993) and looks at the degree of importance attached to different categories of managers at four levels of seniority. It is interesting to note that recent literature mostly considers senior managers as a homogenous group especially with respect to their training and management development needs. Thus, no significant attempts have been made to examine how various levels of management perceive the importance of their required skills, or how the need for skills may vary in accordance with the different demands and constraints experienced by the management team. More important, there seems to be no clear indication in the literature as to how various managerial skills are interrelated.

First, a general hypothesis is made that senior managers at different levels of hierarchy place different degrees of importance to a set of managerial skills and knowledge required for their increased effectiveness. Second, it is hypothesised that the perceived importance of the required categories of managerial skills, as the most essential attributes for effectiveness of senior managers, varies significantly according to the level within the hierarchy of the organisation in which managers are located and perform. Third, it is hypothesised that the higher senior managers climb on the hierarchical ladder the more important they will perceive the self and people related categories of skills for their effectiveness at work. In other words, managers at lower levels of seniority will perceive their effectiveness to be more dependent on task-related skills than on the other two categories. Fourth, and finally, it is hypothesised that there exists a common pattern of interrelationships between the identified set of skills that may actually be different from what is theoretically suggested in the literature.

Methods

Sample

The study in the SII targeted all senior managers (N=98) in two large steel complexes with a total of more than 29,000 employees. A survey was carried out in both organisations by means of a six part questionnaire which was designed and tested for this purpose. Only one part of the questionnaire was designated to managerial skills and knowledge which the participants believed could result in their increased effectiveness. To ensure the validity of the data sought, a combination of open-ended and structured questions were used throughout the questionnaire. Furthermore, it was decided to compliment the questionnaire with a series of semi-structured interviews taking into consideration that a single method of data collection would not be sufficient for 'finding out what people actually want and what their needs are' (Margerison, 1984b). The questionnaire was self administered and in many cases was offered to participants after an informal rapport had been established. In the course of administering the questionnaire, four weeks was spent in each organisation, which provided the opportunity for the respondents to get in touch with the researcher in case they needed explanation to complete the questionnaire. This process proved to be useful in creating the right kind of environment for carrying out the interviews and made it possible to follow up some returned questionnaires as well as gaining access to some secondary data.

In total, 71 useable questionnaires were received which represents almost a 72 percent response rate. This sample of senior management included chief executive directors (N=2), deputy executives and divisional heads (N=13), heads of departments (N=43) and operation senior mangers (N=13), hereafter referred to as S1, S2, S3 and S4 levels respectively. The profile of the respondent senior managers in this study is of a male in his middle ages of 41-45, who is more likely to be an engineer, having 11-15 years of professional experience in the service of his organisation with an average of just above 5 years in his present post. As far as the educational background of senior managers is concerned, 70 of the respondents were university graduates with at least a first degree, predominately in engineering (41) followed by social sciences (17), accounting and finance (6). Graduates in Business Administration are few and far between (7), a new trend and recent infusion in non-production areas like marketing, personnel or corporate planning. Individual senior managers from all functional areas such as Personnel, Finance, Marketing, Purchasing, Research and Technology and Production were included in the sample.

Measures

Synthesising the works of Katz (1974), Mintzberg (1973), Boyatzis (1982), Whetten and Cameron (1980, 1984, 1991) and Analoui (1990b, 1993), 21 management skills were selected and developed to form the statements of the questions. The same question items were used to measure the importance of the required managerial skills, as perceived by senior managers, to their effectiveness. Respondents were then asked to rate the importance of each specific managerial skill and knowledge on a five point-scale anchored from 'low importance' to 'high importance'. It is important to note that in the questionnaire these questions were not presented in predetermined categories so as to increase the reliability of the measurement.

To investigate the validates of the first three hypotheses we first examined the descriptive statistics for the whole data set. The 21 skill items were then grouped, using the above mentioned works, into the three defined categories of : (1) Analytical and self development (seven items), (2) People-related skills (eight items) and, (3) task-related skills (six items). Using factor analysis technique, the existing responses on the same 21 skill items were later used to test the fourth hypothesis of the research.

Results

Table 3.1 represents the rated importance of the 21 skills ranked by the mean value of each specific skill. The mean score ranking also indicates that

Table 3.1
Importance of Managerial Skills Required for Effective
Performance of Senior Managers at All Levels

Summary description of skills	Mean Value	Std. Dev.	Rank Order
Creating organisational climate	4.37	.85	1
Effective time management	4.30	.74	2
Effective communication	4.30	.82	3
Effective decision making	4.21	.84	4
Effective motivation of people	4.18	.90	5
Effective planning of the work	4.17	.99	6
Managing team work and participation	4.15	.98	7
Delegation and resource allocation	4.08	.87	8
Improving one's overall effectiveness	4.04	.93	9
Managing stresses at work	3.96	.96	10
Problem solving and creativity	3.93	1.06	11
Effective appraisal of subordinates	3.86	.78	12
Dealing with conflicts and disputes	3.73	1.00	13
Managing change	3.72	1.02	14
Developing one's own potential	3.65	.99	15
Analysis of the organisation	3.63	.93	16
Working with computer	3.46	1.03	17
Maintaining effective interaction system	3.44	.98	18
Managing one's career development	3.28	1.03	19
Counselling subordinates	3.24	.92	20
Managing financial aspects of work	3.18	1.21	21

Table 3.2
Hierarchy of Important Managerial Skills Required for Effective Performance of Senior Managers at Different Levels of Organisation

Description of the Skills	(Level S1)		(Level S2)		(Level S3)		(Level S4)	
	Mean Value	Rank Order	Mean Value	Rank Order	Mean Value	Rank Order	Mean Value	Rank Order
Effective time management	5.00	1	4.38	2	4.21	2	4.38	4
Managing stresses at work	5.00	1	3.62	9	3.91	9	4.31	5
Effective communication	5.00	1	4.46	1	4.14	5	4.54	2
Effective motivation of people	5.00	1	4.08	4	4.14	5	4.31	5
Problem solving and creativity	5.00	1	3.46	10	3.86	10	4.46	3
Creating organisational climate	5.00	1	4.31	3	4.23	1	4.77	1
Managing change effectively	5.00	1	3.62	9	3.60	13	4.00	7
Effective planning of the work	5.00	1	4.00	5	4.16	4	4.23	6
Effective decision making	5.00	1	4.08	4	4.19	3	4.31	2
Delegation and resource allocation	5.00	1	3.92	6	4.00	7	4.38	4
Dealing with conflicts and disputes	4.50	2	3.77	8	3.53	14	4.23	6
Managing team work and participation	4.50	2	4.31	3	4.02	10	4.38	4
Effective appraisal of subordinates	4.50	2	3.85	7	3.79	11	4.00	7
Analysis of the organisation	4.50	2	3.23	12	3.60	11	4.00	7
Improving one's overall effectiveness	4.00	3	4.08	4	3.98	8	4.23	6
Working with computer	4.00	3	3.23	12	3.42	15	3.77	9
Managing financial aspects of work	4.00	3	3.08	14	2.95	19	3.92	8
Counselling subordinates	4.00	3	3.08	14	3.14	18	3.62	10
Maintaining interaction system	3.50	4	3.38	11	3.30	16	3.92	8
Developing one's own potential	3.00	5	3.38	11	3.65	12	4.00	7
Managing one's career development	2.00	6	3.15	13	3.28	17	3.62	10

senior managers as a whole placed considerable importance on all skills dimensions for their increased effectiveness which meant that the mean value of the least important skills (3.18), is still rated above the mid-point on a five point scale.

The rated importance and the mean score rankings of the skills indicated that senior manager's effectiveness is affected by a combination of diverse set of skills regardless of their positions in the organisations. Table 3.2 indicates the ranked importance of the skills in each levels of seniority. The comparative analysis of the mean scores of the skills across various levels also indicated that senior managers at the fourth level of seniority (S4) attached relatively more importance to the rating of managerial skills than the other three groups (mean value of the least important skill is 3.62 well above the mid-point). Table 3.2, also indicates that the relative importance of task-related skills are fairly similar across all identified levels of seniority except for the chief executive level.

The mean score rankings of the three categories of skills presented in Table 3.3, indicate that, in general, the senior manager's increased effectiveness is dependent more on people-related and analytical and self-related categories of skills than that of task-related skills.

Table 3.3
Importance of Different Categories of Managerial Skills
for Effective Performance of All Senior Managers

Categories of skills	Mean Value	Std Dev.	Rank Order
1. Analytical and Self-related skills	3.89	.31	2
2. People-related skills	3.94	.35	1
3. Task-related skills	3.68	.38	3

Table 3.4
Importance of Required Categories of Managerial Skills for the
Effective Performance of Senior Managers by their Hierarchical Position

Levels of management	Level (S1)		Level (S2)		Level (S3)		Level (S4)	
Categories of skills	Mean Value	Rank Order	Mean Value	Rank Order	Mean Value	Rank Order	Mean Value	Rank Order
Analytical & Self-related	4.14	3	3.74	2	3.87	3	4.19	2
People-related skills	4.81	1	3.93	1	3.82	2	4.23	1
Task-related skills	4.33	2	3.47	3	3.57	3	4.04	3

The mean score rankings presented in Table 3.4, is an indication that the hierarchical position of senior managers has considerable influence on the rated importance of the three categories of skills required for increased effectiveness of senior managers across the four senior management levels. Significant differences were found between the four levels of senior management for all three categories of skills. This result supports the hypothesised influence of the senior management's hierarchy on their perceptions of the required three categories of skills for their increased effectiveness. As shown, in Table 3.4, people-related skills are the most influential categories of skills across all levels except for senior managers in level three (S 3). The results also indicate that the rankings of people-related and analytical and self-related skills change with respect to managerial levels, being either in first or second place, but remain relatively more important than the task-related skills except for the first level in which the task-related skills become more important than the self-related skills. This result again partially supports other hypothesis of the research that senior managers in higher positions perceive the requirement of analytical and self-related skills and people-related skills to be more important to their effectiveness at work than task-related skills.

Discussion

The results of this study so far indicate that the participant senior managers generally hold a high level of commitment to the importance of management development training and the acquisition of managerial skills as the most appropriate means for increasing their managerial effectiveness. The high ratings of the total number of skills for all levels of senior management which ranged between the highest mean value of 4.37 (highest point recorded was 5), and the lowest mean value of 3.18 (above the mid-point), could well indicate an overwhelming support among senior managers in both organisations for management training and development (see Table 3.1). The high ratings may also be interpreted to constitute signals to the validity of the measures employed due to the fact that they have assessed the most tangible aspects of senior managers abilities which were perceived to have great influence on their increased effectiveness.

The findings of this research support the finding of other studies (Analoui, 1993, 1990a; Katz, 1974; Mintzberg, 1973; Pavett and Lau, 1983) and therefore, suggest that the relative importance attached to managerial skills by senior managers varies with respect to the position of senior managers in the hierarchy of organisation. In order to verify this the respondents were asked to rate the importance of the 21 different managerial skills and knowledge which they thought have been the major contributor to their increased effectiveness at work. The objective was to ascertain what categories of skills and knowledge were seen as necessary for performing their managerial roles and functions as well as the degree of importance which the respondents attached to these skills and knowledge.

The degree of importance placed on the various skills can be viewed as a hierarchy of skills which is illustrated in Table 3.1. This list establishes an appropriate body of managerial skills and knowledge which is required for the effective performance of senior managers. The result may also suggest that the senior managers' effectiveness is generally a function of diverse set of skills and knowledge. This hierarchy may well lead us to believe that the prime responsibility of management is to create a conducive organisational climate in which people work willingly and effectively. This overall competency is considered to be the cornerstone of managerial effectiveness and is the key to the improved organisational performance and increased effectiveness which also reflects the overall capability of management to get the job done as effectively as possible (Kakabadse and Margerison, 1985; Mintzberg, 1973; Mullins, 1993). The senior managers at SII were highly aware of their managerial responsibilities and of the presence of the factors which were affecting their effectiveness at work. These were:

- Effective communication,
- Managing time as a resource,
- Making decisions and resolving work related problems,
- Leading and motivating employees at work.

Personal factors such as improving one's own performance and developing one's own potential are considered very important attributes for effective managers. For example, Drucker (1974) believes that, 'one part of the manager's job is to develop people including himself' (p.400). He makes a sharp distinction between the two tasks of management development and manager development, and thus, maintains that, 'development is always self development' (p.427). He argues that as an important part of any manager's job, self development requires that managers learn new skills, knowledge and attitudes in order to perform their jobs effectively. It is increasingly a responsibility for today's manager to develop himself through insight into his strengths and by gaining the required skills and experience on the job, as well as searching for opportunities which lead to greater contribution and superior performance (Drucker, 1974). A self-development model suggested by Delf and Smith (1978), is based on the recognition that successful managers consciously take charge of their own learning and satisfy their development needs without being too dependent on the organisation. An effective manager assures his personal growth and development through feedback on his own performance and by taking advantage of every opportunity to eliminate his weaknesses and strengthen his capabilities. Through this process, the advancement opportunities play an important motivational factor for personal and career development of a manager. At the same time it is the responsibility of the organisation to provide the facilitating means and opportunities for individual growth and advancement.

As indicated in Table 3.1, the importance placed on self and development skills by senior managers is well above the mid-point but lower than other personal factors. As a whole, the mean score for the ability to improve ones own effectiveness was 4.04, and for the ability to assess and develop one's potentials was 3.65. The importance of these skills, to senior managers, varies across the four levels of seniority but the relative range of the distance between the ranking of the two seems to be the same. In assessing the importance of various motivational factors, the opportunity for advancement was perceived as more important than an increase in salary and other financial benefits which senior managers often received for improving their performance.

The importance attached to planning as an ability to set objectives, forecast, evaluate and select the best possible alternatives for doing the job was seen to be considerably high. The mean value for the total number of respondents involved was 4.17, which ranked this skill in sixth place. The mean score varied across the levels (see Table 3.2), tended to decrease in level 2 and 4, but increased slightly for the occupants of the third level. The results again support the findings of Margerison and Kakabadse (1985), which reported that the importance of strategic and short term planning ranked as the third highest factor and was viewed as giving rise to the success of the executives. Other task-related skills such as analysing the organisational structure, maintaining an effective interaction system and managing the financial aspects of the work as well as the ability to manage one's own work with the use of computers have been perceived as equally important by senior managers across all four levels of seniority. This is in line with the findings of Pavett and Lau (1983) who suggest that technical skills were equally important across all three levels of management; top, middle and junior. For the senior managers, as a whole, these managerial skills are perceived as the least important contributing factors to their increased effectiveness though, notably, some were perceived as more important than others.

Categories of managerial skills

The findings of the study supported the hypotheses that the degree of importance which is placed on the three main categories of skills, required for the increased effectiveness of senior managers at work, varies considerably depending on their position within levels of seniority. The results suggest that the need for possession of task-related skills and the perceived importance attached to them in terms of increased effectiveness is generally lower when compared to people-related, analytical and self-related skills (see Table 3.3). The mean score for the Task-related category was 3.68, the lowest, compared with the other two categories. This finding was also supported by the results of another part of the survey's results when we asked senior managers to name and accordingly rate the importance attached to factors which they thought have contributed to their satisfactory performance. Here again, senior managers as a whole, perceived functional managerial skills considerably less important than human ones as determinant factors for achieving results at work. These findings are in agreement with Katz's (1974) argument and Analoui's (1990, 1995) findings that as managers move to higher positions in the organisation, technical skills become relatively less important to them and managerial effectiveness will depend largely on human and conceptual skills. We also noted that although the task-related skills were generally ranked lower in comparison with the other two categories, their importance in terms of getting things done was still rated well above the mid-point by senior managers within all levels.

Interviews with chief executives led to the understanding that the reason for attaching more importance to the task related aspects by executives of both organisations was because they felt that in their positions as top management they had to express their views concerning issues such as their advancement and career development in modest terms. Thus, they devalued any efforts which seemed to proclaim their attachment to these forms of managerial behaviour. This seems to be more culturally and socially determined. This conscious attempt on their part resulted in self and career development being ranked 2.0, the least important of all the skills in our list (see the last row in Table 3.2). It is this low mean score which apparently gave a relative rise to the mean value of the task-related category of skills for S1 in Table 3.4. If we were to ignore this low mean value in calculating the mean score of self-related category there would be a new mean value of 4.5 which would lift the analytical and self related category to second place and drop the task-related skills to third position.

It is also important to note that because of the inevitable small number of respondents in the first level of the seniority, the mean value of all three categories of skills is generally higher for this level. Further the analysis of qualitative data, seemed to support the research hypothesis that task-related skills are generally perceived to be of the least importance to chief executives from amongst the three main categories of managerial skills required for the effectiveness of senior managers at work. Moreover, its relative importance tended to decrease as we move from the top level S1 to the lower positions within the managerial hierarchy. This is also in agreement with the findings of Analoui's (1995) research who reported that the participant senior managers in the Indian Railways placed more importance on their need for task-related skills as they moved lower down in the hierarchy.

The above findings also supports the related research hypothesis that the category of people-related skills is generally viewed, by senior managers, as the most important set of skills when comes to increasing their effectiveness, more remarkably, regardless of their positions of seniority. It has already been learnt, from other studies, that most of a senior manager's time is spent in contact with other people (Carlson, 1951; Copeman, 1963; Stewart, 1967), and that managing people is being increasingly considered as constituting a significant aspect of any senior manager's job (Bolton, 1979; Kakabadse, et. al., 1987; Kotter, 1982). These findings and the results of other studies reported from developing countries (Analoui, 1990a, 1995) implies that the senior manager's effectiveness is, to a lesser or greater extent, a function of competence shown in working with people and that people-related skills, such as communication, interpersonal skills, leadership and conflict resolutions are perhaps the most vital attributes for their success.

Table 3.4 also indicates that in comparison to the other categories, the mean value of the people-related category holds the highest value across all levels. This seems to be true in almost every level of seniority except the third level (with a mean value of 3.82 for S3, which is slightly lower than that of analytical and self-related skills, 3.87). This result was also verified when we asked senior managers to rate the importance of their training needs in the area of people related skills such as communication, co-ordination, control, employees appraisal and development. Again, training on people-related skills was regarded as significant and essential for the increased effectiveness of senior managers at all levels except for third level senior managers.

Self development is considered to be an important part of a manager's job that requires a specific set of new skills and knowledge (Drucker, 1974).

There is an increasing awareness among managers that their effectiveness largely depends on their ability and desire for their own personal growth and development. Senior managers in the SII organisations, placed different degrees of importance, depending on their level and position of seniority, on the category of analytical and self-related skills. The highest mean score for this category is 4.19 which belongs to senior managers in the fourth level. They ranked these groups of managerial skills and abilities as the second most important category of skills needed for their effectiveness.

It is also noted that senior managers (S3) perceived a much greater need for the self-related skills as opposed to task-related skills. The same also seemed to hold true for senior managers at level two and four (S2 and S4). It appears that the analytical and self-related category of skills together with people-related skills are generally perceived as more important than that of task-related ones. These results suggest that the senior managers' own development and growth must be given a high degree of priority in the formulation of human resource development strategies.

Although the felt need for analytical and self-related skills and knowledge were high among all the respondents, it was evident that this need was emphasised more at the lower levels of managerial hierarchy. However, there is a high mean score of 4.14 for the same category at the first level, which seems to make sense when the low number of participants in level S1 is considered. The overall picture suggests that at the higher level of the organisation, specially at the chief executive level (S1), the tendency seems to be more towards a desire on their part for the acquisition of a balanced range of skills from amongst the identified categories while naturally the emphasis is placed more on the people-related ones.

Common patterns and interrelationships

As suggested earlier our classification of different managerial skills is only valid by definition. Therefore, to further test the possible grouping of the skills as identified in the literature and to investigate the existing patterns of interrelationships in the data, factor analysis was considered to provide the appropriate model. Briefly, in a multi-dimensional vector space, as defined by the cases, the presentation of the selected managerial skills (variables) is highly meaningful. The smaller the angle between any two variables (vectors) the closer their association. The common patterns, distinct from each other emerge by passing orthogonal axes through the centre of gravity of possible clusters of variables. Such patterns are defined by the loading of variables on these imaginary axes (factors). In other words the common factors are defined by a set of closely associated variables. Naturally such interrelationships and patterns may differ from industry to industry.

Table 3.5
Vrimax Rotated Factor Matrix for Managerial Skills in SII

Factors:	I	II	III	IV	V	VI	h_i^2
Factor I- People-related skills:							
Managing Team work/participation	**.85**	.11	.22	.02	.13	-.04	.80
Dealing with conflicts and disputes	**.79**	.15	.19	.23	.22	-.13	.80
Counselling subordinates	**.60**	.25	.15	.02	.14	.32	.56
Creating organisational climate	**.59**	.23	.26	.43	-.26	-.03	.73
Problem solving and creativity	**.57**	.46	.08	.33	.27	.17	.75
Effective motivation of people	**.51**	.28	.04	**.45**	.23	.14	.62
Effective appraisal of subordinates	**.48**	.23	.42	-.06	.00	.42	.65
Factor II - Task-related skills:							
Effective decision making	.09	**.80**	.27	.20	.03	-.09	.77
Delegation and resource allocation	.25	**.71**	.18	.21	.16	-.02	.68
Effective planning of the work	.27	**.67**	-.02	-.04	.25	.38	.73
Maintaining interaction system	.37	**.43**	.27	.28	.24	.19	.57
Factor III - Task-related skills:							
Managing financial aspects of work	.26	.14	**.83**	.01	.02	.15	.80
Working with computer	.23	.23	**.63**	.11	.16	.12	.56
Effective time management	-.06	-.05	**.59**	.47	.30	-.12	.68
Analysis of the organisation	.21	.43	**.49**	.08	.15	.12	.51
Factor IV - Analytical and self-related skills:							
Effective communication	.10	.14	.03	**.84**	-.05	.26	.80
Managing stress at work	.31	.27	.18	**.64**	.30	-.12	.73
Factor V - Analytical and self-related skills:							
Improving one's overall performance	.26	.14	.16	-.08	**.80**	.16	.79
Developing one's own potential	.10	.26	.16	.31	**.73**	.08	.74
Factor VI - Analytical and self-related skills:							
Managing one's career development	-.09	-.04	.09	.12	.10	**.85**	.76
Managing change effectively	.36	.30	.36	.08	.18	**.53**	.67
V^t	39.6	7.7	6.5	5.9	5.4	4.8	
Cum V^t	39.6	47.3	53.8	59.7	65.1	70.0	
V^c	56.6	11.0	9.3	8.4	7.7	6.9	
Cum V^c	56.6	67.6	76.9	85.3	93.0	100	

The principal component model of factor analysis was employed for our purpose as we were mainly searching for the basis dimensions of data which would define the total variance. In choosing the number of factors we were guided by a combination of: (i) the magnitude of the eigenvalues, (ii) the percentage of variance accounted for by successive factors and (iii) a relatively significant drop in the percentage of variance accounted for by the last factor left out. These criteria resulted in extracting six factors with eigenvalues greater than 1.00 accounting for 70 percent of total variance. The criterion used for rotation was to look for 'simple structure' in data as this would search for highly interrelated cluster of variables as specific to the cluster as possible. This was expected to make the interpretation of factors more meaningful. Varimax rotation procedure was employed for this purpose. Entries in Table 4.5, aij, with the exception of the last column, reflect the correlation between variable i and the extracted factor j. It follows that $(aij)^2$ is the coefficient of determination and would indicate the percentage of variations in variable i in common with that of factor j.

All loadings of .40 and above are regarded to be moderate to high and have been highlighted, and all loadings between .25 and .39 are considered to be low-moderate. The last column, h_i^2 provides communality for each variable; the square root of each commonalty is equal to the length of the variable-vector in the vector space which remains unchanged through rotation. Each h_i^2 multiplied by 100 gives the percentage of variations in variable i which has been explained by all extracted factors (h_i^2 is analogous to R^2 in regression analysis.) On the whole, most variables have high commonalties, indicating a relatively high degree of explanation offered for them by the extracted factors. The last four rows of Table 3.5 reveal the percentages of total variance (V^t), cumulative total variance (Cum V^t), common variance (V^c) and cumulative common variance (Cum V^c) accounted for by the derived factors. Overall 70 percent of variations in our variables are accounted for by six factors.

Factor I

People-related skills. Factor I accounts for nearly 40 percent of total variance and 57 percent of common variance as explained by all factors. It is clearly dominated by people-related skills variables. Managing team work/ participation has the highest loading, .85, on this factor. This results in a coefficient of determination of more than .72 which indicates the presence of 72 percent common variations between this variable and factor I. Its respective communality shows that 80 percent of variations in this variable is associated with those of, and can be explained by, the derived factors. The next highest loading belongs to dealing with conflicts and disputes, again a people-related, variable. Interestingly, as indicated by its communality, 80 percent of variations in this variable is in common with those of the extracted factors, a very well explained variable. Counselling subordinates, once again a people-related skill, has a high loading of .60 on this factor and the next high loading belongs to creating organisational climate which is another people-related variable. The moderate loading of this variable on factor IV which is basically an analytical and self-related factor is interesting. Technically speaking, this variable, in a moderate way, provides the link between these two factors. Problem solving and creativity has the next high loading on this factor with a rather high communality. Initially this variable was thought to belong to the analytical and self-related skill category, but it seems to have a good loading on factor I. It is interesting to note the moderate loading of this variable on factor II, a task-related skill, and its low-moderate loadings of .33 and .27, on factors IV and V which will later be interpreted as analytical and self-related factors. In other words, this skill seems to be somewhat cutting across the board (a proposition which makes sense.) Effective motivation of people, once again a people-related variable, has a relatively moderate loading on this factor with a rather moderate communality. Again the moderate load of this variable on factor IV which contains communication skill is interesting and its low-moderate loading on factor II, .28, which is a task-related factor is noteable. Finally effective appraisal of subordinates, initially a people-related variable, has moderate loadings on factor I, as well as, on task-related factor III and on analytical and self-related factor VI, again a skill which seems to be moderately associated with three various common patterns. Out of seven skills variables with high loadings on factor I, six measure people-related skills. The low-moderate loading of managing change, a people-related variable, on this factor is also noteable. In conclusion factor I is clearly a people-related factor which in terms of the variations it accounts for, is the most important pattern emerging.

Factor II

Task-related skills (cluster one). Factor II accounts for 7.7 percent of total variance and 11 percent of common variance as accounted for by all factors. The highest loading on this factor belongs to effective decision making skill with a coefficient of determination of .64 and a communality of 77 percent. The low-moderate loading of this variable on factor III is noteworthy. Other variables with high loading on this factor are delegation and resource allocation and effective planning, with maintaining interaction system having a relatively moderate loading. These are all task-related skills. Together they reveal an interesting and highly meaningful pattern in the data. This factor is referenced here as a 'task-related' factor. Once again, the moderate loadings of problem solving and creativity variable (assigned to factor I) and analysis of organisation (assigned to factor III) on this factor are interesting. The low-moderate loadings of effective planning on people related factor I and factors V and VI are also notable. The moderate to low-moderate loadings of maintaining interaction system variable spread across almost all factors, bearing in mind the nature of this skill, is highly meaningful and interesting.

Factor III

Task-related skills (cluster two). Factor III is again a task-related factor. It accounts for 6.5 percent of total variance and 9.3 percent of common variance as explained by all factors. Managing financial aspects of work has the highest loading on this factor indicating that 69 percent of variations in this variable and factor III are in common. The high communality of this variable indicates a high degree of association between this variable and the extracted factors. Working with computer is another task-related variable with high loading on this factor. Effective time management, though initially regarded as an analytical and self-related skill, has a high loading on this factor. In this respect the moderate and low-moderate loadings of this variable on factor IV and factor V, both analytical and self-related factors, are meaningful. Analysis of organisation, another task-related variable, is the last variable with a moderate loading on this factor. The moderate loading of this variable on factor II, which is the previous task-related factor suggests an interesting link. The moderate loading of the effective appraisal of subordinates (assigned to factor I) on this factor is also interesting.

Factor IV

Analytical and self-related skills (cluster one). Factor IV accounts for 5.9 percent of total variance and 8.4 percent of common variance. Two variables have high loadings on this factor. Effective communication and managing stress at work seem to have clustered together. Such a close association seems to suggest that managers with effective communication tend to manage stress at work more effectively, and vice versa. Nearly 71 percent of variations in the first variable is in common with this factor. Initially this variable was considered to be a people-related variable, however, it may be argued to have an analytical dimension. Managing stress at work, an analytical and self-related variable has a high loading on this factor; the low-moderate loadings of this variable on factors I, II and V are noteworthy. Interestingly the commonalties of both variables are rather high indicating that the extracted factors provide rather good explanation for these variables. This factor was regarded as being of an analytical and self-related nature. The moderate loadings of creating organisational climate, effective motivation of people and effective time management on this factor seem very meaningful.

Factor V

Analytical and self-related skills (cluster two). Factor V is responsible for 5.4 percent and 7.7 percent of total variance and common variance, respectively. The two variables with high loadings on this factor are improving one's overall performance, with a loading of .80, and developing one's own potential, with a loading of .73, are both analytical and self-related variables. The low-moderate loadings of the first variable on factor I, the people-related factor, and the low-moderate loading of the second variable on factor II, a task-related factor, are notable. This factor is clearly a self-related factor.

Factor VI

Analytical and self-related skills (cluster three). Factor VI is the last factor accounting for 4.8 percent and 6.9 percent of the total and common variances, respectively. Managing one's career development has a high loading of .85 on this factor with managing change effectively, initially a people-related variable, having a moderate-high loading. The low-moderate loadings of the latter on factors I, II and III, bearing in mind their nature, are interesting. The moderate loading of the effective appraisal of subordinates variable (assigned to factor I) on this factor makes sense. Similarly the low-moderate loading of effective planning skill on this factor is noteable. Overall, this factor was regarded to be of an analytical and self-related nature.

Conclusions and implications

The findings of this research provides partial support for Analoui's model of management development which suggests the presence of hierarchy amongst the categories of managerial skills (1993, p.76). The study at SII, however, has shown that in so far as analytical and self-development skills are concerned the notion of hierarchy of skills hold its validity for levels S2,

S3 and S4. This suggests that the lower the position of senior managers in their organisation the more their perceived need for this category of skills. Task-related skills also tends to follow a hierarchical pattern among senior managers in level 2, 3 and 4. This suggests that senior managers in the lower level of the organisation tend to have greater need for the task-related skills in order to perform their job effectively. This does not, however, suggest that task related aspects of the job of senior managers in higher positions holds little or no importance for them.

One interesting issue which has emerged from all this is that in reality the identified managerial skills are so overlapping that it is difficult to make a clear-cut distinction between the three categories. The line of demarcation therefore, can only be drawn theoretically and only for the ease of analytical purposes. As Katz aptly states, 'in practice these skills are so closely interrelated that it is difficult to determine where one ends and another begins' (1974, p.102). Furthermore, there is clear indication that senior managers irrespective of their seniority, require a comprehensive range of managerial skills for their increased effectiveness. Mintzberg (1975) also claims that the required managerial skills form an integrated whole, thus, implying that no single managerial skill can be ignored if the manager is to do his job effectively. Giving consideration to the three aspects of managerial responsibilities, it may be concluded that managers need to acquire three categories of skills for their effectiveness at work; namely the 'analytical and self-related', 'people-related', and 'task-related' skills. Nonetheless, the results clearly showed that the degree of importance attached to each set of skills tended to vary according to the position of the managers in the hierarchy of the organisation. For the development of senior managers, the implications of the presence of a hierarchy for managerial skills are many.

Within developing countries, the traditional approaches employed for training and developing managers, in particular the senior managers, are consequently not suitable for their effectiveness since it tends to place unproportionate emphasis on theoretical cognitive learning as opposed to the required skills. The findings of this research firmly suggests that there seems to be a perceived need amongst managers for more self-related and people-related skills which are vital for increasing the effectiveness of senior managers. Furthermore, it suggests a real need for a balanced knowledge and skill based management development to cope with the ever increasing demand of organisational problems in developing countries.

These findings also support the view that a contingency approach to training and development must be adopted to reflect the actual training and development needs of senior managers who perform in different levels of the organisation. Moreover, this study may be taken as an empirical evidence that the managerial skills required for effective performance of senior managers would not necessarily vary significantly from one culture to another. The difference in required management training and development needs will probably rest on the degree of emphasis which is placed on the application of the skills in different socio-economic, educational and cultural contexts rather than the skill itself.

The results of the above factor analysis support the proposition that though managerial skills are interrelated, they form various clusters which may be more distinct than the broad categories referred to in the literature. While people-related skills are by far more strongly interrelated, and should be regarded as an integrated set of skills, the same does not apply, at least not to the same extent, to the other two categories of skills. With respect to SII data task-related skills form two distinct patterns, though rather weakly linked, nevertheless two distinct patterns. Similarly, the analytical and self-related skills do not form an integrated single group of skills, rather they seem to form distinct clusters of subsets of such skills, though linked to a low-moderate degree to other clusters of managerial skills. The reader should be reminded that while these results are suggestive in various ways nevertheless they are relevant to the SII senior managers and may differ from industry to industry. However they may provide some insight into a rather complex issue.

References

Analoui, F. (1989), 'Senior managers and increased effectiveness', *Project Appraisal*, Vol. 4, No. 4, pp.215-218.

Analoui, F. (1990a), *An investigation into management training development needs of senior officials in Zimbabwe*, Research Monograph No. 2, DPPC, University of Bradford. UK.

Analoui, F. (1990b), 'Managerial skills for senior managers', *The International Journal of Public Sector Management*, Vol. 3, No. 2, pp.26-38.

Analoui, F. (1993), 'Skills of management', in J.W. Cusworth and T.F. Franks (eds.), *Managing projects in developing countries*, Essex: Longman, pp.68-83.

Analoui, F. (1995), 'Management skills and senior management effectiveness', *The International Journal of Public Sector Management*, Vol. 8, No. 3, pp.52-68.

Bandura, A. (1974), 'Behaviour theory and the model of man', *American Psychologist*, Vol.29, pp.859-869.

Bandura, A. (1986), *Social foundations of thought and action: A social cognitive theory*, New Jersey: Prentice-Hall Inc.

Bigelow, J. D. (1991), *Managerial skills development*, USA: Sage Publication.

Bolton, R. (1979), *People skills*, Prentice-Hall.

Boyatzis, R. E. (1982), *The Competent Manager*, New York: John Wiley and Sons.

Brief, A. P., and Aldag, R. J. (1981), 'The 'Self' in the work organisations: A conceptual review', *Academy of Management Review*, Vol. 6, No. 1, pp.75-88.

Carlson, S. (1951), *Executive behaviour*, Stockholm: C. A. Stromberg.

Copeman, G., Luijk, H. and Hanika, F. (1963), *How the executive spends his time*, London: Business Publications Limited.

Delf, R., and Smith, B. (1978), 'Strategies for Promoting Self-Development', *International and Commercial Training*, Vol. 10, No. 12, December.

Digman, L.A. (1980), 'Management development: Needs and practices', *Personnel*, July-August, pp.45-57.

Hayes, J. L. (1983), 'CEO's in action : January', *American Graduate School of International Management*, Glendale, Arizona.

Jones, J. E., and Woodcock, M. (1985), *Manual of management development*, Gower.

Kakabadse, A., Ludlow, R., and Vinnicombe, S. (1987), *Working in Organisations*, Penguin Books.

Kakabadse, A., and Margerison, C. (1985), 'What management development means for American CEOs', *Journal of Management Development*, Vol. 4, No. 5, pp.3-15.

Katz, R. L. (1955), 'Skills of an effective administrator', *Harvard Business Review*, Jan-Feb.

Katz, R. L. (1974), 'Skills of an effective administrator', *Harvard Business Review*, Vol. 52, September-October, pp. 90-102.

Kotter, J. P. (1982), 'General managers are not generalist', *Organisation Dynamics*, Spring, pp. 5-19.

Livingston, J. S. (1971), 'Myth of the well-educated manager', *Harvard Business Review*, January/February, pp. 79-93.

Locke, E. A. (1976), 'The nature and causes of job satisfaction', in M. D. Dunnette (ed.), *Handbook of industrial and organisational psychology*, Chicago: Rand-McNally.

Luthans, F., and Davis, T.R.V. (1979), 'Behavioral self-management: The missing link in managerial effectiveness', *Organisational Dynamics*, Vol. 8, No. 1, pp. 42-60.

Manz, C. C. and Sims, H. P., Jr. (1980), 'Self-management as a substitute for leadership', *Academy of Management Review*, Vol. 5, No.3, pp.361-367.

Margerison, C.J. (1984a), 'Chief executives' perception of managerial success factors', *The Journal of Management Development*, Vol. 3, No. 4, pp. 47-60.

Margerison, C. J. (1984b), 'Where is management education and development going - some key operations', in A. Kakabadse and S. Mukhi (eds), *The future of management education*, England: Gower.

Margerison, C.J. (1985), 'Achieving the capacity and competence to manage', *The Journal of Management Development*, Vol. 4, No. 3, pp. 42-55.

Mintzberg, H. (1973), *The nature of managerial work*, New York: Harper Collins.

Mintzberg, H. (1975), 'The manager's Job: Folklore and fact', *Harvard Business Review*, July-August.

Mullins, L.J. (1993), *Management and organisational behaviour* (3rd ed.), London: Pitman.

Mumford, A. (1984), 'Effectiveness in management development', *Journal of Management Development*, Vol. 3, No. 2, pp. 3-16.

Mumford, A. (1986), *Handbook of Management Development* (2nd ed.), Gower.

Pavett, C.M., and Lau, A.W. (1983), 'Managerial work: The influence of hierarchical level and functional specialty', *Academy of Management Journal*, Vol. 26 No. 1, pp. 170-177.

Rummel, R.J. (1970), *Applied factor analysis*, Northwestern University Press.

Stewart, R. (1963), *The reality of management*, London: Heinemann.

Stewart, R. (1967), *Managers and their jobs*, London: Macmillan.

Waters, J.A. (1980), 'Managerial skill development', *Academy of Management Review*, Vol. 5, No. 3, pp. 449-453.

Whetten, D.A., and Cameron, K.S. (1980), *An assessment of salient management skills*, Working Papers, University of Wisconsin School of Business.

Whetten, D.A., and Cameron, K.S. (1983), 'Management skill training: A needed addition to the management curriculum', *The Organisation Behaviour Teaching Journal*, Vol. 8, No. 1, pp. 10-15.

Whetten, D.A., and Cameron, K.S. (1984), *Developing management skills*, USA: Scott, Foresman and Company.

Whetten, D.A., and Cameron, K.S. (1991), *Developing management skills* (2nd ed.), New York: Harper Collins.

4 Behavioural and causal influences of the individual managerial effectiveness in Ghanaian public sector

Dr Farhad Analoui

Introduction

Much attention has been given to the effectiveness of the senior managers' and their performance by recent theorists, management researchers, developers and practitioners, in developed, Developing Countries (DCs) and Developing Economies (DEs) (Copeman, 1971; Kotter, 1982; McCall and Lombardo, 1983; Margerison and Kakabadse, 1984). This organisational phenomenon, illusive in nature (Mores and Wagner, 1978), has been known and labelled as a concept which is difficult to quantify (Brodie and Bennett, 1979) and even more difficult to measure (Dunnette, 1971; Drucker 1988), yet it is often talked about and has also attracted much interest, from lateral and multi-lateral agencies, and has also been acknowledged by serious researchers such as Mintzberg (1973), Kirchoff (1977), Longford (1979), Margerison (1984), and the World Bank (1994).

The concern for understanding managerial effectiveness within DCs and DEs however, has hitherto evolved mainly around, not the managers, but the organisational setting (Charsley, 1986; Mullins, 1993) social, cultural and political contexts (Jones, 1988; Kiggundo, 1989; Analoui 1995, 1997) and has been debated within the boundaries of an open system theory (Willcocks, 1992). The recent surge of interest from academia points to the managers' own choices, and the contentious issue that managers performance is inevitably contingent upon and affected by the casual and behavioural influences within their immediate and wider socio-economic and cultural settings (Stewart, 1982, 1991). This includes their own perception and understanding of what constitutes effectiveness in a particular context (Kakabadse et. al., 1987; Analoui, 1997).

Senior managers are believed to make a major contribution towards the well being and development of their nations in a particular economy (World Bank, 1991; Blunt, 1992; Labbaf and Analoui, 1996). The questions and issues which have not been adequately addressed, especially within DCs and ECs' contexts, concern the causes and sources of influences, including managers' own perception, which influence the degree of effectiveness of the individual senior managers and executives and arguably their organisation and nations as the whole.

This chapter is based on the findings of a recent pilot study, funded by the Department of International Development (DFID) into the behavioural and casual influences of the senior managers' effectiveness within the public sector in Ghana. First, the study, its scope, methodology and the nature of the data collected are outlined, and the underlying methodological assumptions including choices available to senior officials, managers and executives have been dealt with. Then, the eight major clusters of influences, referred to here as 'parameters', of managerial effectiveness namely, the Senior Managers' Perception; Skills and Knowledge; Organisational Criteria; Motivation for Effectiveness; Constraints and Difficulties: Choices and Opportunities; Inter-organisational Relationships, and finally Dominant Managerial Philosophy are discussed briefly. Based on the above, relevant conclusions are reached and the need for further research and the adoption of a holistic approach to public sector reform as a means of achieving increased managerial effectiveness are emphasised.

Scope and objectives of the study

This first time study into managerial effectiveness, was planned and carried out in the Ministry of the Environment, Science and Technology (MEST), a major component of the Ghanaian Public Sector. The preparation for this initiative commenced in 1995 and was successfully completed in 1997. This pilot research, funded by Economic and Social Committee for Overseas Research (ESCOR)[1], forms the basis for a proposed cross-cultural and comparative study, into the factors and influences which determine the effectiveness of the senior officials and managers with the aim to improve managerial effectiveness within Developing Countries (DCs). It has been administered by the Development and Project Planning Centre (DPPC), University of Bradford, UK.

The primary purposes of this study were;

1. to identify the different behavioural and causal variables necessary to determine the effectiveness of managers/officials within DCs' institutions and organisations;
2. to elaborate on the construction and future use of appropriate methods to be used for the collection and generation of relevant data concerning the managerial effectiveness in different cultural contexts.

The identification of the causal and behavioural influences will pave the way for the planned comparative work within DCs and/or in a number of Developing Economies in the near future. What makes this research almost unique is that, the study of the behavioural influences and casual influences for senior managers' effectiveness have never been systematically attempted and the result will therefore make a significant contribution towards understanding the way senior managers perceive their effectiveness and what are the determinants for their effectiveness at work.

Choice and meaningful action

The works of Silverman (1970), Stewart (1983, 1991) and Kakabadse et. al., (1987) have posed the questions, do managers, during the course of their daily activities, exercise a choice? If so, how is their choice of a particular behaviour and/or action being affected? How do senior officials and managers perceive their effectiveness? What is the criteria for senior managers' effectiveness in public sector organisations? These studies have particular methodological relevance and implications for the present research.

Senior managers during their daily activities have been shown to exercise a choice from amongst a repertoire of what they consider to be effective behaviour (Kakabadse, 1983; Analoui, 1997) The issue of 'choice' and also 'meaningful action' raises other questions such as the degree of awareness, motivation and constraints and opportunities with which senior managers are faced. More importantly, it leads to the realisation that senior managers are not mere respondents to events but that they continually act, interact and negotiate the reality of working in the public sector culture and attempt to define, redefine, modify and even change the socio-cultural and political realties (Mangham, 1979; Kotter, 1982).

Consideration which was given to the above issues meant that the study could be seen by some as contentious and as an attempt to break away from the traditional boundaries of normal paradigm (Ravetz, 1971). The researcher's attempt to avoid basing the study on heavily pre-determined conceptualisations (Silverman, 1971; Burrel and Morgan, 1979) has meant that there was a need to consider managerial effectiveness as it is and not as it is assumed to be within DCs and DEs (Blunt, 1990; Analoui, 1997).

The researcher's recent work within the public sectors of DCs including Zimbabwe (1990), India (1995) and Romania (1997), all pointed to the presence of an 'awareness' of and the need for increased effectiveness on the part of the senior managers/officials, and that this increase in effectiveness was feasible. These studies also provided a basis for understanding the situation in Ghana. However, it is important to add that throughout the public sector in Ghana, separate initiatives have begun to address the issue of improving public sector performance through 'reform', 'restructuring' and 'improved performance programmes' of which the present work is not a part. These attempts have all originally gained momentum from the document Vision 20/20 which was prepared by the President and which pointed to the significant role of the public administration and set out the strategy for better performance by reform of the public sector in Ghana within the next millennium.

Methodology and the nature of the data

The fieldwork phase of the research began in early 1996, and included planning, several fieldwork visits to various organisations, administering the survey questionnaire and conducting semi-structured interviews. A total of 80 percent (N= 217) of the senior managers and executives of the entire ministry were included in the survey, of which 59.4 percent (N= 129) responded.   Of this 129 respondents, 71 (83 percent) were eventually interviewed.

The organisations within the MEST involved in the study were:

1. Town and Country Planning Department (TCPD)
2. Environmental Protection Agency (EPA)
3. Council for Scientific and Industrial Research (CSIR)
4. Ghana Atomic Energy Commission (GAEC)
5. Ghana Regional Appropriate Technology Industrial Service (GRATIS)
6. Development and Application of the Intermediate Technology (DAPIT)

Apart from the TCPD and DAPIT all the other organisations consist of several organisations and departments spread throughout Ghana. For example; the CSIR consists of 17 research institutes and has the largest number of employees. The Environmental Protection Agency has its headquarters in Accra and acts as an umbrella for 10 departments which are located throughout the regions.

Profile of the respondents: position, gender and age

A large proportion (N=107) of the managers (83 percent) were male and only a small proportion (N=19) were female. This was due to the general trend of male occupancy of managerial positions within the public sector. Of the 19 female managers almost half (N=9, equivalent of 7 percent) were from the CSIR where the scientific nature of the work provided more opportunity for the qualified female respondents to work alongside their male counterparts. The remaining female respondents were occupying senior positions within MEST and GAEC, where again the work culture seemed not to distinguish between the respondents based on their gender. It is however, important to bear in mind that, apart from CSIR where female scientists did occupy roles such as Director or Heads of Departments, most senior positions were occupied by male respondents. All directorates of the Ministry were male, however the fact that at the time of the study the Minister was female seemed to generate confidence amongst the female respondents in so far as their career development was concerned (See Table 4.1).

Table 4.1
Distribution of the respondents based on gender

Organisation		Male	Percent	Female	Percent	Total	Percent
CSIR	A	43	83	9	17	52	100
EPA	B	12	92	1	8	13	100
GAEC	C	17	85	3	15	20	100
MEST	D	14	64	5	23	19	87
GRATIS	E	13	93	1	7	14	100
TCPD	F	8	100	0	0	8	100
No Response						3	13
Total		107		19		129	

As explained earlier, most respondents targeted were holding executive and highly senior positions. Nearly 30 percent of the respondents were Executive Directors, Directors, Assistant Directors and Heads of Departments (N= 43). The differences in the structures of the component organisations meant that respondents labelled with the same role occupancy were positioned in different levels of the hierarchy in their respective organisations. For example, Directors of research stations tended to occupy a lower position in comparison with the respondents in charge of the Directorates in the main Ministry organisation. The senior managers as the whole accounted for 73 percent of the respondents, though some described their title as higher or lower depending on the years of experience in their present position (See Table 4.2).

Table 4.2
Respondents organisational position within the ministry

Position in Organisation	Total	Percent
Director	10	8.1
Deputy/Assistant Director	17	13.7
Head of Department/ Co-ordinator	16	13
Deputy H.O.D.	2	1.6
Chief Senior Officer	6	4.8
Senior Officers (Category)	73	58.4
No Response	5	3.9
Total	129	100

The age range of the respondents was varied with the youngest manager at 23 and the oldest executive at 63 years old. Most respondents were in their 40s (33 percent). A large proportion were between 30 and 40 years old (49 percent) and a few were below 30 or above 50. Although seniority seemed to constitute a major criteria for determining the significance and importance of the individual managers' contribution, in most organisations senior managers showed an appreciation of professionalism and acknowledged the improved work performance of their junior staff or colleagues.

Analysis and emergence of parameters

Attempts were made to generate data and information which met both criteria of 'adequacy' and 'relevance' (Ackroyd and Hughes, 1982; Gummesson, 1991). A three-part questionnaire was designed which consisted of 21 questions, a mix of open and closed questions.

The open questions, eight in all, explored the views of the respondents by asking the senior managers to provide a maximum of five responses in order of priority to them. Based on the order of priority, the responses obtained were allocated values, from '1' (for the first priority) and '0.2' (for fifth priority) accordingly. Application of this method, not only signified their order of priority for the Frequency Analysis, it also provided a basis for tabulation and comparison between different categories of the data.

The closed questions, 6 in all, measured the degree of importance which was placed by the senior respondents on a scale of 1 (Little Importance) to 7 (Great Deal of Importance) to issues related to managerial effectiveness such as awareness, career development and the relationship between management development and increased effectiveness.

The semi-structured interviews evolved around the issues which emerged from the responses to the open questions in the questionnaire and which concerned individual, organisation and wider external influences such socio-economic, political and cultural origins. The opportunity to meet with the senior managers also yielded data which because of its sensitivity could not have been included in the questionnaires.

The most time consuming aspect of the data collection was related to conducting the interviews especially amongst the most senior participants in the survey. Often the Director being interviewed felt that they wished to spend more time with the researcher but the need to participate in scheduled committee meetings and unexpected demands from their superior forced them to spend most of their time doing 'what everybody does in the ministry' attending meetings! The combination of the above resulted in the collection and generation of qualitative and quantitative data which has been subjected to grouping, frequency analysis and tabulation.

The analysis of the data resulted in the identification of groups of causal and behavioural influences, independent as a category but interdependent on one another. Each revealed one aspect associated with managerial effectiveness. The subject of the research were subsequently referred to as 'parameters' of managerial effectiveness. These parameters pointed to individual but also internal and other external contextual factors which as a whole determined the senior managers effectiveness. These are:

Perception of effectiveness (first parameter)

The senior managers and officials were asked to consider, 'How would you describe an effective manager?' This query was aimed at exploring the perception of the senior managers of their own effectiveness and at discovering what characteristics and qualities they thought an effective manager should possess. The responses provided ranged from 'ability to supervise', 'being a good leader', to being concerned with 'deadlines', 'honest', 'experienced' and 'able to deliver goods on time'.

The description provided also varied according the type of organisation the managers belonged to. Such perceptions also represent the characteristics of a manager whom they often referred to as 'ideal'. Did managers say something about themselves or did they describe an ideal manager? The data collected indicated that on the whole, managers have in mind an image of an effective manager whom they wish to be or more importantly who they wish their superior to be. It was particularly interesting to discover that in situations where the managerial control exercised was complete and which left little room for expression of discontent, the managers used such occasions (the questionnaires or interviews) to describe how they felt about their organisations and their immediate superiors.

Table 4.3
Effectiveness / Perception

PRIORITY	DESCRIPTION	TOTAL Response
1	Set and achieve results/output/objectives/being output orientated	24
2	To organise and achieve objectives/results, task within time limit	17
3	Get work done through teamwork/participation/ relating well to people	13
4	Ability to delegate	12
4	Plan, motivate and control subordinates	12
4	A good listener	12
5	A good motivator of people/inspiring	11
6	Plan work, schedule, organise, execute to perfection	10
6	Hard working and disciplined	10
7	Ability to supervise/leadership	9
7	Allocate resources efficiently (people, materials)	9
7	Knowledgeable in fieldwork, technical knowledge, know how	9
8	Responsible, conscientious and focused	8
8	Initiator, pro change, innovative, making things happen, solve problems	8
9	Perform tasks satisfactorily, promptly	7
10	Plan, organise, achieve policy framework, knowledge of policy, developing organiser	6
10	Meet objectives, targets, demands of the job	6
10	Take decisions, decisive, without fear or favour	6

The more senior the managers, the easier they found it to provide a description of who and what they thought an effective manager should be. However, no respondent ever directly criticised their superior, but suffixed their answers with comments such as 'we could do with a few of these people in this organisation'.

Analysis of the data, in the ministry as the whole, indicated that the following 10 groups of attributes, in their order of priority, were stressed as the most important qualities (See Table 4.3).

The respondents' perception of an effective manager is that of a multi-faceted individual who possesses a varied mix of abilities and personal characteristics. Evidently, it is expected that an effective senior manager will be capable of planning, organising and achieving policy framework, one who can develop the organisation as the whole. It was interesting to see that most managers referred to their superiors as those who can not organise and generally ignore policy and legal framework. The second and third qualities attributed to effective managers revealed even more disturbing yet not wholly unexpected characteristics of the type of manager that can be found in these organisations. The 'ability to delegate', 'supervise and lead' clearly questioned the abilities of the present top management.

On the whole, the qualities which were described portrayed a manager who is able to both carry out the task and deal with people at work. However, most emphasis seems to have been placed on the need to understand subordinates, and motivate and lead people at work. It was also noted that managers felt that they ought to be able to perform tasks with little or no supervision all. When they were specifically asked whether this is their expectation from their subordinates or was it that they felt that they were constantly being supervised, most expressed the former rather than the latter.

Despite the impression given that effective managers require qualities which are more people related, the terminology used to describe these qualities, such as planning, organising, scheduling, disciplining and the like are indicative of the functional image of the manager as described by early management theorists.

The impression given is that, it is not enough to be able to get the job done, simply because managerial positions also require the ability to work with people. The fact that most managers were critical of the way they were being managed or the way things are in their organisation is indicative of their frustration and dismay with the present system within the public sector.

Managerial skills (second parameter)

Senior managers and executives were asked to suggest between 3 and 5 managerial skills, in order of priority to them, which in their view were essential for ensuring increased effectiveness. The responses collected were weighted according to their corresponding order of priority. A total of 32 levels of skills and expertise were identified. The different descriptions of skills which were provided encompassed almost all aspects of management. These skills, depending on the priority assigned to them by the senior participants were then tabulated and categorised into five major skill categories for each organisation.

Further analysis showed that from amongst the numerous skills, knowledge and abilities which were reported to be essential for increased managerial effectiveness, the 10 most important ones were, by and large, referring to the people related and analytical categories and not the task related ones (see Table 4.4). Skills such as delegation, being a good planner, organising ability, good human relations and leadership skills were indicating that, as expected, senior managers are more in need of 'interpersonal' and 'analytical skills' rather than 'informational' and 'decisional' as has been described in the available literature. Three important issues have emerged from the data. These are;

- There seems to be a similarity between the characteristics attributed to an effective manager and the skills which are required to remain effective. This consistency in the responses given has important implications for the way managers perceive themselves and others, in particular their superiors.
- People related and analytical skills seems to be the most important skills required by managers for their effectiveness at work. While most skills tend to equip the managers to become more successful in their interaction with others, the self related skills seem to be needed in order to compensate for the lack of attention and supervision expected by them.
- Again the responses were partly expressing the managers expectation of others, in particular the leadership of the organisation and partly providing what they thought were the main ingredients for being effective. Data generated through interviews indicated that in most cases respondents felt that possession of these skills would 'hopefully' lead to more effectiveness at work but in reality they felt that the situation may never change. In many cases the list of skills provided seems to be projection rather than accurate self assessment.

The responses provided largely concur with the findings of previous studies of the senior managers in developed and developing countries. Senior managers become more and more aware of the need and necessity for possession of skills which enabled them to work with people, simply because an awareness is gained that one can not be effective unless he or

Table 4.4
Managerial skills required for increased effectiveness

Pri	Description	CSIR		EPA		GAEC		MEST		GRATIS		TCPD		TOTAL	
		F	V	F	V	F	V	F	V	F	V	F	V	TF	TV
1	Good planning skills	22	16.4	8	4	9	6.2	6	3.8	4	3.4	3	2.4	52	36.2
2	Effective communication	20	13.2	8	4	9	6.2	6	3.6	4	3.2	3	1.8	50	32
3	Good human relations skills	26	14.8	6	3.2	10	5.6	1	0.4	4	2.6	3	2	50	28.6
4	Organising ability	16	11.6	7	5.2	5	2.6	5	3.6	2	1.6	4	2.8	39	27.4
5	Supervisory skills	15	10			5	3	2	2	3	1.6	3	1.4	28	18
6	Delegation	9	4.6	6	2.8	2	1.2					4	2.8	21	11.4
7	Time management	3	3	3	1.4	1	0.4	3	1.2	3	1.8	2	2	15	9.8
8	Leadership skills	3	1.2	4	1.4	2	2	2	2	2	1	1	0.4	14	8
9	Analytical skills	5	3	1	0.8			3	2	3	1.4	1	0.2	13	7.4
10	Loyalty/dedication	6	3	5	2.4							1	0.2	12	5.6
10	Ability to motivate others	2	0.4	1	0.8	2	1.2	3	1.8	2	1.2	1	0.2	11	5.6
TOTAL		127	81.2	49	26	45	28.4	31	20.4	27	17.8	26	16.2	305	190

Pri: Priority   F: Frequency   V: Value

69

she can work with or through people, namely colleagues, peers and subordinates. It is probably not surprising to report that senior managers require as much if not more 'management development' than 'management training'.

Organisational criteria (third parameter)

Managers were asked what were the criteria for effectiveness in their organisations. As expected, in each organisation a list of factors was produced which was not exactly the same as those from the other organisations. Evidently, each organisation because of its cultural specifications deriving from the nature of the work, its history, size and the like, tended to support the basis for a particular way of working and standard with which effectiveness was measured.

From a list of 38 criteria used to determine effectiveness, the ten most widely used criteria throughout the ministry, ranged from 'meeting targets' (34.8) the most important to 'increased productivity' (8.2) the last in the list of priorities. Meeting targets usually referred to what was expected from the employees. In organisations such as EPA, Research Institutes (CSIR) and GAEC, periodically projects were discussed and targets were set. Most senior and executive managers expressed the opinion that the most important indicator to them of their effectiveness was that their staff were achieving targets. However, it became clear that targets were often 'set' for the subordinates, with little degree of involvement in the setting of those targets on the part of the employees concerned.

Criteria such as 'publications' may appear to be unusual as the second most important factor for determining effectiveness from an organisations point of view. The reason for this is largely due to the large number of research institutes and scientific research departments within the CSIR, EPA and GAEC. Basically, scientists who are also senior managers, because of the nature of their job, were expected to be able to publish the results of their research. In these organisations, it was evident that those who published enjoyed a rather higher degree of status amongst their colleagues, peers and in the organisation as the whole. Being able to publish and offer the results of the research to seminars and international conferences was seen as a basis for becoming known amongst the scientific community and maybe ultimately 'getting a job abroad' (See Table Five).

Other Criteria such as self discipline (17.8), achievement (15) and self motivation (12) as well as managing time (9.4) and punctuality and quality

Table 4.5
Organisations criteria for increased effectiveness

Prio	Description	CSIR		EPA		GAEC		MEST		GRATIS		TCPD		TOTAL	
		F	V	F	V	F	V	F	V	F	V	F	V	F	V
1	Meeting targets	17	10.4	10	8.6	4	1.6	11	9	3	2.4	3	2.8	48	34.8
2	Publications	14	13.2	1	0.4	9	7.8							24	21.4
3	Self discipline	8	6.8	1	1	8	4.8	3	2.4			3	2.8	23	17.8
4	Good achievement	9	8.2	2	1.6	2	1.4	2	1.8	4	2			19	15
5	Self motivation	4	2			4	2.4	4	2.4	6	4.6	1	0.6	19	12
6	Planning abilities	3	3	1	1	2	1.6	4	1.4	3	2	2	1.4	15	10.4
7	Time management	1	0.2	2	1.8	3	2	4	3.4	3	2			13	9.4
8	Good and punctual report writing	7	6.2	3	1.6	2	1.2			1	0.2			13	9.2
9	Well motivated staff	6	3.2	1	0.6	1	1			3	2.4	1	1	12	8.2
9	Training	2	0.8	2	1.4	3	2.4	1	0.8	3	2.8			11	8.2
9	Increased productivity			1	1	4	3	3	2	2	1.2	1	1	11	8.2
Total		71	54	24	19	42	29.2	32	23.2	28	19.6	11	9.6	208	154.6

Prio: Priority   F: Frequency   V: Value

71

in terms of report writing were seen as important criteria and were indicative of the expectations from top managers of their subordinates. Regardless of the difficulties, demands and constraints with which managers were faced, the organisation expectation was an ability to 'get on with it' and 'get the job done'. Most work which was carried out in these departments took the form of projects and programmes, therefore the ability to prepare the research report and providing it in time were seen as being of the utmost importance. Reports and other written documents were seen as the means of verifying the achievement of targets. Managers are expected to plan, self motivate and achieve targets. These were expectations very similar to the characteristic used by the managers to describe an effective manager. It could be argued that all managers were aware of what was expected from them and that their views and opinions concerning managerial effectiveness has been partly, or even to a large extent in some cases, formed by the dominant value system of the organisation.

As far as the top management is concerned, as shown in the literature, there is a tendency on the part of the senior managers and executives to identify with the core values of the organisation and what was observed in the Ministry confirmed the stated belief.

Motivation (fourth parameter)

As suggested earlier, in order to understand effectiveness attention has to be paid to all parameters of the phenomenon, in particular the motive behind the actions undertaken by managers. The analysis of the quantitative data revealed, not surprisingly, that the motivators were those factors which were not all ready present at work.

The fact that remuneration (46.4), was seen as the most important motivator was due to the inadequate presence of 'Hygiene Factors' in the Ministry as a whole. By far remuneration, salary and economic incentives seems to constitute the root of ineffectiveness at work. The 'budgetary system', as was described by the respondents and senior executives was seen as the main 'culprit'. All managers reported that, their effectiveness is adversely affected by the low level of remuneration since they had to 'think about' how to compensate for the lack of it, and/or spend time outside of the organisation, often on 'projects of some sort to feed their family'.

Top management showed deep dissatisfaction with the 'worsening situation'. 'How can we (senior managers) motivate our employees? We have no control over it at all'. It was therefore understood that employees from time to time need to 'earn some money', therefore, their absence from the organisation was not complained about seriously.

On average, it was reported that the monthly salary of a manager would only 'take care of a third of their monthly expenses'. Almost all managers supplemented their monthly remuneration with some sort of second earning, which in many cases took them away from their work place and even periodically their country.

The most interesting point however, is one which goes beyond 'remuneration' or in this case the lack of it. Motivators, such as 'recognition from superiors' (25.4), 'job satisfaction' (24.8) and 'training and self development' (21.6) were reported as the main motivating factor towards effectiveness. These and the other remaining factors such as 'promotion' and 'good team work' seem to be symptomatic of the following issues (see Table 4.6).

- The reward system within the public sector acts as a demotivator and adversely affects their effectiveness at work.
- Managers feel that they do not receive recognition for work well done.
- The managerial style adopted by the top management is responsible for this.
- Job satisfaction, especially amongst scientists seems to be the most important motivator for remaining in their posts.
- Achievement of targets set also added to a sense of job satisfaction and thus acted as a motivator in their work. Those managers who were responsible for challenging work found the challenge to be motivating and the main reason for their effectiveness at work.
- Provision of resources and team work were suggested to work as motivators.

It was interesting to note that what was expressed as the motivators were indeed the problem areas and the main sources of discontent and frustration on the part of the senior managers. Devaluation of the currency, inflation, a substantial decline in the purchasing power of the managers together with organisational structural reform adds to the worsening situation as far as the motivation for effectiveness is concerned.

Demands and constraints (fifth parameter)

It is difficult if not impossible to deal with the issue of effectiveness at work without considering the 'constraints and demands' with which managers are faced. Realistically, managers are not free floating agents, allowed to do

Table 4.6
Main factors which motivate towards increased effectiveness

Priority	Description	CSIR F	CSIR V	EPA F	EPA V	GAEC F	GAEC V	MEST F	MEST V	GRATIS F	GRATIS V	TCPD F	TCPD V	TOTAL F	TOTAL V
1	Remuneration	34	25	3	2	5	3.4	13	11	6	4.4	1	0.6	62	46.4
2	Recognition from superiors	19	13.6	6	4.2	4	2.8	2	1	2	2	3	1.8	36	25.4
3	Job satisfaction	14	10	5	4.4	1	1	4	2.6	2	2	5	4.8	31	24.8
4	Training/self development	11	6.8	3	1	11	7.6	7	4.2	3	1	2	1	37	21.6
5	Provision of resources	11	7	5	2.8	2	1.8	5	2.4	2	1.2	1	0.6	26	15.8
6	Promotion	15	11					2	1.6	2	2			19	14.6
7	Good teamwork/co-operation			2	1.2	3	1	6	4.6	8	5.8	1	0.6	20	13.2
8	Contribution to development of institute/nation	11	6.4	1	0.6	2	1.2			1	0.8	4	1.6	19	10.6
9	Reward for good/hard work	3	0.6	4	2.8	1	0.6	3	2	3	2	2	1	16	9
9	Achieving set goals/targets	4	4	1	0.4	2	0.6	2	0.8	1	0.4	3	2.8	13	9
Total		122	84.4	30	19.4	31	20	44	30.2	30	21.6	22	14.8	279	190.4

F: Frequency   V: Value

what they desire. In almost all organisations, there are inhibiting forces which slow down the progress and need to be managed, removed or negotiated. In line with an open system approach towards understanding managers, their works and effectiveness, the managers were asked to report the obstacles, difficulties, demands and constraints at work. Analysis of the data provided a list of 40 factors which were reported as having an adverse affect on the effectiveness of the managers, though managers in each organisation naturally experienced different sets of difficulties.

'Inappropriate resources', 'shortage of appropriate staff' and 'lack of/or inappropriate training' As shown in a summary (see Table 4.7), despite the differences between the organisations and the difference between the degree of emphasis placed on the identified factor, a cluster of factors tended to be shared amongst the organisations.

The most important demands and constraints were 'Inappropriate Resources' (48.2). This however, did not solely cover the often talked about resources such as money, computers and the state of the art equipment, rather, managers felt that inappropriate human resources made their work and life difficult. The issue of 'shortage of appropriate staff', although fourth (16.6) in the list is clearly related to the issue of inappropriate resources.

In some organisations such as EPA, the inadequacy of the human resources and the inappropriate 'staff' seem to contribute to the apparent ineffectiveness. In other organisations, especially the more technical and scientific ones the absence of trained staff, especially in the field of management is noticeable. Therefore, the general lack of resources in addition to inappropriate resources created a 'headache' for both middle and senior management.

In organisations such as CSIR, the sheer number of managers and technicians who required training both in the technical as well as managerial fields posed a constraint for the Human Resource Unit. The slow and painful way in which funding agencies responded towards the need for more appropriate resources has of course added to the already established list of difficulties and constraints present at work.

Whilst, the 'lack of or inappropriate training was regarded as relatively less acute, it is easy to see the relevance of this important factor, or indeed the lack of it, for the increased effectiveness of the managers in the organisation. All these and other difficulties have been contributed to by a 'lack of funding'. This however, is not unique to the Ministry or indeed to Ghana. Throughout the developing world, a lack of funds is being blamed for the lack effectiveness which is being observed.

Table 4.7
Demands and constraints which affect effectiveness

Price	Description	CSIR F	CSIR V	EPA F	EPA V	GAEC F	GAEC V	MEST F	MEST V	GRATIS F	GRATIS V	TCPD F	TCPD V	Total F	Total V
1	Inappropriate resources	22	17.6	6	5	13	10	10	6.4	7	4.8	7	4.4	65	48.2
2	Poor remuneration	10	7.6	5	3.6	9	5.8	5	4	5	4.2	2	2	36	27.2
3	Lack of funding	17	12.2	1	0.6	9	8.4			1	1			28	22.2
4	Shortage of appropriate staff	13	8.6	3	1.8	2	1.6	3	3			3	1.6	24	16.6
5	Lack of motivation	8	5	2	1	7	4.6	6	3.8	3	2			26	16.4
6	Inadequate data/information flow	8	3.6	3	2.2	6	3.6	2	1.2	1	0.6			20	11.2
7	Lack of transport	5	2.2	1	0.8	6	3.4			1	0.2	4	3.2	17	9.8
7	Unrealistic targets	3	3	4	3.2			4	2.6	1	0.2	1	0.8	13	9.8
9	Lack of teamwork	3	1.2	2	1.4	2	0.4	3	1.8	3	1.8	3	2.4	16	9
10	Inappropriate training	3	1.8	1	0.2	3	2.4	2	1.6	5	2.8	1	0.2	15	9
Total		92	62.8	28	19.8	57	40.2	35	24.4	27	17.6	21	14.6	260	179.4

F: Frequency   V: Value

'Poor remuneration', 'lack of motivation', 'lack of teamwork' It is not surprising to see the 'poor remuneration' (48.2) as the second most important constraint with which managers are faced. Earlier it was explained, that the present 'budgetary system' or reward scheme in the public sector, whether in Asia or Eastern Europe is commonly perceived as problematic. Salaries are generally low and are not 'calibrated' to the needs of the staff.

It is almost expected that managers in almost all organisations should report a 'lack of motivation' (16.4) as another major culprit. While, the lack of motivation clearly posed questions related to 'maintenance' factors, in particular 'salary and reward', it is also related the effectiveness of other organisational and managerial matters.

In a sense, a 'lack of teamwork' mentioned by almost all managers including the very top executives, is an indicator that 'things are not well'. As one aptly put it, 'there are other issues besides money which count as incentives...a word of thanks would do....but only a few of us who have understanding superiors can expect some recognition and concern'.

The managerial attitudes and approaches seem to see functions such as organising and co-ordinating as a matter of distribution and not as the 'delegation' of tasks amongst staff. However, it needs to be said that the presence of motivators such as 'responsibility', 'recognition' and the like can not replace the basic hygiene factors such as adequate remuneration. The above however, becomes meaningless unless they are seen within the context of the deteriorating state of the economy, raging inflation and an uncontrolled pricing policy. The second most important problem in relation to the lack of remuneration is the issue of housing. It is seen as almost impossible for the managers to possess their own accommodation. The expensive and unaffordable housing in the market has forced managers, especially those with large families and extended family responsibilities, to move out of the capital.

It is also important to recognise that in Ghana, like many other developing countries, possession of owned accommodation is seen socially as an indication of effectiveness at work and success as a whole. Most managers have to relay on 'projects' to supplement their salary and seek opportunities outside working hours, such as training, research, consultancy and even a second job in order to 'buy a plot' and 'gradually build on it'.

Working abroad and over and above the regular hours has repercussions for the incumbent and more importantly for the effectiveness of the organisation as the whole. It is not unusual to see junior and middle managers using the work as a 'resting place for recuperation'. The added stress and a lack of attention to the physical and psychological well being results in frequent illnesses and a further loss of productivity and effectiveness.

'Lack of transport', 'unrealistic targets, 'inadequate data and information'
A lack of transport' at the individual level, coupled with a lack of 'proper, adequate and reliable' public transport' is unanimously regarded as a major constraint. Almost all organisations involved in the study reported the undesirable effect of this issue on their own and others effectiveness. It was noted that, the majority of the senior managers do possess personal transport or have the use of an organisation or 'project' vehicle.

The prevalence of the 'role' culture within the public sector means that managers are almost powerless without their subordinates. This is largely due to the presence of the commonly adhered to belief that 'managers' should not do what is not their job'. The late arrival of the already demotivated administrative staff who have had to spend three and half hours travelling before they reach work, undoubtedly has an adverse effect on the effectiveness of their superiors. As one top executive explained, 'all you need is one rain fall and you lose more that 50 percent of your staff. Worse than that even are those who make it to work and then after recovering need to leave early to get home before it is too late: a vicious circle'.

It was discovered that senior managers are now provided with incentives such as interest free loans, transport maintenance expenses and other means to overcome the transport difficulties. This has reduced the problem of transport at least amongst the senior staff. Ironically however, senior staff who may benefit from these incentives already have access to 'project or organisation vehicles'. Some organisations such as EPA have adopted a policy of providing transport for their staff, at least on main routes, which has proved successful.

A lack of transport, at the organisational level is a much greater concern. Almost all vehicles available to public sector organisations have been procured through a grant, a loan or are leftover from a project or programme. However, the most startling discovery relates to the inappropriate distribution of resources amongst the organisations concerned. Some organisations seem to possess many vehicles, whilst others such as GAEC have none. Therefore, it is not surprising to hear staff and managers speak of 'such an unfair and thoughtless distribution of resources' as a source of discontent and demotivation at work.

In at least one organisation, the top management of the organisation were reported to have under their control between three and five 'project' vehicles, including 'four wheeled drive', whilst at the same time three teams of scientists who work for GAEC have to share one set of equipment and use public transport to visit hospitals in order to monitor the X-Ray equipment.

It may seem unrelated but a 'lack of data and information flow' (11.2) in some ways has been the cause of the presence of these constraints. Top management often are not aware of the extent of resources available in the organisation as the whole. Such inadequacies and shortcomings lead to high expectations and unreasonable targets. At the individual level, the flow of information is extremely slow. In most cases the secrecy and use of information as a source of power is an indication of classical management philosophy at work which leads to frustration and the wastage of valuable time.

The constraints and demands, whether those already identified and briefly discussed or those which are never mentioned, such as attending funeral proceedings on Wednesdays and Fridays can not all be mention here, but there are many other interrelated demands. Such clusters of demands at an individual, organisational and a wider social level leave the managers with very little chance to determine their own level of effectiveness.

Choices and opportunities for effectiveness (sixth parameter)

Stewarts (1982, 1991) suggests that choices open to managers in order to be effective at work are primarily determined by the degree of demand placed on them and the constraints in their job. A total of 35 factors related to the choices available have been identified, from which the 10 most important ones are listed below (see Table 4.8). The responses of the senior managers point to solutions and ways of dealing with the present situation in order to become more effective. As one explained, 'this is not the ultimate solution by any means but what we can do in these circumstances is limited to training and improving the working condition as much as possible'.

Almost all departments and organisations considered training as one of the most important factors for increased effectiveness (70: 63.4 FxV). This was particularly evident in organisations such as CSIR, EPA and GAEC where the main proportion of the staff were scientists. They generally believed that training would increase their effectiveness, though most qualified this by adding that, 'but not by Ghanaian Institutions'. It was interesting to see that most senior managers showed very little confidence in the effectiveness of the training which is provided locally, in particular the Centre for Management Development (CMD) and the Ghana Institute for Public Administration (GIMPA). It was widely believed that the course

Table 4.8
Choices and opportunities

No.	Choices and Opportunities Description	CSIR F x V	EPA F x V	GAEC F x V	MEST F x V	GRATIS F x V	TCPD F x V	Total
1	Training (Self)	29= 27..2	5 = 4	13=11.4	3 = 3.4	12=11.4	8 = 7	70=63.4
2	On-the -job training, part-time study	13 = 9	2 = 1.8	1 = 0.2	9 = 5.4	2 = 2	6 = 4	33=22.4
3	Necessary resources/equipment	12 = 7.2	4 = 3.6	5 = 4.4	3 = 1.6	2 = 0.8		26=17.6
4	Team work/ co-operation	5 = 2.6	4 = 2.4		2 = 1	4 = 1.6	3 = 1.4	18 = 9
5	Better remuneration	1 = 0.2	1 = 0.8	1 = 0.4	3 = 2	5 = 3		11 = 6.4
6	Funding	5 = 3.8		2 = 1.8		1 = 0.6	1 = 0.8	9 = 7
7	More appropriate staff	6 = 4	2 = 1.4	1 = 0.6				9 = 6
8	Visit other units/establishments	3 = 2.4	1 = 1	1 = 0.2	1 = 0.2	2 = 1.6	1 =0.6	9 = 6
9	Effective/regular communication	3 = 2.4	1 = 0.4	1 = 0.4	1 = 0.8	3 = 1.6		9 = 5.6
10	Relevant literature/library	4 = 2.2	1 = 0.8	2 = 1.6			1 = 0.4	8 = 5
	Total	81 = 61	21=16.2	27 = 21	22=14.4	31= 22.6	20=14.2	210=148.4

F = Frequency   V= Value

(content and structure) and the trainers were not able to meet the needs and demands of the senior managers. Examples provided by all organisations illustrated this point.

Apparently, one of the conditions of the service is to take a three month training course at GIMPA prior to commencement of duties in the public sector and there is very little evidence as to whether GIMPA has the institutional capacity to either provide 'Public Sector Management' training or be able to accommodate all such demands. To make the matters worse, theoretically, all officers are expected to attend refresher courses at GIMPA after being in service for a while.

There was some damning evidence as to the ineffectiveness of the present training facilities and opportunities. As one explained, 'I took a course at GIMPA 11 years ago, I have kept the training material and even the time table. Last year, my wife who is also a public sector employee took a training course at GIMPA, but not the same one, or at least the title was different (trying not to laugh but emphasising the point). Yes, you guessed it. The same course, same material has been taught under a different name to different group of people'.

The consensus was that, courses organised with foreign consultants seem to be more 'modern' and 'useful'. As for the rest, 'Well, they can be a waste of time, that is certainly for senior staff. Though for the senior ones it means a free meal and a chance of getting away from here (pointing to the offices)'.

Most senior managers sought training abroad as one of the possibilities rather than opportunities open to them to become more effective. There seems to be an implicit order and schedule for staff to take 'foreign visits'. 'May be towards the end of '98 it is my turn to go to Canada'. These training courses served as motivation. One which was expected as a right rather than based on proper and systematic training need analysis.

The absence of an appropriate appraisal system, meant that opportunities were generally shared and often instead of training, senior staff were sent away on Masters' and even PhD programmes abroad.

The more realistic view was that, in the absence of external opportunities for training, more internal and on-the-job training should be arranged. It was felt that a combination of part-time study and on-the-job training (33: 63.4 FxV) may provide better value, a point which was not acceptable by all.

There were two other major factors which were regarded as opportunities for improving effectiveness: one was referred to as resources, better working conditions and equipment and the other was referred to as the organisational and managerial processes. Most scientists, especially those at the Ghana Atomic Energy Commission, felt that 'their effectiveness could be almost double, if they had more resources'. The point which was frequently mentioned was that, a more equitable distribution of resources could improve the work of the Ministry and the effectiveness of its staff.

Organisational and leadership processes such as, communication, delegation, incentives, team management and the like, were mentioned as solutions rather than opportunity. 'If only we could...' suffixed most such suggestions. Wherever, there was a discussion concerning effectiveness, training and availability of opportunities, it was repeatedly mentioned that: 'Those who REALLY need the training for increased effectiveness are the very top management of the Ministry and the organisation. They are the policy makers...' a point which some top management agreed with and some resented intensely.

The opportunities were in a sense related to demands and constraints. It appears that the presence of the constraints and demands were forcing senior managers to think of a 'way out'. Sadly, in most cases and only in interview situations, senior managers revealed that, training, part-time study and full-time secondment, visits abroad including attending seminars, conferences and other scientific venues were seen as ultimately enabling the senior managers to move up, move away or one day be able to work for international agencies.

It was clear that the presence of 'role-culture' and lack of motivation 'has forced' some managers 'to think of themselves'. Therefore, the exploration of choices perceived as being available to them, indirectly showed the presence of a strong belief in what could only be regarded as the main reason for 'person-cultures' in the Ministry.

Nature of inter-organisational relationships (seventh parameter)

Implicit and explicit remarks were frequently made where the overall subject of managerial effectiveness was being discussed. All respondents saw their effectiveness as being affected, if not determined by the overall effectiveness of the organisation. It was evident that the respondents were aware that there is a two way relationship between their effectiveness and the organisation that was determined partly by their organisation's relationship with other organisations and agencies, both nationally and internationally.

At national level The Ministry, the co-ordinating Headquarters, seems to be the focus of attention for senior managers from other agencies. It was generally believed that for a variety of reasons, the Ministry tends to influence the potential for effectiveness of the other departments. In other words, there was a wide spread belief that the inadequacies of the Ministry become stumbling blocks for the agencies and related organisations. Interestingly, amongst the agencies and departments, there seemed to be little problem in terms of identification of the level of the desired action, but it was the procedure that once the Ministry became involved, delays and other related problems tended to occurred. Following are the main reasons for the inadequate and ineffective inter-organisation relationship between the Ministry and the other agencies.

History the Ministry is relatively new and in fact, is only a few years old. The policies, procedures and regulations are either absent or are in the process of being prepared. The related agencies have already been established with a history and accumulated organisational knowledge. This creates tension between the members of the agency and the Ministry when they feel that they are being controlled by an organisation which is new and as some put it, its staff 'don't know what they are doing'. It was quite apparent that the ministry can not co-ordinate its activities and may be does not wish to do so. What, however was clear was that, the Ministry seeks to control other agencies whether or not that control is needed. This had serious implications in so far as trust and the effectiveness of the agencies and their managers were concerned.

Work culture The Ministry by its very nature was operating on a bureaucratic basis, with role culture as a dominant influence on the behaviour of its staff. Whereas the other organisations, apart from the DAPIT, were mainly task-related and resourced with scientists whose main preoccupation was 'getting the job done and finding rules or regulations for not delaying it or stopping it from happening at all'.

Shortage of resources The Ministry is operating with less than half the resources it was originally envisaged it would have in order to meet its guiding, co-ordination and monitoring functions. The Directorate of the Ministry were over worked and under staffed and the morale was decisively low. The irony of it became evident when the researcher discovered that the recruitment and selection at the Ministry is not carried out independently. The Ministry had no control over who should work for their department and how long they may remain with the Ministry. The resources which are available to them have been taken, or brought but certainly not recruited, from other organisations and ministries. So, it was not surprising to see that even when projects were completed on time, they still had to wait to receive the approval of the Ministry, which due to the shortage of staff caused further delays and despair for the senior managers of both camps.

Lack of training, funds and control Evidently, the Ministry could not have access to international funds in the same way as other the agencies, such as the EPA, especially in so far as training and development were concerned. However, from time to time, members at the Ministry managed to secure funds and training abroad and thus left the ministry, which was already short of staff, for a long period of time. What often occurred, because the Ministry has no control over nor the policy concerning the 'retaining' of its staff, when an individual moved away, was either promoted or found a better place to work, their position was filled with inexperienced staff who required training and thus could not meet the requirements of the agencies. Hence, less effectiveness all around.

The best example of the lack of a coherent human resource policy (not on paper but in operation) and clearly agreed upon objectives is the case of the Assistant Director, Human Resource Directorate;

> During the 15 months of the study, I have noticed that the Assistant Director, with whom I worked, took part in a number of training courses, one which was for at least three months duration, in the field of human resource development. However, shortly after my last visit to the field she was gone. Promoted, I was told. The new individual in charge requires training.

Meetings and more meetings The culture of the Ministry was dominated, as it was expected, by meetings. Firstly, senior managers and executives in the Ministry felt that whenever there was an opportunity and the Ministry and its varied activities needed to be represented it was they who had to attend a protocol or meeting and not their colleagues in the agencies. Second, there seemed to be a need to attend meetings which did not result in actions, or if they did, there were not adequate resources to implement the decisions. Third and the most important one was 'being on call by the Minister', this meant 'dropping anything and going to attend a meeting'.

Visitors, consultants, meetings in other ministries, radio and television interviews took most of the valuable time of the top executives of the agencies and the staff at the Ministry. As a result, there seemed to be a consensus amongst the senior managers involved in the survey that despite the good intentions of the Ministry, their interrelationship can be best described as problematic and at worst as disastrous. Most managers felt that the central ministry is becoming a hindrance to their effectiveness.

The government policy of restricted recruitment and the budgetary system of rewards and promotion meant that often agencies and the Ministry found themselves at the mercy of the 'Government' and its policies. Most managers questioned the logic of the necessity for the presence of a ministry with monitoring, co-ordination and leadership functions which it could not sufficiently perform.

At international level During the last few years there has been a shift of policy on the part of the aid and international funding agencies, who have diverted funds to projects and/or directly to agencies. Both the World Bank and DFID have provide funds and loans to different agencies of the Ministry. For example, EPA and CSIR. It believed that this direct action will result in greater benefit and that in this way the bureaucratic line ministries can be circumvented. The consequences of this policy are as follows:

External agencies such the World Bank do affect the capability of the agencies and their senior managers' effectiveness. A comparison between the Ghana Atomic Energy Commission and EPA or CSIR illustrates the above point. A lack resources, training and funds for projects in the Ministry and GAEC are largely due to the intervention of the outside agencies.

The Ministry has effectively no control over the funding and the relationship between the agencies and the funding organisation. This has led to uneven distribution of the resources throughout the Ministry.

Although the funding agencies policy of the injection of funds directly to the agencies seems to work and there appears to be a logic for it, since the Ministry, for the reasons stated above, seeks to keep constant control, the overall degree of the effectiveness expected may not be realised.

Each funding agency seems to have their own policy and agenda as to where the ground for development lies. Thus, their intervention is based on an implicit agenda which may not make sense to the senior managers in the field. In one agency it was evident that the problem was not the funds available but how 'to get rid of it (spending) according to the plan'.

The concentration of funds and opportunity into one or two agencies has resulted in low morale and feelings of envy and jealousy amongst the others. Senior managers at the agencies who have benefited from this inter-organisation relationship with international agencies felt that such a relationship has a direct effect on their own and their organisations effectiveness.

The relationship between, research stations, agencies, the NGOs, universities and other scientific organisations seems to contribute to the effectiveness of the individual managers and the effectiveness of the organisation as the whole.

Dominant managerial philosophy (eighth parameter)

It has been established that the dominant managerial philosophy in an organisation does influence the operations which are carried out in it and the roles performed, and generally it influences the flow of information and the informal and structured relationships amongst the people in the organisation. The leadership of the organisation provides the standard for the patterns of behaviour and therefore have proven to be a decisive factor in determining the effectiveness of the managers in the organisation.

The data, whether in qualitative or quantitative form, has been tainted by the presence of this influence of the managerial philosophy and style of the top executives of the Ministry and its related agencies.

The traditional preference for 'politically correct administration' as opposed to management has resulted in many instances in the ineffectiveness of the individual managers and the organisations as the whole. However, this ought to be seen in context in that, all executives in charge of the agencies, departments and the Directorates of the Ministry have been appointed as opposed to being specifically recruited or selected.

The appointments are made by the higher organisation, often from the Presidential Quarters. The qualifications for such an appointment are not necessarily the managerial ability of the individual concerned, but their compatibility with the requirements of the post, including their political orientation, as envisaged by the higher authority. In the case of the Ministry of the Environment, Science and Technology there seems to be no consistency in the nature of the appointments. Comments have been made about the fact that none of the senior managers at the level of strategic apex have experienced formal management training and therefore, the traditional style of manager seems to prevail.

In all organisations, there seems to be a tendency on the part of management for centralisation, top down management, over emphasis on control and managerial decision making. In most cases it was observed that executives did not delegate and therefore in their absence major decisions could not be made, there were some exceptions to this general rule amongst the executives. Distrust between the subordinate and the superior appeared to be the norm. Favouritism and victimisation were reported be the norm rather than the exceptions.

The degree to which the executives and senior managers adhered to traditional management, or to correct administration principles varied from one organisation to another. However, apart from a few top senior managers and executives who did feel that there is a need for change of attitude and policy, the others seemed to remain insistent that being at the top justifies the lack of need for management training and the adoption of the participatory approaches to their management of task and people at work.

Conclusion

Managerial effectiveness is a complex multi-facet organisational phenomenon. The 'awareness' shown and the required abilities and competencies alone can not sufficiently explain the nature of managerial effectiveness. As shown here, there is also a need for consideration of other parameters such as individual and organisational criteria, the motivation and the constraints and demands which determine the choices of behaviours and degree of effectiveness in a particular context.

It is evident that there is a need and necessity as well as scope and potential, for carrying out studies of this nature within the public sector in DCs and DEs. It is now recognised by lateral and mutli-lateral aid and funding agencies that success of the development project in particular and development as a process is largely determined by the effectiveness and development of the Human Resources, of which executives and senior manager play a significant part. In DC's where the public sector is held almost solely responsible for the realisation of development and progress, it is vital that the management of these organisations, especially the effectiveness of its senior members is made the focus of any serious analysis or intervention.

The methodology employed has played a major role in the realisation of the aim of the study. The exploration of senior managers views, adopting participatory methods, the greater involvement of the respondents, the use of open and semi-interviews and sharing the data and results at all stages have guaranteed access to rich and qualitative as well as quantitative data.

The most pertinent conclusion reached relates to the presence of the above parameters and identification of the behavioural and causal influences as their constituent components. These factors point to the significance of the role of the senior managers as individuals, the organisational context and dominant managerial philosophy in operation as well as the external socio-economic, cultural and political influences.

Of the myriad of factors identified the most influential one is undoubtedly the prevailing organisational and managerial attitude and practices. The results of this pilot study, in part, point to the outdated organisation structure and culture and the need for improving leadership styles, delegation and human relations at the workplace.

The five parameters of effectiveness within public sector organisations also point to a mirror image of the characteristics of each dimension. That is to suggest, what forms the motivation for greater effectiveness is also indicative of what the constraints and demands are which control, inhabit or completely paralyse the individual concerned. The perception of the individual managers of their own and their colleagues effectiveness is also related to the skills and abilities attributed to the effective manager. And, most important of all, the organisations expectation of its managers is reflected in the nature of the criteria for effectiveness which is held by the organisation.

Inadequate 'hygiene' factors at work, namely the salaries and inappropriate working environment are difficult to address simply because their solution rests outside the organisation and within the sphere of the authority and power of the policy makers and public sector governing body. As for the absence of 'motivators', it is the bureaucratic and traditional managerial approach in operation, with emphasises on the 'task' at the expense of 'people', which is largely to be blamed.

Changes of attitudes and values are hard to achieve since it requires much planned intervention, long term investment and commitment on the part of the policy makers and executives and senior managers involved. Therefore, it is almost impossible, if not naive and simplistic, to envisage reform and restructuring the public sector in Ghana with the aim to increase effectiveness unless attention is paid to the complex myriad of influences and causes which form the very parameters of this organisational phenomenon.

Note

1. The Department of International Development (DFID) is the British Government Department which supports programmes and projects to promote international development. It provides funding for economic and social research to inform development policy and practice. DFID funds supported this pilot study and the preparation of the summary of findings. DFID distributes the report to bring the research to the attention of policy makers and practitioners. However, the views and opinions expressed in the documents do not reflect DFID's official policies or practices, but are those of the author alone.

Reference

Ackroyd, S. and Hughes, J. (1982), *Data Collection in Context*, (2nd edition), Longman, New York.

Analoui, F. (1990), 'An Investigation into Management Development training Needs of Senior Officials in Zimbabwe', Research Monograph, No.2, Development and project Planning Centre, University of Bradford.

Analoui, F. (1995), 'Management Skills and Senior Management Effectiveness', *International Journal of Public Sector Management*, Vol. 8, No. 3, pp.52-68.

Analoui, F. (1997), *Senior Managers and their Increased Effectiveness*, Avebury, Aldershot.

Blunt, P. (1990), 'Strategies for enhancing Organisational Effectiveness in the Third World', *Public Administration and Development* Vol. 10, No. 2, pp.299-313.

Blunt, P. (1992), *'Managing Organisations in Africa'*, Walter de Gruyter and Company, Sweden.

Brodie, M. And Bennett, R. (1979), (eds), *Managerial Effectiveness*, Thames Valley Regional Management Centre, Thorne and Stace Ltd., Sussex.

Burrell, G. and Morgan, G. (1979), *Sociological Paradigms and Organisational Analysis*, Arena Publishing Company, England.

Charsley, W.F. (1986), 'Effective Management - So You Think You Have Got it Right?' *British Journal of Administrative Management*, Vol. 1, November, pp.11-12.

Copeman, G. (1971), *The Chief Executives and Business Growth*, Leviathan House, London.

Drucker, P. F. (1988), *The Effective Executive*, William Heinemann, Paperback Edition.

Dunnette, M. D. (1971), 'Assessing managerial performance', *Proceeding of a one-day seminar*, Independent Assessment and Research Centre, August 1970, London, pp.38-53.

Gummesson, E. (1991) *Qualitative Methods in Management Research*, Sage, London.

Jones, M. L. (1988), 'Management Development: An African Perspective', *Management Education and Development*, Vol. 17, No. 3, pp.202-216.

Kakabadse, A. P. (1983) *The Politics of Management*, Gower; Nichols Publishing Co., New York.

Kakabadse, A. Ludlow, R. and Vinnicombe, S. (1987), *Working In Organisations*, Published in Penguin Books.

Kiggundo, M. (1989), *Managing Organisation in Developing Countries*, Kumarian Press Inc., Texas, USA.

Kirchoff, B. A. (1977), 'Organisational Effectiveness and Policy' *Research, Academy of Management Review*, July, Vol. 2, No. 3., pp.347-355.

Kotter, J.P. (1982), 'General Managers are not Generalists', *Organisational Dynamics*, Vol. 10, No.4, Spring, pp.5-19.

Labbaf, H. and Analoui, F. (1996), 'Management Development and Managerial Effectiveness: The Case of Senior Managers in the Steel Industry in Iran', *Discussion Paper*, No. 63, (December) Development and Project Planning Centre, University of Bradford.

Langford, V. (1979), 'Managerial Effectiveness: A review of Literature', in Brodie, M and Bennett, R., *Perspectives of Managerial Effectiveness*, (ED), Thames Valley Regional Centre.

McCall, M.W. Jr and Lombardo, M.M. (1983), 'What Makes a Top Executive?' *Psychology Today*, February.

Mangham, I. (1979), *The Politics of Organisation Change*, Associated Business Press.

Margerison, C. J. And Kakabadse, A. P. (1984), How American Chief Executives Succeed: Implication for Developing High potential Employees, An American Management association Survey Report.

Margerison, C. J. (1984), 'Chief Executives' Perception of Managerial Success Factors', *The Journal of Management Development*, Vol. 3, No. 4, pp.47-60.

Mintzberg, H. (1973), *The Nature of Managerial Work*, Harper and Row, New York

Morse, J. J. and Wager, F. R. (1978), 'Measuring the Process of Managerial Effectiveness', *Management Decision*, Vol. 21, No. 1, pp.23-35.

Morse, J.J. and Wagner, F.R.(1978), 'Measuring the Process of Managerial Effectiveness', *Management Decision*, Volume 21, No.1, pp.23-35.

Mullins, L. J. (1993) *Management and Organisational Behaviour*, Pitman 3rd Edition.

Ravetz, J. R. (1971), *Scientific Knowledge and It's Social Problems*, Oxford University press.

Reddin, W. J. (1974), 'Managerial Effectiveness in the 1980s', *Management by Objectives*, Vol. 3, No. 3, pp. 6-12.

Silverman, D. (1970), *The Theory of Organisations*, Heinemann, London.

Stewart, R. (1982), *Choices for the Manager*, McGraw-Hill.

Stewart, R. (1991), *Managing Today and Tomorrow*, Macmillan.

Willcocks, S. G. (1992), 'Managerial Effectiveness and The Public Sector', *International Journal of Public Sector Management*, Vol. 5, No. 5, pp.4-10.

World Bank (1991), *World Development Report*, Oxford University Press.

World Bank (1994), *Trend in Developing Countries*, A World Bank Book, Washington, D.C. USA.

5 Social implications of compensatory discrimination in public services: the case for scheduled castes in Bihar (India)

Dr Rajalaxmi Rath

Introduction

Castes are the building blocks of the Hindu social system. The traditional society in India is based on a hierarchy of castes each with an ascribed occupation. The caste-system is elaborate, rigid and relatively immobile. This social order has continued for over three millennia primarily due to the sanction of religion behind it. In the past some of the castes performing menial works were considered 'polluting' by touch. These so-called 'untouchables' were not originally conceived as part of the socio-religious order, but were created subsequently as castes outside the Chaturvarna system of the Hindu society. Due to the stigma of pollution attached to their occupation, they were compelled to live a life of social ostracization and economic deprivation. Consequently they suffered from social disabilities due to long years of exploitation, deprivation and social segregation.

The process of industrialization and urbanisation had practically little impact on the rigid social system in the country. The situation hardly changed even during the British rule in spite of some half-hearted efforts by the Government as well as voluntary and reformist movements. Inspired by the ideals of Mahatma Gandhi and other reformers, the leaders of the independence movement in India held out hopes of a brighter future for these Dalits (depressed classes). After the achievement of Independence in 1947 the makers of the Indian Constitution strove to fulfill the pledge of building a new social order based on the principles of liberty, equality and fraternity. While considering the claims and counterclaims of the various backward communities and ethnic and religious minorities in India there was universal and unreserved acceptance of the need of providing special and protective safeguards in favour of the most disadvantaged communities in India as atonement for the sins inflicted upon them in the past by the society.

The preferential treatment was considered necessary to bring the depressed classes at par with the rest of the Indian society. The various constitutional guarantees for the 'Adivasis' and 'Harijans' include economic, educational and social programmes of development as well as the policy of reservation of seats in legislatures and of posts in public service both under the Union and the States. On the basis of the social disabilities and backwardness various groups belonging to the 'Harijans' were designated as Scheduled Castes (SC). Under the relevant provisions of the Constitution quotas of posts were reserved for them in all public services on the basis of their population in the particular State of the Indian Union.

The scenario in the state of Bihar

Social structure in Bihar is characterised by high degree of rigidity and very low social mobility. Although untouchability has been abolished by law, the scheduled castes still suffer from inferiority complex and social disabilities imposed upon them by the upper castes. The rigidity of the caste system is glaring in the rural areas of Bihar, where practically no social change has taken place. The society is still basically feudal and exploitative. The phenomena of bonded labour, atrocities on weaker communities, social segregation, orthodox practices are still prevalent. However, the situation is better in the industrial and urban centres where there is some evidence of increased social interaction among all communities.

With 14.6 percent of scheduled caste population, Bihar accounts for a large chunk of the communities who deserve preferential treatment for their social emancipation. It is interesting to note that the degree of economic and social backwardness is different even among these communities. In Bihar 23 castes have been scheduled by the Constitution (see Appendix 1). The castes like Dusadh, Chamar, Dhobi and Pasi are more advanced among the scheduled castes. The condition of castes like Dom, Mehtar, Mushar, Nat, Turi is miserable and pathetic. The most backward groups among the scheduled castes have not been able to acquire the minimum level of reservation in public services. Bihar with its semi-feudal socio-economic condition, years of under-development, exploitative social and rigid caste system presents an appropriate area for study of the process of social transformation taking place among the Harijans (dalits) due to the reservation of jobs in public service.

This chapter focuses on the social implications due to job reservation on the beneficiaries as well as the general population. The theoretical basis of reservation and the guarantees enshrined in the Constitution to usher in a new social order need to be tested by the results of the implementation of the policy. Although the task appears to be nearly impossible in terms of the high expectations, which the lofty ideals of the Constitution have aroused, yet the experience of nearly five decades of State intervention in providing compensatory discrimination in favour of the depressed classes is not wholly unrewarding.

Provisions in the constitution of India

Article 14 made 'Equality' a Fundamental Right. But the principle of 'equality' is a double-edged weapon. It places the strong and the handicapped on the same footing in the race of life. To treat unequals as equals is to perpetuate inequality. The humanness of a society is determined by the degree of protection it provides to its weaker, handicapped and less-gifted members. It was in view of this that Constitution makers made special provisions in Article 15 (4), Article 16 (4), and Article 46 for the scheduled castes and scheduled tribes.

Article 15 states 'The State shall not discriminate against any citizen on grounds only of religion, race, caste, sex, place of birth or any of them' Clause (4) of Article 15, which was added by the Constitution (First Amendment) Act, 1951 says 'Nothing in this article or in clause (2) of Article 29 shall prevent the State from making any special provision for the advancement of any socially and educationally backward classes of citizens or for the scheduled castes and scheduled tribes'.

The safeguards, which pointedly deal with the reservation of jobs in public services are Article 16 (4), 320 and 335. Article 16 gives equal opportunity to all citizens in matters relating to employment or appointment to any office under the State without discriminating on grounds of race, caste, sex, descent etc. Clause (4) of Article 16 specifically states that 'Nothing in this article shall prevent the state from making any provision for the reservation of appointment or posts in favour of any backward classes of citizens which, in the opinion of the State, is not adequately represented in the services under the State'. Article 320 makes it the duty of Union and State Public Service Commissions to conduct examinations for appointments to the services in the Union and States but clause (4) of Article 320 specifies that it shall not be required for the Public Service Commission to be consulted as respects the manner in which any provision referred to in Clause (4) of Article 16 may be made or as respects the manner in which effect may be given to the provisions of Article 335.

Under Article 335, 'The claims of the members of the scheduled castes and the scheduled tribes shall be taken into consideration consistently with the maintenance of efficiency of administration in the making of appointments to services and posts in connection with the affairs of the Union or of a State.'

It is important to note that the preferential treatment under Article 335 is accorded to members of the scheduled castes and scheduled tribes only, and not to members of 'backward classes' in general, as does Article 16 (4).

Article 17 says 'untouchability' is abolished and its practice in any form is forbidden. The enforcement of any disability arising out of 'untouchability' shall be an offence punishable in accordance with law. Article 25 (b) provides for social welfare and reform and the throwing open of Hindu religious institutions of a public character to all classes and sections of Hindus. Article 46 of the Directive Principles of State Policy directs the State to promote with special care the educational and economic interests of the weaker sections of the people in particular the scheduled castes and scheduled tribes.

Compensatory discrimination versus meritarian principle

There is a contradiction between the legal system designed under the Constitution and the existing social order. Whereas, the equality provision of the Constitution promises basic equality of all human beings as an ideal yet the existing social structure is basically unequal. Law can only indicate the general direction in which members of a society are expected to move but the nature and character of the social structure will ultimately determine whether the change envisaged by law will be effective or not in a given period of time.

Equality in the simple sense does not take into consideration the differences existing among various groups in society. It is based on the principle that, 'Every man to count for one and no one to count for more than one'. But in reality there are differences among groups and at the same time there are differences among individuals in the same group. Some individuals are more meritorious and capable than others, whereas there may be individuals in society whose merit and capabilities may be lower because of various factors. The 'meritarian' principle recognises only the merit of an individual and seeks to reward the individual on the basis of his merit alone. On the other hand, the 'compensatory principle' recognises the need of the individual and takes into account any special disability or hardship being faced by the individual in the social set-up. It may be necessary to provide for such compensation, but enough precaution has to be taken in determining the quantum and beneficiaries of compensation. At the same time sufficiently strong reason has to be advanced to depart from the principle of equality in the simple sense while applying the principles of compensation based on need and special disabilities.

Every society is characterised by a certain division of labour through which the various activities are carried out. This kind of division provided the society with its defining features. The division of labour is found not only in rural or traditional societies but also in modern industrial societies. There are sharp differences of opinion among sociologists about the justification of the division of labour. Some sociologists consider division of labour as a necessity for any society, Marx was very critical of such division. He argued that the division of labour is capitalist in nature and therefore undesirable. In the Marxist point of view the futuristic society will have such a structure that no individual would be tied down to a particular profession or occupation but each individual would move freely from one occupation to another according to his choice. Marx and Engels argue that such a society cannot be created out of the existing social order unless a new society is created by revolutionary methods.

Our constitutional framework does not seek to do away with the division of labour but aims to regulate such division of labour among the individual members of the society in a fair and equitable manner. It provides for 'careers open to talent'. There is no compulsion for any individual to take up one particular occupation as was happening in the caste-based traditional society. There is an attempt to assess the capabilities of individuals and assign tasks suitable to them irrespective of their past background. There are many obstacles to implement the principle of careers open to talent in our social set-up. Nevertheless, it is possible today for individuals from the deprived groups to attain the highest position in society, in spite of the rigidity of the division of labour and the occupational pattern of the individual members of the society.

The meritarian principle requires a free competition among all the individuals so that each person can occupy his proper place according to his merit . The approach behind the compensatory principle is different in that this principle expects the State to intervene in a positive way in favour of the weakest in order to ensure that the competition is not just free but also fair and equitable. The first principle is satisfied if discrimination and barriers are only lifted but the second principle goes further by providing for safeguards against the excesses of free market competition since such competition will be prejudicial to the socially disprivileged groups.

The Constitution attempts to strike a balance between both these principles. The Fundamental Rights lay emphasis on the meritarian principles, whereas the special provisions in the Fundamental Rights along with the Directive Principles emphasise need based discrimination in favour of the disprivileged communities. However, in applying the meritarian and compensatory principles enough precaution must be taken. It would be erroneous to presume that meritarian principle is resourceful enough to take care of the requirements of the modern society. A modern society must strike a balance between the two principles instead of relying solely on either of these principles. If everything is left to be decided on the basis of the merit of the individual then we may end up with competition among unequals leading to further distortions in the social structure. On the other hand, the intervention by the State in pursuing the compensatory principle in favour of the weak must be specific with defined limits otherwise there is a risk of the system getting increasingly dependent on official patronage and bureaucratic interference. It must be borne in mind that the compensatory principle is basically discriminatory in nature. Therefore, the discrimination must be used very carefully so that while destroying old inequalities new distortions in society are not created.

Rationale of the policy of compensatory discrimination

It is a recognised fact that individuals differ in respect of their merits and capabilities. If there are historical factors like prolonged deprivation, segregation and other social disabilities then the differences among the individual members of society tend to get more pronounced and accentuated. In such a situation of social inequalities it is unfair to treat all members of the society on the same footing and leave them to compete freely with others for filling up positions of power and prestige.

The various constitutional guarantees which strive to give preferential treatment to these communities are violative of the principle of equality. Nevertheless, the Constitution gives a clear direction to the State to intervene in favour of the backward communities by the various special provisions. These provisions aim at compensating for the injustices inflicted upon the socially disabled communities, but at the same time are discriminatory in nature since they deprive the communities who are more developed. This system has been termed as 'compensatory discrimination' by Marc Galanter. There is also an underlying implication that such deliberate policy of discrimination will cease when preferential treatment leads to correction of the age-old distortions in society.

The scheme of compensatory discrimination as envisaged in the Constitution consists of a wide array of statutory and directive provisions in favour of the scheduled castes. The provisions relate to reservation of seats in legislature, reservation in academic institutions and reservation in public services. Besides, certain preferences are also provided to these communities like scholarships, stipends, legal aid, health care, and special schemes for their development. The measures include ban on land-alienation, abolition of bonded-labour, provision of minimum wages and various safeguards against atrocities on these sections. In the process of planning and development of the national economy many schemes have been introduced for the benefit of the scheduled castes with the objective of raising their economic status.

According to Marc Galanter the provision of reservation in government employment is the 'paradigm case of the Indian policy of compensatory discrimination'. It is the 'core' of the governmental policy for bringing about greater social integration. 'Government in India is regarded, not as just another employer, but one that affords a degree of security, prestige and authority not obtainable elsewhere' (1984). As there is no reservation in the matter of employment in the private sector, the educated candidates among the scheduled castes depend heavily upon the government for getting employment. Moreover, induction into the government not only provides employment but also give them access into the administration. Their presence in the government offices is likely to ensure a greater degree of sympathy and understanding towards the problems of the backward group.

Experience of other countries

India is not the only country facing the challenges of safeguarding the interests of minority and weaker sections of society. Such problems have existed and are continuing to engage the attention of governments in advanced countries also including the western democracies. United States is basically a country of minorities. The country received immigrants from almost every race and ethnic group of the world and continues to receive them even today.

The development of minority protection has been greatly influenced by a single minority group namely the Black Americans whose tragic history provides the moral foundation of such protective policy. Over a period of two centuries a pattern of legal and institutional framework has emerged to protect the rights of the blacks.

The policy of 'affirmative action' which was initiated by President

Kennedy and further pursued by President Johnson sought to include proportions of minority workers of certain specified races and ethnic groups according to their 'availability' and was to be administered under government supervision. According to this policy the employer must count his employees by race and type or level of employment, determine the 'degree of under-utilization', and then make every effort to reach the prescribed standards that approximates the proportions of employees of each group and in each job category, which a complex analysis shows as being theoretically available. The policy of 'affirmative action' like the policy of reservation or reverse discrimination' in India, has also given rise to a lot of controversies and criticisms right from the beginning. The defenders of the policy argue that this policy is necessary to counter widespread discrimination and that compensatory action in favour of the oppressed groups is fair. On the other hand the opponents argue that it is unfair to sacrifice the rights of the individuals for equal treatment by introducing discrimination in employment and that such policy would undermine standards of achievement in education, the professions and employment.

As in the United States affirmative action in Canada represents a strategy to overcome the effects of 'institutional discrimination'. This policy has led to increased participation of minorities in the Canadian public services. Canada is a nation of immigrants. It was a 'mosaic', a society formed by different ethnic groups. Minority protection in Canada is both in the form of eliminating unwarranted discrimination and also in the form of positive collective rights. The former provides for the equality of economic opportunity as well as equal access to the social, cultural, and political affairs of the society as a whole. Legislative enactments also prohibit discrimination in such areas as education, employment, housing and commercial service on the basis of race, religion, ethnic origin or language. The latter encompasses collective rights political, cultural, or linguistic accorded by Canadian government (federal or provincial) to minority groups.

The Canadian government keeps on making 'special legislative enactments' for increasing 'quantitative and qualitative participation of native peoples'. In 1978 the federal Government, the public service commission, together with native groups' consultation made efforts to launch new programmes, which would ensure more native participation. Federal departments were ordered to:

review their existing practices governing the design of jobs, recruitment and selection, training and career development of employees, in order to identify and systematically eliminate any such practices which discriminate against and/or present barriers to indigenous persons who are public servants or are candidates for positions in the public service (Wirsing, 1981, p.59).

The British society has also been brought into contact, through immigration, with a number of quite distinct groups, commonly the West Indians and the Asians. Researchers who have conducted interviews of both 'blacks' and 'whites' in both the public and private sector have some interesting samples of answers. There were white workers who resented the very presence of blacks, to the extent that they were prepared to leave the area even at great financial loss to themselves. The blacks in Britain are also protected by law against discrimination. Enactments also keep a certain portion of jobs reserved for the non-whites. The white workers felt that 'blacks increased unemployment'. A corollary of this belief is the view that 'we are becoming second class citizens in our own country'.

Social transformation through job reservation

While evaluating the performance of the policy of reservation in the process of social transformation in India it must be borne in mind the grounds on which the policy was formulated as well as the goals aimed at. Since the policy is discriminatory in nature and deprives many aspirants from getting the benefits of government services all care must be taken to ensure that the discrimination neither exceeds the limits prescribed by the framework of reservation nor becomes ineffective due to improper or inadequate implementation. Under the Constitution the authority of the State was directed to intervene in favour of the disadvantaged groups with a view to remove the stigma of unattachability and social isolation imposed upon them for centuries. There is a deliberate effort to protect them from the forces of free competition in an environment of inequality. Instead they were promised a fair and equitable opportunity to improve their lot by entering the coveted ranks of bureaucracy. There was a presumption that by the induction of members from these communities into the ruling elite changes could be brought about in the existing social structure. The new elite was expected to play the role of a catalyst of social change in their communities. The ultimate objective of the Constitution was to create a secular society where individual dignity is assured irrespective of his caste or creed.

The policy of reservation among scheduled castes has undoubtedly created an impact on the social set-up in the four decades of its implementation in the State of Bihar. By virtue of reserved quota many candidates from among them have secured entry into various levels of administration in the State Government. It is not uncommon to come across Harijan (Dalit) officers occupying high offices where they can play a decisive role in the affairs of the State. The policy has had a significant role in bringing about some amount of modification in the social structure in Bihar.

Although the practice of untouchability was abolished by a constitutional provision yet much greater social effort is necessary to bring about a change in the outlook of the general population. The difference between the legal order envisaged in the Constitution with its emphasis on equality and the existing social order, which is full of inequalities is too glaring in the society in Bihar. It goes to the credit of the policy of discrimination that many of the so-called 'untouchables' are at the helm of affairs in the government. This has created a definite change in the psychological reservations of the general society against the scheduled castes. Harijan officers are holding influential positions and deciding important administrative matters. This by itself has given a fillip to these SC's and acted as a morale booster for their public image, however, it must be mentioned that a change in the attitude towards the scheduled castes is confined only to the big towns and to some extent also in small urban centres in Bihar but the wind of change has not permeated the society effectively in the rural areas. In the villages the new elite among the scheduled castes still receive less generous treatment than allowed to them in the urban society. The image of the depressed person of the past holds on to the scheduled castes official when he visits the rural areas. His past image still comes out vividly in the minds of the villagers if he undertakes his occasional though less frequent visits to his native village. The service-holder thus faces the paradox of divergent image and treatment at the two different places namely at his place of posting and his native village.

There is enough evidence of social mobility taking place among these communities. The rigidity of the caste-system is so elaborate and deep-rooted that it is not so easy to overhaul the system. Nevertheless, it is found that a perceptible dent in the system has been achieved over the years, which is becoming more and more evident with the passage of time. A contrast of treatment meted out by society to three generations makes the point quite clear. In the case of the first generation service-holders among these communities generally it was found that the previous generation had suffered from many discrimination and social disabilities, whereas, the next generation consisting of their children were more acceptable in the general society. In fact, the children of the beneficiaries felt less inhibited and could mix freely with children of all communities. The status of the first generation service holders is in the nature of a transitional phase from an era of underprivileged position to an era of more secular social communion. There are no doubt some exceptions but by and large this is the general trend emerging in the case of the job holders in these communities.

There is also a growing tendency among the job holders to aspire for upward social mobility through the process of Sanskritisation. Many of them have adopted the Hindu religious practices like worshipping gods and goddesses, celebrating important Hindu festivals and observing certain Hindu rites on the occasion of marriage, birth and death. Most of them hold progressive views on social practices like child-marriage, dowry, small family norm, inter-caste, inter-community marriages and status of women. In fact, many of them are found to be as open minded and cosmopolitan in their outlook as members of any other community. There is a growing sense of self-confidence, determination and social awareness visible among them.

The emergence of the new elite is a significant development in the process of social transformation among these communities. The ultimate objective of the egalitarian ethos of the Constitution is to attain a social order in which the interests of various communities are taken care of by adequate representation in the administration. The State intervention in favour of the weaker section has succeeded in broadening the base of the ruling elite by the deliberate introduction of representatives from these communities into the ruling class. The new elite among the Harijans have made their presence in almost every department of the government and due to their mere presence they are able to ensure two things. Firstly, it is no longer possible to ignore the interests of their communities while plans, projects or general government policies are being formulated. Secondly, by their presence in positions of authority they ensure induction of more and more members of their communities up to the level of reservation prescribed so that the constitutional provisions are properly implemented. By their presence in the government they work as watch dogs to protect their group interests. Although this is the general trend among the new elite there are a few who prefer to remain aloof and uncommitted to protect and promote the interests of their less fortunate fellow men. Their indifference can be attributed to their selfish desire to extricate themselves from the unhappy and miserable life in their communities in the past and their efforts to project an image of sophistication. Barring these upstarts the privileged members of the scheduled castes who have gained entry into the seats of power have sympathy for their communities and try to do as much as they can for their development.

Social implications of protective discrimination

The discrimination introduced by the policy of reservation in favour of the scheduled castes has resulted in different types of antagonistic reactions in different groups and communities. As the policy has deprived many meritorious candidates of other communities from entry into the portals of power and prestige, a certain amount of bitterness, jealousy and hostility is noticeable among them. The beneficiaries of reservation generally feel that they are treated as usurpers by others. Many of the job holders feel that they do not receive cooperation from their superiors or subordinates. There is a lurking fear in their mind that their superiors being members of the upper-castes may report adversely against them in the annual confidential remarks, which may be detrimental to their promotional prospects. Such jealousy and bitterness is not confined to the upper castes only. Even the other backward classes (OBC) in Bihar are sore against the Harijans in two ways. Firstly, the OBCs in Bihar were granted reservation up to 20 per cent in 1978 after a prolonged agitation whereas the scheduled castes have been enjoying these facilities even before Independence. Secondly, the OBCs could get only 20 per cent reservation whereas, the scheduled castes only have been given 14 per cent reservation although the OBCs far out number them.

The jealousy against the members of scheduled castes who have benefitted by job reservation is noticed even within their own communities. Most of the reserved posts have been siphoned off by the more dominant and developed sections among these castes. It is observed that candidates from four dominant scheduled castes namely the Dusadh, Pasi, Dhobi and Chamar have taken a lion's share of the reserved posts leaving a small pittance for other castes. In fact, castes like Nat, Mehtar, Dom, Mushar, Turi have almost no representation in the administrative machinery of the State. These sections who have remained socially most backward and live in sub-human conditions of existence have every reason to be aggrieved. The various constitutional guarantees have neither any meaning for them nor hold out any hope for the future unless radical measures are taken in their favour.

The vagaries of free competition inherent in the meritarian principle were sought to be taken care of by the principle of protective and preferential treatment to the weaker sections. The caste has been taken as the enabling factor for the purpose of reservation. In doing so all individuals among these communities have been presumed to have equal and similar capabilities and were expected to compete fairly well. But the study reveals that such a free competition within these communities in turn has resulted in greater skewness and distortions in the process of development of members of these communities. The groups who were better off socially and economically have stolen a march over the weaker groups. If this process continues, a situation may be envisaged where greater social inequalities are created among the scheduled castes themselves while striving to end the old inequalities in society between them and the upper castes. In order to check this trend certain corrective measures will have to be introduced before it is too late. It may even be considered that providing for some kind of 'reservation within reservation' so that a certain percentage of posts may be reserved for those Scheduled Castes who are grossly under-represented in the public services. If necessary the qualifying marks may also be further lowered to accommodate candidates from these groups. A special scheme has to be taken up to spread education among the weakest sections. Greater awareness has to be brought about among them to motivate them to take advantage of the various facilities available.

When reservation was introduced for the first time in India in favour of the scheduled castes the provisions were valid for a period of ten years. Subsequently the policy was extended for a further period of ten years and finally till the turn of the century i.e. 2000 A.D. It is interesting to note that Dr. Ambedkar who championed the cause of the scheduled caste was himself not in favour of the continuance of reservation for an indefinite period. He wanted the special safeguards to be temporary so as not to prevent the integration of scheduled castes with the rest of the society. Shri H. V. Kamath a leading public figure and social activist also wanted a time bound programme. He said; 'indefinite extensions of the policy of reservation is contrary to the spirit and letter of the provision enshrined in the Constitution and will tend to perpetuate the caste system'. The late Sri Jagjivan Ram the Harijan statesman of eminence has gone on record saying, 'the problems of a poor Brahmin and a poor Harijan are the same' (Statesman, 1980).

There is no denying the fact that the number of jobs are few and the target groups too many. It will certainly take quite a long time before we can say that enough has been done to justify discontinuance of preferential treatment. It would probably be desirable in the given situation to allow these provisions to continue till the turn of the century and perhaps a decade beyond, so that there would be a feeling among the weaker sections that ample time had been given to them to gather themselves up and achieve a fair degree of upward mobility.

It is more important to achieve greater spread of the benefits among various groups among the scheduled castes. To achieve this end certain bold measures will have to be introduced. Firstly, reservation should be granted only to two generations at the most. It has been observed that there is a fair degree of upward mobility even among the children of the first generation beneficiaries; hence it is reasonable to expect the social disabilities to disappear or at least be minimised after two generations in a family having entered government service. Secondly, it may be desirable to introduce the criteria of economic status also along with the social backwardness since some sections among the Harijans are economically better off. In order to ensure greater coverage and to bring relief to the more deprived groups among these communities such criteria will be necessary in view of the limited number of jobs. Thirdly, the education and awareness of the most backward of these cases should be brought at par with the general sections to enable them partake of these benefits. Of course, successful implementation of the policy will ultimately depend upon a responsive administration, and proper work ethics will have to be evolved to ensure greater sympathy and consideration towards the scheduled caste candidates both at the time of recruitment and promotion. The government must choose dedicated officers who have adequate sympathy and commitment towards development of the weaker sections and post them in key positions where they can be effective in translating the various safeguards into realities.

Conclusion: limitation of the policy

The policy of reservation of jobs in public services as an instrument of social change suffers from some drawbacks. It has raised hopes and expectations among the communities to a level which is unrealistic, judged both by the possibilities of emancipation of these communities through this policy as well as by its performance, as manifest in the process of its implementation. The reserved jobs are too few compared to the vast multitude of aspirants waiting to avail of the benefits. Moreover, high level of education has to be imparted to a large number of members of these communities so that they can enter the bureaucracy at a relatively higher level. Otherwise they can neither enjoy a higher social status nor can they play a decisive role in the administration. In the long run excessive dependence on this policy may prove to be not only costly but also lead to increasing sense of revolt among the other communities as well as disenchantment among large number of educated youth of the weaker sections due to their failure to succeed in the limited job market. Needless to say the policy promises nothing to the vast multitude of illiterate scheduled castes who form the overwhelming majority of these communities.

Greater stress will have to be given both by the administration as well as by voluntary non-governmental effort so as to accelerate the pace of all-round development of the poorest sections of the society who mostly belong to these castes. Much more has to be done to create an impact for faithful implementation of the various anti-poverty programmes, which will benefit these sections of society. It is felt that this is the only way to halt the growing tension in society particularly in the rural areas between the haves and the have-nots. Effective implementation of laws relating to minimum wages, land reforms, provision of better credit facilities and implementation of special programmes for the economic development of the SCs will go a long way to create a more harmonious social order.

The success of the democratic system visualised in the Constitution depends upon the creation of a social structure based on fraternity, mutual trust and above all the dignity of all the citizens irrespective of their caste, creed and race. The State can become strong and enduring if social life is made free of strife and tension, and all communities are provided with the means to enjoy the fruits of development.

Appendix one

Scheduled castes (Bihar)

1. Bantar
2. Bauri
3. Bhogta
4. Bhuiya
5. Bhumi (Excluding North Chotanagpur and South Chotanagpur Divisions and Santahal Pargana District)
6. Chamar, Mochi
7. Chaupal
8. Debgwi
9. Dhobi
10. Dom, Dhanged
11. Dusadh, Dhobi Dharhi
12. Chasi
13. Halalkhar
14. Hari, Mehter, Bhengi
15. Kanjari
16. Kurariar
17. Lalbagi
18. Mushar
19. Nat
20. Pan, Sawasi
21. Pasi
22. Rajwar
23. Turi

References

Abraham, A.S., (1979), 'Centers move for early decision on job reservation', *Times of India*, 12 December, Vol. 1, pp.2-3.

Abraham, A.S., (1985), Going beyond reservation: Framework for a wider policy, *Times of India*, 20 April, Vol. 8, pp.3-5.

Abraham, A.S., (1980), 'Limits to reservations: Policy divorced from Social Reality', *Times of India*, 19 September Vol. 6, pp.3-5.

Apte B.P., (1985), Only half of reserved jobs are filled, *Link*, Vol.27, No. 36, April, pp.7-8

Apte, B.P., (1982), Our Constitution and Reservation Policy.

Basu, D.B., (1983), *Constitutional Law of India. New Delhi*, Prentice Hall of India Pvt. Limited.

Beteille, A., (1983), *The Backward Classes and The New Social Order, Delhi*, Oxford University Press.

Bihar Govt. Publication, (1979), Compilation of circular of Scheduled Castes and Scheduled Tribes, Bihar Government.

Bottomore, T.B., (1964), *Elites and Society*, Penguin Books.

Editorial, (1988), Combating Tribal Poverty, *Sun Times*, May 28.

Faridi J., (1980), Job reservation: How much, for whom and how long? *Hindustan Times* (Magazine), 2-3 November.

Gallanter, M., (1984), *Competing Equalities, Law and the Backward Classes in India, Bombay*, Oxford University Press.

Ghurye, G.S., (1961), *Caste, Class and Occupation, Bombay*, Popular Book Depot.

Govt. of Bihar Publication (1979), compilation of circulars of welfare and protections of Harijans, Adivasis and other Backward Classes (pt.1).

Govt. of India Publication (1985), Report of the working group on the Development of Scheduled Castes, During the Seventh Five Year Plan.

Govt. of India Publication (1982), Report of the Commissioner for Scheduled Castes and Scheduled Tribes

Goyal, B.R., (1981), *Educating Harijans. Haryana*, Academic Press.

Isacs, H.E., (1965), *India's Ex-touchables*; Asia Publishing House, Bombay.

Jha, Chetkar, (1979), *Reserved Representation*, Seminar No. 243 November, pp.29-30.

Jha S.N., (1979), Seminar No. 243 *In Public Services*, pp.18-21

Khanna, M.C. (1979), 'Plan for job reservation given up', *Times of India*, 20 November, Vol. 1, pp.2-3.

Khanna, K.C., (1981), Policy on Reservation: Need to correct distortions, *Times of India*, 21 April, pp.83-5.

Khanna K.C., (1981), 'Panel for review of reservation policy', *Times of India*, 25 April, Vol. 1, pp. 5-6

Kuppuswamy, B (1968), *Social Change in India*, Vikas Publications.

Makwana, Yogendra, (1985), Reservation : Does it promote Class War, *Link*, Vol. 27, No. 36, April, pp.9-11

Mishra S.N. (1981), Job Reservation and Intensification of Social Conflict: A case study of North Bihar Village, *Gandhi Marg*, Vol. 3, No. 2, May, pp.98-107

Rai S.K., (1980), Problem, Seminar 268 December, 108p.

Reddy, G.S. (1980), Whither Scheduled Caste Reservations? *Mainstream* Vol. 18, No. 40, May, pp.15-18.

Reddy G.S., (1983), Scheduled Castes and the struggle against Inequality, *Social Action*, Vol. 33, No. 4, October-December, pp.462-63

Sachchidananda, (1974), *Education among the Scheduled Castes and Scheduled Tribes in Bihar*, Vol. 1, School Students, Patna, A.N.S.I.S.S.

Saksena, H.S., (1981), *Safeguards for Scheduled Castes and Tribes; Founding Fathers' views*, New Delhi, Uppal Publishing House.

Shah G., (1981), Gujarat Anti-reservation Agitation, *Mainstream*, Vol. 19, No. 28, March, pp.33-34

Shah G., (1985), Caste and Class Reservation, *Economic and Political Weekly*, Vol. 20, No. 3, January pp.132-136

Sharma, B.A.V. (Ed.) (1982), *Reservation Policy in India. New Delhi*, Light and Life Publishers.

Sheth D. L., (1985), Grant Reservation Debates, IE pp.1-8

Sheth D. L., (1987), Preservation Policy Revisited, Seminar Paper Reservations: Objectives and Policies.

Singh. P., (1982), *Equality, Reservation and Discrimination in India New Delhi*, Deep and Deep Publications.

Srinivas, M.N., (1966), *Social Change in Modern India. Bombay*, Allied Publishers.

Taub, R.P., (1969), *Bureaucrats under Stress*, Calcutta, Firma K. L. Mukhopadhyay.

Vidyarthi L.P. and Mishra, (1977), *Harijan Today*, New Delhi.

Wirsing R.G., (ed) (1981), *Protection of Ethnic Minorities, Comparative Prospective*, U.S.A. Pergamon Press.

6 Developing effective communication for project managers in developing countries

Dr Ali R Analouei

Effective communication, an optimum balance of science and art, is essential for the effective management of the human resources within organisations and projects. Arguably the success of the managers is determined, if not wholly, partly by the degree of their effectiveness in relating to others in the workplace environment or the clients as the case may be (Analoui, 1997a). The communication system, within an organisation, resembles the nerve system of a complex biological entity. Its prime function is to relate the parts together and ensures the co-ordination of their efforts and outputs which is essential for the survival and well being of the parts and of the organism as a whole (Handy, 1985; Analoui, 1991).

In the project context, as Borman aptly remarks, the 'the flow of information achieves a community of understanding to provide objectives, divide work, develop morale, evaluate performance and mobilise the resources of the organisation' (1982, p.14). Since project managers are charged with the responsibility for the achievement of the set objectives they are therefore, required to establish an effective communication system and remain an effective communicator throughout the implementation stage and beyond.

This chapter, first explores the importance of communication for the project managers and the successful implementation and operation of the project. Then, in a subsequent discussion the major forms and characteristics of communication, namely; formal, informal and interpersonal and their relevance for the human resource development and project managers, in particular, will be dealt with in some detail. Finally, in a summary the importance of adopting a holistic attitude to communication for managers is emphasised and salient conclusions are drawn.

Communication and effective project implementation

Different organisation structures, namely; Functional, Matrix or Projectised could be used for the purpose of project implementation (Gobeli, 1987). The management in the organisations are responsible for carrying out several activities and functions. These include; planning, organising, staffing, directing and controlling (Goodman and Love, 1980). All these activities require the development of effective communications skills on the part of the human resources within the organisation and in particular by the managers. It has been argued that project management is about a series of management activities which go on throughout the life of a project and which involve the use of communication through a variety of different communication channels (Analoui, 1997b).

The major difference between the implementation phase and the operation process is that the former phase involves critical and uncertain activities with a relatively fixed span of time and resources to manage them. To implement a project, normally, a project team is formed and the team members are either recruited from inside or outside of the existing structure (Analouei, 1998). The activities, to be carried out, could be entirely new to some of members. The project's organisational set-up may also be new to the project. Within the developing world, especially where public sector projects are concerned, transfer from one organisation or department to another charged with the responsibility of a new project is a frequent and familiar affair. Often the political issues rather than the manager's personal attributes and work experience are the main determinants for choosing the manager. Even under these unfavourable circumstances, it has been observed that managers with effective communication skills, especially the ability and skill to relate to others at the interpersonal levels, tend to influence the outcome of a negotiating process to a large degree (Kakabadse and Brovetto, 1989; Analouei, 1998).

Whatever the selection process may be, the manager, once in charge of the project, requires prompt and regular reliable feedback in order to be able to take appropriate actions for their own and the projects survival. The project manager often faces political, economic, environmental and technical difficulties and pressures from both inside and outside the organisation (Baum, 1985). To resolve these difficulties, a network of external and internal communication links ought to be established and maintained. Preston (1981) goes as far as suggesting, '... Control communication ... and you are in control' (p. 3).

Of course, the nature of the task to be implemented, varies from one project to another and from one region to another. These differences necessitate the use of different communication networks and systems. Since, most projects within developing countries are being implemented through national institutions the management of the project are naturally expected to follow 'orders'. A tradition which is prevalent in public sector work-cultures (Handy 1985; Analoui, 1991, 1997). Consequently, as expected, the communication system of the project becomes an extension of the slow, inflexible and often one way system which is already in operation within the Ministry or department. It is not surprising, therefore, if recently it has been observed that donor agencies insist on the formation of a separate structure preferably outside the public sector organisations to implement the projects. This approach known as a 'projectised structure' will result in the use of different managerial styles and a more effective communication system within the project organisation.

Project managers, whether in public or private sector organisations and projects, are expected to provide strong leadership, especially in human resource mobilisation; political interaction; motivation of staff, clients, sponsors and potential beneficiaries; building a network of organisational support; and creativity in solving problems (Rondinelli, 1979). To do this, it is essential for them to establish a variety of different formal and informal communication chains both within and outside of the project organisations.

The formal system

The formal communication channels are to be established by the management in the first instance and according to the organisational objectives and policies. This form of communication is popular amongst the practitioners who subscribe to the principles of the Classical Managerial School as it allows the use of near absolute authority and unquestionable control over the subordinates (Handy, 1985). Therefore, the activities within in the operational phase of the project are largely controlled with the aide of procedures and rules. Because most activities in this phase of the project implementation are more or less pre-planned and are of a routine nature, the formal channels of communication such as written reports, memos, notices, and minutes of meetings are liberally used to transmit the information, albeit mechanically, from a source to the receiver (Smith et. al., 1985). From this managerial prospective, people within the project organisation are assumed to be not socially inter-linked with each other thus they are expected, while working on the project, to use the already established formal communication networks in organisations.

During the implementation phase, which is typically characterised by the involvement of various agencies, the use of a formal communication network becomes essential to assign the role of each group or individual and to keep the track of all the actions and the level of the progress of the project activities. This form of communications assures that the required information is being transmitted consistently. As Morss (1988) suggests although a project design document can sketch the broad outline of an information system, the manager should develop the plan for implementing it. These information bases which contain Work Breakdown Structures (WBS) or scheduling, detailed designs and procedures and the organisational policies or other relevant information which are required to be passed on formally and on time to the specific individuals or groups through the existing channels such as;

1. written forms, for example, memos, letters, reports, handbills, questionnaires, pamphlets, manuals and the like;
2. verbal channels for example, meetings, individual and group presentations, conference and seminars.

In a traditionally organised project organisation, information usually travels downward on an hierarchical basis in order to pass on organisational objectives, rules and regulations, notices, directives and instructions to attain common organisational goals. This form of communicating is widely used in mechanistic organisations with centralised decision making and controlled bodies (Pilcher, 1992). Such structures tend to place disproportionate emphasis on the presence of a strong vertical specialisation and control mechanism, unlike the organic organisations which are characterised by decentralised structures and a two way flow of information within and amongst their sub-systems (Analoui, 1993).

Using report is another form of formal communication which is expected from the managers throughout the project, albeit periodically. The manager requires periodic progress reports which could be daily, weekly, fortnightly or monthly. He or she has to provide information to the related agencies or top ministries in the form of a report. These reports may take different forms and have several different names such as working paper, project status, annual evaluation report and so on (depending on the nature of the project and the receiver of the information).

In theory, the use of a formal channel of communication coincides with the time when the project manager feels that an idea or a project requirement needs to be carried out by a related task group or an individual. The manager inevitably uses relevant jargon which encodes the message and then proceeds to transmit the message either verbally or in written forms. The message then is conveyed through the available and/or chosen channels like fax, electronic mail, telephone, a meeting or a presentation to the receiver(s). The receiver, once in possession of the message, decodes the content and proceeds to act accordingly. However, in practice, this seemingly simple process proves to be much more difficult and problematic.

As Handy (1985) aptly asserts, we never communicate as effectively as we think we do. For effective communication, Mitchel (1982) suggests that messages should have similar meaning(s) to both the sender and the receiver. Hence, the message should be simple, clear and consistent. The credibility of the communicator, scarcity and reliability of the message are also important factors for ensuring effective communication. To achieve this, ultimately, it must be ensured that the message has been fully and correctly understood by the receiver, thus some form of feedback is essential to the effectiveness of this process. This implies that a two-way channel of communication is essential for sending and receiving information, in particular where it concerns important and scarce information. Project managers can then be assured that their messages have been understood, acted upon easily and that the manger will get the appropriate feedback on the decision made (Hanna, 1985).

Barriers to effective communications

The information to be communicated may be distorted or even completely halted by different barriers. Preston (1981) suggests three main barriers to effective communication. These are ;

1. Semantic barriers,
2. Serial distortions, and
3. Problem of communication load.

Semantic barriers could be avoided by judging accurately the state of the sensory factors of the receiver. Age, sex, educational and economic levels and regional and religious background, their interpretation of different body gestures, all affect the receiver's level of perception (Albers, 1974).

The serial distortions could be minimised by reducing the number links in the communication chain or the levels within the organisational hierarchy of the communication network (Handy, 1985). The message should therefore be sharp with more emphasis on the important points and scarce data. Urgency should also be incorporated into the message in order to avoid further delay during its transmission.

115

The communication load poses a barrier to the effectiveness of the communication. It is of two main types; 'overload' and 'under-load'. The overload tends to create stress and anxiety which in turn frustrates the receiver and ultimately would result in damage to the quality of the work environment of the organisation. Hence, the information could be ignored, given low priority or even filed.

Sometimes, it could be advantageous to managers to speed up the work by reducing its quality or by delegating some portion of it to others. Under-load creates boredom on the part of the receiver and in extreme cases the sender may loose credibility and control. In these cases more information should be provided to increase the effectiveness of the communication.

The major problems associated with formal communication are those associated with the process being very slow and/or being due to purely task oriented factors. In projects where teams are utilised the formal system can not be entirely relied upon to receive or send information and feedback.

Informal communication

Dichter (1989) refers to three theories or approaches to the management of human resources or otherwise in the work organisations. He states that the first theory known as Theory 'X' refers to a relentless application of hierarchical, top-down management, which incidentally heavily relies upon the use of formal communication as discussed above. The Theory 'Y' is based on the assumptions that people in work organisations are capable of exercising a choice and are willing to take responsibility for what they do. Thus, the rules and regulations are loosened and defined in such a way that it allows for more decision making on the part of the workers. Finally, Theory 'Z' refers to a style of management used in Japan which incorporates motivation and organisation in cultural terms. The latter two theories could only be implemented successfully by allowing the use of more informal communications.

Since the 1950s, use of informal communication channels has gained an unprecedented popularity especially in organisations which intend to optimise their efficiency by involving and using the human resources more effectively. In order to achieve this managers resort to the use of less centralised means of control and decision making in order to get the things done more efficiently through others. In this way employees receive advice, from the managers and peers involved, through informal communication channels. Smith et. al., (1989a) observes that managers don't spend their time planning, organising and controlling. They spend a surprisingly high proportion of their time in lubricating the human mechanism of the organisation by discussion, informal and unplanned meetings, attending to colleague's and subordinate's personal problems, dealing with crises and dealing with outsiders who want or can grant favours.

Informal Communication

Informal communication allows for the transmission of information in any direction regardless of the formal position of the sender in the organisation. In this respect, informal communication can take many patterns such as star, chain, Y shape or wheel. Informal communication is fast and does not necessarily have to obey the set organisational procedures for communication.

Mintzberg (1979) observes that rich networks of informal communication supplement and sometimes circumvent the regulated channels; and decision processes flow through the organisation, independent of the regulated system. It has the potential to facilitate the communication amongst the organisation members and thus enable them to send and receive information to and from lateral and diagonal sources along with the top/down formal communication networks (Smith, 1982b). The lateral source could be labelled as colleagues in the same department and diagonal sources may be described as their counterparts on the other departments. The messages could be conveyed easily and efficiently by using personal relations to speed-up the communication process. Pilcher (1992) contends that informal relationships are often used as a basis for communication where the formal system tends to be too slow and ponderous to deal with situations that demand quick responses.

The use of channels of informal communication is actively encouraged during the process of building teams and quality circles which are used mostly during operational and implementation phases (Analoui, 1997b). Quality circles which was initially developed in the West has been widely used in Japanese organisations and nowadays it is being incorporated into different organisational cultures in the West (Jones and Woodcock, 1985). The work groups informally meet and discuss the quality of their service, product and their work life as a whole and thus suggest ways to improve them. The decision making process is generally based on the quality of the feedback which is receive in order to improve the efficiency of the organisation and the quality of the product. Adair (1989) defines quality circles as the gathering of the wisdom of people. He indicates that, in 1980, Toyota Corporation had 46,000 workers and the corporations received

587,000 suggestions from the work force to improve the quality of the products across the projects.

There are, however, disadvantages to sole use of the informal communications, in particular the information available from the grapevine of the organisation. The messages and information could be distorted or prejudiced as they pass from one person to another simply because people differ in terms of their frames of references, cultural values, personal fears, aspirations and opinions, the language they use, their degree of understanding and the degree of interpretations included in the original message (Kakabadse et. al., 1987). People's differences in terms of status, personality and pre-occupations means that they tend to understand the message as they perceive it. Often the information is understood according to the receiver's own expectations (Smith et. al., 1987). While it is impossible to get rid of grapevine altogether, it would be possible to improve the work-culture of the groups by creating more trust and confidence amongst the team members. This will reduce the distortion caused through the grapevine and thus allows for speedy communication to a lot of people at different levels of the hierarchy (Mitchel, 1978).

Interpersonal skills for project managers

It is nowadays believed that 'interpersonal communication' is one of the essential requirements for effective management of the projects.

Interpersonal Communication provides the managers with an opportunity to pass and receive information and to establish sound and healthy working relationships (Analoui, 1993, P. 184).

The project managers spend a large proportion of their time communicating with people who are in some ways attached or associated with the project. It is essential for the project managers to complete the task in time and within the allocated resources by exercising a reasonable degree of control over the work processes. This means interacting with a variety of people both within and outside of the ambit of project to, for example, ensure that the task has been carried out according to certain specifications or simply to satisfy the donor, client and the public as the whole. These intricate decisions can not be made and the various managerial functions can not be smoothly carried out unless managers possess appropriate interpersonal communication skills (Mintzberg, 1973).

To achieve this level of competence a manager has to begin by accepting that the human resources, both within or outside of the project, those who are associated with the project whether employees, colleagues or contractors, all have certain socio-psychological needs which they actively strive to satisfy (Bolton, 1979). These needs vary from the desire for 'inclusion', to exercising 'control' over their work and the need for 'affection and affiliation'. Interpersonal communication often provides the main channels for expressing and conveying these needs to others as well as providing means for their partial or complete satisfaction. The traditional image of the project manager as a simple implementer places emphasis on the mechanical aspects of the project manager's role thus ignoring the socio-psychological aspects of the managerial work (Analoui, 1989). The expression of interpersonal needs can also create clashes of interests between different individuals and work groups and ultimately harm the progress of the project. Hence the managers, including those in charge of the projects and programmes, have to develop interpersonal skills such as 'effective listening', 'assertive behaviour', 'conflict-resolution' and 'problem-solving' to meet the socio-psychological needs of the people and work situations to optimise efficiency (Turner, 1983; Analoui, 1993).

The situations in which skillful interpersonal communication is called for are many. Individuals and team members need to be encouraged and motivated. Managers play an important role in creating the 'shared value' and a feeling of 'us' amongst the individuals and work group members (Kakabadse, 1983) and ensuring their commitment to the goals of the project by getting them 'involved' by listening to their comments and suggestions.

Project managers, from time to time, need to communicate with the general public, the client, who could be affected by the project either in economic or social terms. These beneficiaries also need to be informed about the impacts of the project on their lives as well as ensuring that their points of view are considered. The managers are often expected to discuss the different aspects of the project with the team members and the public to achieve the goals accordingly. Conflict-resolution and problem-solving skills are essential to fulfill these functions and are increasingly required to make things go as specified and as scheduled between different the agencies involved in the project.

The contractors and consultants could be the most difficult people to deal with in the developing world as they try to get the things done according to the interest of the project. From time to time issues related to specifications, scheduling and payment procedures are brought up which are potentially conflictual in nature and require diplomatically handling. The manager ought to be interpersonally skillful enough to deal with these conflicts without wasting further time and resources, thus avoiding harm to the project (Reilly, 1987).

Conclusions

Effective communication is essential for the successful implementation of the projects. Project mangers play an important role towards achieving this goal and in maintaining reasonable control and discipline within the organisation. Project implementation, with stress on task oriented teams necessitates the use of strong and efficient formal communication channels to set out the procedures and inform those involved in the project implementation about their individual or group assignments, responsibilities and progress.

It is important to ensure that directives and guidelines issued are coherent, clear and precise. During the implementation and operational phases people are required to perform their tasks and roles in co-ordination with others. An established and well tried procedure could prove beneficial in terms of reducing uncertainty as well as providing direction.

Informal communication could be effectively used to improve the operational phase by introducing quality circles and the formation and maintenance of task groups more effectively. The implementation phase is very critical and therefore it requires different informal links to avoid delays by solving internal and external problems quickly. The interpersonal communication channels are also required to motivate people and satisfy their psycho-social needs which are necessary for their development. Skillful communications also helps one to work effectively with different people from different backgrounds with different values, beliefs, and interests. Hence, interpersonal communication is the need of the hour to implement formal and informal channels effectively; improve the organisational culture; encourage the involvement of the local people; and make the most of the available resources, in particular the human resources of the organisation.

References

Adair, J. (1988), *'The Effective Communicator'*, Industrial Society, London.

Analoui, F. (1997a), *Senior Managers and Their Effectiveness*, Avebury, Aldershot, England.

Analoui, F. (1997b), *Project Management Manual*, Government of Romania Department for European Integration.

Analoui, F. (1993), 'Skills of Management', in Cusworth, J. and Franks, T., *Managing Projects in Developing Countries*, (eds), Longman Scientific and Technical, UK.

Analoui, F. (1991), *Towards Achieving the Optimum Fit Between Managers and Project Organisation*', in Project Appraisal, Vol. 6, No. 4, December.

Analouei, A. R. (1998), 'Use of Task Groups and Teams for Management of Human Resources', in F. Analoui *Human Resource Management Issues in Developing Countries*, (ed.), Avebury, Aldershot, England.

Bolton, R. (1979), *People Skills*, Prentice-Hall, USA.

Bormann, E. G. (1982), *Interpersonal Communication in the Modern Organisations*, 2nd edition, Prentice-Hall, New Jersey.

Baum, W. C. and Tolbert, S. W. (1985), *Investing in Development: Lessons of World Bank*, 1st edition, OUP, New York.

Dicher, T. W. (1989), 'Development Management: Plain Orfancy: Sorting Out Some Muddles', in *Public Administration and Development*, Vol. 9, No. 13, Summer.

Gobeli, D. H. (1987), 'Relative Effectiveness of Different Project Structures', in *Project Management Journal*, Vol. 18, No. 2.

Gariers, R. and Roland, A. (1991), 'Management By Projects: The Management Strategy of the New Project-oriented Company', in *International Journal of Project Management*', Vol. 9, Part 2.

Goodman, L. J. and Love, R. N. (1980), *Project Planning and Management: An Integral Approach*, Pergamon, New York.

Handy, C. B. (1985), *Understanding Organisations*, Penguin, Harmondsworth.

Hanna, N. (1985), 'Strategic Planning and Management', in *World Bank Staff Paper*, No. 751, IBRD.

Herman, A. H. (1974), *Principles of Management*, 4th edition, Wiley, London.

Jones, J. E. and Woodcock, M. (1985), *Manual of the Management Development*, Gower, London.

Kakabadse, A., Ludlow, R. and Vinnicombe, S. (1987), *Working in Organisation*', Penguin Books.

Kakabadse, A. and Brovetto, R. (1989), *Management and The Public Sector*, (eds), Avebury, Aldershot, England.

Mintzberg, H. (1979), *The Structuring of Organisation*', Prentice-Hall, London.

Mitchell, T. R. (1978), *People in Organisations*, McGraw-Hill.

Morss, E. R. and Gow, D. D (1988), 'The Notorious Nine Critical Problems in Project Implementation', in *World Development*, Vol. 6, No. 12.

Piltcher, R.(1992), *Principles of Construction Management*, 3rd Edition McGraw-Hill, London.

Preston, P.(1981), *Managerial Communication*, Goodyear.

Reilly, W. (1987), 'Managerial Constraints to Rural Development in Africa', in *Agricultural Administration Extension*, Vol. 26.

Rondinelli, D. A. (1979), 'Planning Development of Projects: Lessons From Developing Countries', in *Long Range Planning*, Vol. 12.

Smith, P. (1989), *Management in Agricultural and Rural Development*, Elsevier Applied Science, London.

Smith, M., Beck, J., Cooper, L.C., Cox, C., and Ottaway, R. T. (1982), *Introducing Organisational Behaviour*, Macmillan.

7 Work cultures and change of attitude in public sector

Suzanne Fogg

Iceberg or onion? What is culture?

Sometimes referred to as 'an onion', sometimes referred to as 'an iceberg', culture has been studied and discussed by many people in many walks of life, ranging from sociologists and anthropologists to economists and chemists! It is as essential for the life of the organization, ever present, yet as hard to understand or describe due to its sheer nature and lack of physical character. This chapter will begin by defining a working meaning for the term 'culture'. Having explained the idea of a 'present dominant culture' and showed that it can exist at a national level, at a specific moment-in-time as well as at an organisational or institutional level, the characteristics of two contrasting types of cultures will be analysed; the role culture and the task culture. These, though often taken in abstract, will be used to illustrate the issues that arise when attempting to bring about a change of attitudes in public sector organisations.

'Culture' has become a popular word in everyday management language. As it is not immediately obvious what is meant by culture, many authors writing on the subject have developed their own interpretations and definitions. Trompenaars believes culture 'is the way in which a group of people solves problems' (1993, p.6). This explanation appears somewhat simplistic, yet he goes on to explain that like 'an onion', culture comes in layers and in order to understand it, you have to peel it layer by layer. This is interesting in that it clearly breaks down the level of consciousness in our behaviour (for solving problems), with the outer layers consisting of the products of culture. Explicit, like the skyscrapers of Manhattan, they are expressions of deeper values and norms that are further in the 'onion heart' and require more time to understand as they are more difficult to identify.

Other explicit expressions of culture may be seen through language, food, architecture or clothes for example, but these appear to be purely symbols of culture rather than actual beliefs.

In the middle layer of the symbolic 'onion' Trompenaars describes norms (i.e. what is right and wrong for a group) and values (i.e. what is considered good and bad ideals within a group) and distinguishes these as how one *should* behave as opposed to how *one aspires* to behaving. The concept of 'desire' is fundamental to his belief of how people behave, and a stable and shared understanding of this 'desire' results in a cultural tradition being developed and elaborated (1993, p.26) or not. At the core of the 'onion' lie the implicit assumptions that underlie all human action which are based on the need to survive. Though Trompenaars believes these to disappear from human consciousness, they remain at the heart of the system on which the outer onion layers are based upon, and it is these absolute assumptions which are probably most difficult to change when a culture shift is attempted.

Broms and Gahmberg (1982) also believed it to be necessary to go to the level of the subconscious in order to find values. In the same way as 'culture means values', for them, 'values mean images' (p.30) and the 'ethics of a group is located in images and symbols, which are kept alive as long as the group exists'. The idea of images representing values in the subconscious was also proposed by the philosophers Jung and Cassirer, not in order to bring mysticism and abstract ethical concepts into the realm, but for a scientific explanation for human decision making and planning.

Where Watson (1994) discusses the need for culture, he defines it as;

> the system of meanings which are shared by members of a human grouping and which define what is good and bad, right and wrong and what are the appropriate ways for members of that group to think and behave (p.21).

Watson bases this on two key ideas; human nature to wish to find meaning in one's life (with people free to make choices over particular actions) and that the world is an essentially ambiguous place in which humans can not realistically make detailed plans. These ideas mean that 'culture', while in part morally based, helps people construct their own identities. He emphasises that culture is 'human-made', and that rather than being moulded by their culture, humans engage with it and constantly re-make it (p.23).

Even though determining what is good from bad, and right from wrong, is difficult in relation to human behaviour these notions seem fundamental to all views of culture. The Collins English Dictionary (1986) definition is succinct in summing up these ideas and defines culture as 'the total of the inherited ideas, beliefs, values and knowledge, which constitute the shared bases of social action'. Understanding these different views of culture and the idea of it as an 'Iceberg' where the explicit part is based on a much larger implicit part beneath the water is important. The dictionary interpretation has been adopted here as a basis for discussion.

Present dominant culture?

The 'present dominant culture' referred to in the question could be understood as existing at several different levels. Trompenaars (1994) describes the highest level of culture as 'national' or regional, the French or West Europeans versus the Singaporean or oriental (p.7). Much literature exists that analyses cultures present at this level, especially with a view to improving business links at an international level. Often very general and stereotyped, these descriptions provide an insight into other cultures and identify fundamental differences that could otherwise result in miscommunication and loss of business. The logic, structured and rational culture of north Europeans has been contrasted to the Euro-Latin's person-related and sensitive culture (Trompenaars, 1994). These are relatively minor cultural differences when compared to the four dimensions (power distance, uncertainty avoidance, individualism and masculinity) studied by Hofstede (1986) in over forty countries where IBM had employees.

The concept of culture can also be understood in terms of the changing 'fashions' in 'schools of thought' at various points in time. In the management world, like in the clothes industry, fads exist and different theories of best practice are adopted and later rejected as new ideas come on the market. Where personnel management was the norm in the 1980s, human resource development has now overtaken.

The idea of culture developing and becoming dominant in an 'organisation' will be the focus of this paper. Having defined culture as the behaviour (or 'social actions') 'within' a group that results from 'the inherited ideas, beliefs, values and knowledge' it appears to be a tautology to say 'this' is 'influenced by the present dominant culture'. Culture, in terms of the organisation has been described as the 'hard to define rules that spell success or failure' (Business Week, October 1980). Though hard to define, the principal factors that influence the choice and the structure of a culture have been described by Handy (1993) as, 'history and ownership, size, technology, goals and objectives, the environment and the people' (p.192). These factors have varying degrees of influence; for example size, have proved to be the most important variable influencing choice and structure of culture with large organisations on the whole more formal and authoritarian. Similarly, for technology, factories involved in mass production, with routine and programmable operations will tend to be better suited to well developed technology than businesses involved in non-continuous discrete operations.

The objectives of any organisation will contribute significantly to the culture, that develops, but these are not always clear-cut. Where the aim is clear, such as increasing share value, the culture will be focused and respond to that core aim requiring a high profit ratio. The employees will usually have a focused attitude to reach their targets following set rules and regulations, with direct accountability to their superiors.

Objectives will determine the direction taken and the 'strategy' chosen by an organisation. The underlying philosophy, or culture, of the organisation will determine any plans for the future. Whether these are then suited to the organisation will determine their success or failure. An 'intended' strategy may not necessarily be suited to the organisation and its culture, or the environment, therefore the 'realised' strategy (in practice) may be quite different from the theoretical strategy chosen initially.

A 'strategy' will usually be in keeping with the ideology behind the organisational culture as it will be conceived by the owners, bosses or original creators. Devising a strategy represents a deliberate attempt to 'shape' an organisation. Shaping an organisation is usually an attempt to bring about long-term survival and requires careful management. Watson believes that for survival an organisation must explicitly set out to develop a 'strategic intent' (1994, p.87) and hope for a 'winning culture'.

Culture pure or mixed?

The factors which contribute to a specific culture forming have been shown to be diverse, yet four main types of culture have been identified by Harrison (1972). These are;

- power culture   (spider's web)
- role culture   (temple)
- task culture   (fisherman's net)
- person culture   (galaxy of stars)

126

Each type of culture has been associated with a 'form' or an organisational 'structure', for example fishermen's net or spider's web.

Though characteristically very different, it is unusual for an organisation to follow one single type of culture only. More commonly, an organisation is associated with a specific form, yet shows features that are possibly best described as a mix of culture types to suit their specific needs and objectives. The role culture and the task culture will now be described and analysed as contrasting examples of two types of culture. The service culture will then be briefly looked at, as a new fifth culture.

Role versus task culture

The role based organisational culture, as its name indicates, is based on the fundamental idea that within any organisation the 'role' of a person is of paramount importance. This applies for the cleaners as much as for the accountants in a role based organisation. More important than the individual himself, the part he plays within the structure of the temple is his purpose for being. The structure of the organisation is based on a strict hierarchy, with all roles joined in an orderly manner. A clear division usually exists between the higher and the lower echelons of the workforce. The bosses are respected, in a paternalistic way, and authority comes from the top and moves down the ranks.

From the employees point of view, each employee has a specific function, be it little or large, up-front or back-stage, for which he is suited to and has the necessary skills, therefore training is not considered necessary. As requirements (expectations) on the individual are clear, the work to be accomplished is also predictable. It is also easily controllable. Each employee is accountable to a superior, who controls and supervises the work. As all responsibilities within the organisation are clearly defined, theoretically each post is filled and each job is taken care of. Jobs tend to be fairly secure if performance satisfies the basic requirements.

Communication within a role based organisation follows the formal structure of the temple, with specific channels and specific rules and regulations relating to the information flows. The rigid structure of the temple, or role based culture, provides it with a firm foundation, in which innovation and flexibility are not welcome, but security and regularity are guaranteed. In this 'reactive' closed environment, tradition is maintained in line with the beliefs and values of the propounders of the classical school in management.

The task based organisational culture is quite different from that of role culture. The individual is essential in the fisherman's net framework. Tasks, or goals, are the driving force for the organisation as a whole and require working together and co-ordination for mutual benefit. This results in commitment to the cause of the organisation. Each individual is equal to his/her neighbour and considered on an identical level, resulting in mutual respect. Equality and democracy are paramount. Consultation and communication are extremely important in all directions.

No greater responsibilities are given to one employee rather than to the next. Each individual employee is flexible and can adapt to the task of another. Ability is the determining factor for any task rather than superiority. Training is important to guarantee flexibility and adaptability at all times, while being responsive to needs.

The strength of the net comes from its flexibility and self-control. Rather than an environment of rigidity, the role-based culture encourages creativity and innovation as it is for the greater good of the organisation. Rules and regulations have no place. Lack of control from the higher ranks can result in chaos and disintegration if the situation is not suitable, for example where resources are in shortage and no senior individuals have the authority to give orders nor to take control. This 'pro-active' open environment is encouraged by the 'Modern School'.

The service-based culture is a more recently developed concept. It is in accordance with the view to improving the efficiency and effectiveness of the service industry, where a large number of employees are in direct contact with the customers (rather than a factory, where only the boss or employees working in marketing actually have this contact) and therefore their role is very important in the success of the company. The process of feed-back is crucial to the survival of the organisation as this is how it adapts and innovates according to the needs of the market. The role of the managers is then to facilitate and encourage the processes in the organisation rather than to control them. The dynamic and open environment created in a service based culture enables the organisation as a whole, to continuously adapt to change as and when necessary.

An interesting comparison between the different culture types has been illustrated by the different Greek Gods. Zeus, the God of harmony, is supposed to reflect the role culture, preferring stability and predictability, while Athena, Goddess of war represents camaraderie and support for the task culture. Zeus with his force and Dionysus, with his craft, are supposed to represent the power and person cultures respectively (Handy, 1993).

Attitudes in the public sector

The public sector in most countries comprises many different services ranging from education, transportation, waste disposal and highway maintenance, to libraries, police and fire services, recreational facilities and social services. As 'services' provided by the government, the dominant 'culture' has usually been based on the key idea to provide assistance to the population, without making a profit. In many countries, the unusual objectives, the enormous size, the lack of 'ownership' and long complicated history, as well as the lack of resources and technological inputs of the public institutions, have all contributed to developing a 'unique culture', that can not realistically be compared to any private sector organisations.

Public sector organisations are traditionally seen as fitting into the 'role culture' model, where each individual works within a greater temple, unaware of the goings on in other parts of the temple. The sheer size of most public institutions results in a high level of hierarchy and control, with little room for innovation and flexibility. For the purpose of this discussion, the assumption made is that a change in culture, if desired would be from a closed role culture towards a more open task culture.

The issue of 'whether' change is necessary, or even 'wanted' needs to be discussed. Change, whether in original objectives, work methods or behaviour, if initiated internally is usually a reaction, or 'strategic response' to some crisis or opportunity (Williams, et. al., 1989, p.65). Though in crisis in many countries, the public sector services are not fighting for their survival (against competitors) as they remain monopolistic institutions in the market. Yet, with 'efficiency' a key word for the 1990s, and greater transparency and accountability (for example, to the tax payer), change in performance of the public sector institutions has now become viewed as necessary and the opportunity is there to be taken, when resources permit.

It is important to point out that whereas in developed countries, individuals are generally selected (be it at national election or local community level) on the basis of their qualifications and experiences, their ideas and their knowledge, the situation in developing countries tends to be different. Traditionally, individuals will be selected for their age and authority. This fundamental difference is based on strong cultural differences. As with the elders in a village community, the environment in many public organisations is based on respect and power, with little questioning of authority. This subservient deferential culture results in great obedience yet with this, change is extremely difficult to bring about.

Change: a means to an end

The means by which change can be brought about, have been written about at length, and according to Williams, et. al., (1989, p.72) who describe the practical techniques, there are six main methods:

1. changing the people (through recruitment, selection and redundancy),
2. changing places (reshuffling and moving people into key positions),
3. changing beliefs and attitudes (with workshops, meetings, quality circles, teams, communication, participation, counselling and role models),
4. changing behaviour (through training in new skills and techniques),
5. changing structures, systems, technology, (functional groupings, networks, reward schemes, budgeting systems, appraisal and monitoring for performance changes),
6. changing corporate image (name, logo, employee involvement for identification).

Change should not be considered an end in itself, but a means to an end. Where organisations have set out to implement a new strategic direction, by introducing new objectives, methods, systems, structures, training and people, they have quite often fortuitously changed their culture as well. Change must be carefully planned 'not to occur in a vacuum' but rather to be linked to organisational effectiveness via strategic planning (Williams, et. al., 1989, p.66).

Though possibly over-exaggerated and over-simplified, the features of the traditional role culture described above, have contributed to a clear division of labour (like in the temple structure) in which civil servants are administrators and implementers, while politicians are in power, making laws and important decisions.

The issue of 'power' is fundamental to this dominant culture. As Williams, et. al., (1989) explain 'the concept of power refers to the ability to cause others to perform actions that they might not otherwise perform... therefore to change the behaviour of others' (p.99). They further emphasise the need, when managing change, to understand not only 'who' are the people who influence change, but 'what' are their sources of power. Power may come for a civil servant from his status, having access to privileges, or from an individual's position in relation to information. Abuse of power often comes from within unsatisfied cultures, for example low pay leading to corruption.

The police force and the public administration

Different departments in the public sector require different kinds of culture mixes, and different degrees of culture change. The public administration, is traditionally rigid in structure, with high levels of control and little individual responsibility. This has often led to many demoralised employees and low performance. Any changes must have as their prime consideration 'being of service'. This is not incompatible with the formation of teams (both vertically and horizontally), co-operation and dialogue. A decentralised organisation where individual's have incentives to perform to their best and find their jobs challenging and interesting, will require a significant shift in culture. Flexibility is not necessarily easy to operate, especially where money is concerned, as transparency and accountability are not based on judgement but require good financial management. Certain rules and regulations will need to be enforced for efficiency purposes.

The police force has traditionally been based on a strong hierarchical structure, and behavioural procedures have suited the 'law and order', objectives... However, change has become necessary as the objectives (or problems) have changed. Where previously a militaristic culture of authority and rules dominated, modern policing now requires more thought and adaptiveness, as criminals become more inventive. Teams and co-ordination across borders, are becoming the norm as drug-smuggling and law-evasion increases in scale of operation. Preventing and outwitting organised crime is the aim rather than simple response.

In both situations, the shift is from a closed to a more open organisational culture. Problems arise when there is not sufficient communication and with this a lack of understanding and suspicion as regards the new ideas. Though responsibilities may change, some individuals find it hard to let go of their specific roles. Flexibility of task responsibilities for them is difficult, and adapting to a less controlled and accountable environment means they must be more self-disciplined and self-controlled in order to perform to their optimum capacity. Trust becomes vital where previously the employees relied only upon themselves.

Watson (1994) identifies, for the public service, one of the eight characteristic concepts mentioned by Peters and Waterman in their book 'In Search of Excellence': the simultaneous loose-tight control. This is based on the idea that people are not tightly constrained by supervisory surveillance or by rules, yet tightness comes from people choosing to do what is required of them because they wish to serve the values which they share with those in charge (p.16). To stifle change an individual would maintain their control, of everything, following bureaucratic procedures to slow down all action, keeping all issues secret and generally creating a difficult work environment, to the point of sabotaging work for all to suffer.

Conclusion

Attempts have been made to illustrate the 'complexity of bringing about 'change', especially with regards to 'culture' which itself is not a straightforward and easily definable concept. Change in any institution, be it private or public, requires a great deal of planning and for a change in 'shape' to be successful, a 'strategy' must be devised. Taking time, change can be brought about through the use of many different mediums; with communication crucial at all levels. Though very gradual, change within the public sector, is becoming more common and efficiency and effectiveness are slowly becoming core implicit assumptions in the heart of the organisations.

References

Broms, H. and Gahmberg, H. (1982), *Mythology in management culture*, Helsingin Kauppakorkeankoulun Julkaisuja.

Collins Paperback English Dictionary (1986), (ed). McLeod, W. Collins, London.

Handy, C. (1993), *Understanding organisations*, Fourth Edition, Penguin Books, St Ives.

Hannagan, (1995), *Management concepts and practices*, Pitman Publishing, London.

Harrison, R. (1972), 'How to describe your organisation', *Harvard Business Review*, September.

Hofstede, (1986), 'Culture consequences', in Handy, C. (1993) *Understanding organisations*, Fourth Edition, Penguin Books, St Ives.

Larson, C. E., LaFasto, F. M (1989), 'Team Work; what must go right/what can go wrong', *Sage Series Interpersonal Communication 10*, Sage Publications, London.

Schermerhorn, J.R. (1996), *Management*, Fifth Edition John Wiley and Sons, Inc. New York and Toronto.

Schein, E. H. (1985), *Organisational culture and leadership: a dynamic view*, Jossey-Bass Publishers, San Francisco.

Trompenaars, F. (1994), *Riding the waves of culture: understanding cultural diversity in business*, Nicholas Brealey Publishing. London.

Waddington, M. E., (1996), 'The Managing manual', School of Business, Huddersfield University.

Watson, T. (1994), *In search of management; culture, chaos, and control in managerial work*, Routledge, London and New York.

Williams, A., Dobson, P., Walters, M. (1989), 'Changing culture: new organisational approaches', Institute of Personnel Management, Trowbridge.

8 Transfer of farm power technology for agricultural mechanisation in Bangladesh: the need for change and training

Dr R I Sarkar

Introduction

The agricultural sector employs over 40 percent of the country's population, produces about 30 percent of the GDP and earns about 30 percent of the foreign exchange by exporting various agricultural commodities and products. Over 10 million farm households earn their livelihood and share the total cultivable land area of 9.6 million hectares. Thus the key to sustained economic development for Bangladesh lies in raising the productivity of agriculture sector.

Agricultural operations in Bangladesh are still overwhelmingly muscle and animal powered. Land preparation (LP) or tillage of millions of fragmented and scattered small-sized farms is traditionally done by draught animals (DAs). Draught animal power (DAP) demands increased since the introduction of high yielding varieties of rice (HYV) in the sixties. Increased draught availability through the improvements in tillage implements and tools were attempted but failed as DAs in Bangladesh are very small and weak (producing only about 0.35-0.40 hp per pair). Presently the draught power shortage is about 30-35 percent throughout the country and the shortages are acute during the peak periods. In some parts the peak period shortages rise upto 45 percent.

On the other hand increasing demands for food and fibre for the country's vast population of 120 million, growing at the rate of 2 percent per year, also put pressures on land for production increases through double or triple cropping. This demands a change for more farm power inputs per unit area and farmers are looking for mechanical power sources as an alternative to meet shortages. But the selection and the transfer of appropriate alternative technology for farm power for the smallholders in Bangladesh would need a careful analysis of technical, social (human resource aspects) and economic factors. In this chapter an attempt is made to select appropriate farm power technology and suggest ways for the transfer of technology for the vast number of small farmers of Bangladesh.

Agricultural development and mechanisation policies

Agricultural production of over 20 million metric tons (MMT) of food grains (mainly rice) is needed to meet the present food and nutritional deficiencies of the country. The government of Bangladesh (GOB) had given top priority to develop agricultural sector in all the past four five-year plans since independence in order to meet food self-sufficiency, to solve the problems of employment of rural labour forces and to alleviate the poverty level.

Past development plans and strategies

The country followed a course of planned development since its independence in 1971 with a view to inducing fast and appropriate development. All the past three five-year plans had poverty alleviation, economic growth, population control, higher literacy, etc. as main plan objectives. The third five-year plan (TFYP) for 1985-90 emphasised on literacy and intended explicitly to promote human resources development. Meeting basic minimum needs of the people, their productive employment and food self-sufficiency were incorporated to the national development effort in the fourth five-year plan (FFYP) for 1990-95. The distinct emphasis with regard to the availability of food and nutrition for the vast population who are in a situation of large scale unemployment and under-employment has heightened the concern on reducing absolute poverty level through increased agricultural productivity. The FFYP plan also envisaged to raise food production to about 22 MMTs. In short the broad objectives of the agricultural sector during TFYP and FFYP were to:

- expand production base of promising food;
- maximum use of land and, water resources inputs;
- improve employment situation and farm income; and
- higher production of forestry resources.

Emphasis on the crop diversification and mechanisation through private entrepreneurs were some of the additional objectives in the FFYP to stabilise outputs.

Past mechanisation policies and strategy

Tractorization was very low in the sixties and seventies. Animal power was the main source of farm power until 1970. As multiple cropping with modern varieties of rice intensified the demand for more draught power (DP) increased. The DP constraints over the years led to pressure for mechanical power sources. The trend of increased imports of tractors and power tillers (PTs) continued since independence to make good of the losses of DAs in the wars, cyclones and floods of 1971, 1970 and 1988 respectively. After the devastating cyclone and floods in 1987 and 1988 GOB had reduced import taxes and tariffs on PTs and other agricultural machinery in response to the acute farm power shortages brought about by the losses of millions of DAs. Power tillers (7-12 KW) of various makes and models were imported since 1988. But there were no extension advice relating to the optimum size of PTs and tractors to various farm sizes.

In the FFYP which ended in June 1995 emphasis had been given to agricultural mechanisation by the following statements:

- to rapidly expand minor irrigation coverage,
- to promote competitive markets,
- to create employment opportunity,
- to educate farmers and dealers on the use of inputs,
- to maintain current waiver on duties and taxes of small (1-20hp engines).

These objectives were not achieved and no training programme to improve the skills of farmers and dealers were undertaken in the FFYP.

Present status of agriculture and mechanisation

Bangladesh is blessed with fertile soil and water resources. About 9.6 million hectares of cultivable land is intensively used by over 10.0 million farm households. But 65 percent of land area is subject to flooding of different depths at some periods of the year. Rice is grown on about 80 percent of the cropped area to meet foodgrain deficiency of Bangladesh. HYV winter rice is grown during dry season (December-March) with irrigation from both surface and ground sources. Early and late wet season

Table 8.1
Area irrigated by different methods ('000 ha)

Methods	Five year averages				Annual Data			
	1970/75	1975/80	1980/85	1985/90	1986/87	1988/89	1990/9	1992-93
Modern:	569	769	1357	1721	1798	2340	2510	2858
Power Pumps	486	574	708	609	660	658	657	687
Tube Wells	55	137	501	963	982	1512	1677	2013
Canals	28	59	148	149	156	170	176	159
Traditional: (Doons, Swing buskets & others)	691	686	533	377	402	399	427	396
Total:	1260	1455	1890	2098	2200	2739	2937	3254
Modern (%)	44.7	52.8	71.1	82	81.7	85.4	85.5	87.8
Traditional (%)	55.3	47.2	28.9	18	18.3	14.6	14.5	12.2

Source: BBS (1992)

rice is grown during April-July and August-November periods with no or little irrigation. Area irrigated by all the methods has increased from 1.26 million hectares in 1970/75 to 3.25 million hectares in 1992/93 (BBS, 1995). Irrigation area coverage under different technologies or methods are presented in Table 8.1.

Farm size and distribution Nearly 80 percent of the rural population are dependent on agriculture for their employment, income and food. The agricultural census of 1983/84 estimated the total number of farm households as 10.00 million. The percentage of agricultural labour households was 39.8 and they are dependent on wage income mainly working as casual labour on other farms. Table 8.2 shows land ownership, farm size and distribution between 1960 and 1984. It shows that the number of rural households increased by 40 percent over the period. The increase in the number of households in the marginal category (less than 0.5 ha) from 24 to 41 percent over the period shows a growing trend at marginalisation of peasantry. This functionally landless category farmers rely on off-farm wage employment and supply casual labours for others. The problem of under or unemployment is more severe in this category during off peak periods.

Land utilisation and labour productivity The land utilisation in Bangladesh has reached its maximum as it can be seen from the census data. Table 8.3 shows the trends of land use for different crops in Bangladesh. The index of multiple cropping increased to about 164 percent in 1990/91 from 138 percent in 1971/72. Per hectare productivity increased substantially from the adoption of modern technology. Agricultural labour force increased at the rate of over 1.2 percent over the 30 years period as shown in Table 8.4. Labour productivity grew at the rate of 1.4 percent during the same period and crop output per agricultural worker increased by over 3 percent.

Crop Production Improvement in agricultural production required major modifications in the cropping environment. Modernisation of irrigation and water control was one of the key effort to the intensification of agriculture during the dry season. Today, the most important mechanical technology in agriculture is associated with irrigation. The contributions of other inputs like chemical fertilizer and pesticides, HYV seeds, extension advice, agricultural credits and improved management were substantial in increasing agricultural production. Contributions of all the inputs together resulted in an increase in cropping intensity, and land and labour productivity. Table

8.3 shows trends in crop production, cropping intensity and per ha yields over the same periods.

Table 8.2
Land

Household type	1960	1977	1983/84
Rural households	8.24	10.87	13.82
Farm households	6.14	6.26	10.05
Near landless house-holds (owning less than 0.2 ha)	0.80	0.34	2.42
Landless and nearlandless	2.90	4.96	6.19

Farm size (ha)	Percentage of Farms			Percentage of land		
	1960	1977	1983/8	1960	1977	1983/8
Up to 0.44	24.3	15.9	40.5	3.2	2.7	7.8
0.45 to 1.00	27.3	33.8	29.9	12.9	16.3	21.2
1.10 to 3.00	37.7	40.9	24.7	45.7	49.4	45.1
Above 3.00	10.7	9.4	4.9	38.1	32.7	25.9

Agricultural employment Bangladesh agriculture today appears to be employing over 55 percent of total labour force of both sexes, thus giving employment opportunity to over 34 million rural people in agricultural sector (BBS, 1995). Average number of days of employment per person per year vary in different regions of the country. Khan (1980) earlier reported 115 days of employment in agriculture activities per year. Employment rate Per ha of cropped area was about 185 man-days during 1989-90. This number has increased since then for a number of reasons. It has recently reached about 200 man-days/ha. Rice crop is the highest employer of the rural labour force. Changes in cropping patterns, high cropping intensity, introduction of HYV and modern inputs, farm sizes, tenancy, land ownership, cultural practices and level of mechanisation inputs have positive influences on increase or decrease of employment of labour force. Table 8.4 shows the year-wise employment trends of rural labour forces.

Table 8.3

Acreage, production and cropping intensity of major food-grains (1979-90)

Year	Area ('000 ha)	Rice Production (mm tons)	Av.Yield per ha (kg)	Area ('000 ha)	Wheat Production (mm tons)	Yield per ha (kg)	Cropping Intensity (%)
1970/75 *	10,026	10.89	1100	126	0.11	865	136
1975/80 *	10,253	12.62	1220	182	0.43	1710	142
1980/81	10,540	13.88	1320	604	1.09	1808	153
1983/84	10,780	14.51	1340	538	1.21	2250	154
1984/85	10,278	14.39	1430	677	1.44	2130	152
1985/86	10,402	14.8	1445	540	1.03	1898	154
1986/87	10,614	15.16	1453	585	1.07	1836	159
1987/88	10,327	15.73	1492	598	1.03	1724	166
1988/89	10,225	15.3	1520	560	1.01	1796	167
1989/90	10,483	17.86	1703	592	0.89	1503	167
1990/91	10,440	17.85	1710	599	1.01	1676	171

- Five year average data

* Five year average data

Source: BBS and Ahmed, M (1988)

141

Present status of mechanisation

The constraints of agricultural mechanisation and technical issues will be highlighted in this section to describe the current status of agricultural mechanisation.

Table 8.4
Agricultural labour force and employment

Characteristics			Years		
	1969/70	1975/76	1981/82	1985/86	1989/90
Agricultural labour force * (million)	14.19	15.15	15.4	17.4	15.45
Employment in crop prod. (mil. man days)	1868	1848	2050	2366	2653
Employment per worker per year (days)	132	122	133	136	172

* Male Labour force only
Source: *Ahmed M (1988) and BBS*

Current mechanisation strategies

Agricultural mechanisation policies and strategies are often confounded by considerable controversy about labour displacement and inequality aspects and benefits. But concern for food self sufficiency dominated the country's past and present development strategies and policies. Higher level of inputs use needs more investments and greater incentives to resource poor farmers. Similarly high population growth, poverty, unemployment and low incomes are major obstacles to investments in modern agricultural inputs. In the absence of proper mechanisation strategy in the country Khan (1990), a consultant appointed by FAO, prepared guide-lines for an agriculture mechanisation strategy. The salient points of the strategy regarding meeting DP shortages are as follows:

- increase the number of DAs
- improve breeds and health of DAs
- use of power tillers and tractors

He suggested that the use of mechanical power is more appropriate in the short and medium terms and simultaneously programmes should be implemented to improve the health conditions of DAs. But the strategy should not resort to increasing the number or population of cattle. The strategy also emphasises on (i) custom-hire services of mechanical power technology; (ii) local manufacturing capacity development through removing taxes on imported raw materials or levying taxes and tariffs on imported machines; (iii) education and training of all persons involved in the use of mechanisation inputs; (iv) private sector involvement in machinery supply, sales and distribution; (v) credit facilities development on easy terms; and (vi) research and development (R&D) programme on adoption, modification and development of appropriate machinery and tools for specific problems facing farmers.

Constraints of agricultural mechanisation

The following in short would seem to be the major constraints which have led to low adoption rates of agricultural technology in the country.

1. High cost of agricultural machinery;
2. Controls of importation;
3. Inappropriateness of imported machinery;
4. Lack of standardisation of products;
5. Lack of trained man-power and appropriate transfer mechanisms;
6. Lack of mechanisation extension advice/services; and
7. Lack of long-term mechanisation programmes.

It would be unrealistic to attempt to formulate mechanisation strategy or establish an appropriate framework for mechanisation development without giving due attention to the above points and other complex economic and social variables affecting decisions. Other sectors should necessarily work together to ensure right atmosphere for mechanisation.

Farm power for land preparation

With increasing irrigation and cropping intensity, the problem of a shorter turn-around time between the harvesting and planting of the subsequent crop draught power shortage is becoming more serious. There are indications of a growing farm power shortage in many areas to the extent of 45 percent. Major sources of farm power are briefly described below.

143

Animal power Majority of farmers still use DAP for tillage and other farm activities. The capacity and draught availability from the local herds are very low and usually 30-40 days are needed to prepare seed beds for 1 ha. This is because of the poor health, breed and low quality feeds. They can produce draft force about 0.25-0.35 KW. The cattle population in Bangladesh are declining due to many factors thus making the draft power situation worse. The draught cattle population in Bangladesh including work buffaloes (see Table 8.5).

The draught animal requirement for about 9.6 million hectares of cultivated land with 160 percent cropping intensity, assuming no constraint on timeliness, would be 8.0 million pairs or 16.0 million cattle (with 2 ha capacity per pair of bullocks). The latest Livestock Census (BBS, 1986) quoted the number of working animals as 11.2 million. On this basis a shortage of 5 million DAs (45 percent) exists in the country. According to Gill (1981) average land cultivated by a pair of bullocks is 4 acres (1.62 ha) and the shortage of draught animal is over 8 million (above 80 percent) on this estimation.

Table 8.5
Cattle population in Bangladesh

Species	Population (million)
Adult Male	**21.176**
Adult Female	8.154
Young Stock (<3 Years)	8.404
Draught Cattle :	4.622
Buffaloes:	**10.9**
Adult Male	
Adult Female	0.457
Young Stock (< 3 Years)	0.266
Draught Buffaloes:	0.33

Source: BBS (1986)

Power tillers The use of PTs (PTs) or single axle tractors has increased rapidly since the import duty was removed from small diesel engines of less than 15 KW in 1988. Table 8.6 shows the import trends of PTs since 1988. From 1960 to the mid 1980s about 6500 PTs were imported and sold to the private sector with credit subsidised by the government. Under the tax relief provision private sectors are recently importing over 25,000 PTs annually and the number is expected to exceed 100,000 by 1995 (Sims, 1993). The high capital investment required to own PTs is prohibiting small farmers from owning and operating them. Contact hire by small farmers is preferred. The timeliness and reduced time for soil preparation are considered as added advantages of PTs.

Table 8.6
Power tiller imports in Bangladesh

Year	Numbers
1988	3,500
1989	7,000
1990	10,000
1992	35,000
1994	60,000

Source: Sutton D S (1993) and Sims B G (1994)

Tractors Tractors are not currently a major power source in Bangladesh agriculture and are likely to be declining. D.H.Sutton (1993) reported a total of 5,200 tractors in the country. The sale of tractors are below 100 a year and most of the imports have been to government organisations through aid programmes. The tractors not only have higher capacity but have very high costs compared to PTs (10 to 12 times higher). The rural infrastructure also does not permit tractors to be widely used for tillage purposes.

Local manufacture of agricultural machinery and tools Manufacturing of sophisticated agricultural machinery and tools is very limited in Bangladesh. All the handtools and animal drawn implements are made locally by village blacksmiths and artisans. Small and large irrigation pumps (upto 2 cusecs), plant protection equipment and power threshers are all made locally. Some small-scale fabricators and manufacturers are making indigenous agricultural machinery and spare parts with limited facilities and investments. The quality of locally made equipment and spares is very poor but they are cheaper in many cases.

Training, transfer and research

To ensure that mechanisation contributes to agricultural development, measures must be taken to train farmers on technical skills and extension workers in the management and transfer of technology. Besides for the successful transfer and adoption of mechanisation technology, institutional development as well as infrastructure development at local levels are very crucial. These will include promotion of appropriate community level skills and services such as blacksmiths, carpenters and mechanics with appropriate workshops and supplies of spare parts and materials. Training to improve the range of skills and to increase knowledge of technology options are presently imparted at several vocational institutions throughout the country but these are not available for the village level farmers, blacksmiths and carpenters. There is also the lacking of extension services for the dissemination of skills and knowledge of mechanised agriculture.

Agricultural engineering departments of the universities and institutions in Bangladesh have in the past undertaken some research and development (R&D) projects. These are usually confined to development or adoption of existing tools, implement or simple machines. As often is the case many of these developments are not proven on the farmers fields. More research and development efforts on multi-purpose use of PT engine for milling, pumping, transport, etc. needs to be done. Besides the need to collect, collate, publish and disseminate information to the farmers, mechanics and extension workers and to train them is more important in order to transfer technology to the unskilled farmers.

Selection of farm power technology for land preparation

Selection of appropriate mechanisation system is a complex procedure. An in-depth study on the subject is beyond the scope of this paper. Theoretically, the selection of any technology starts with an assessment of the job to be done e.g. tillage, planting, etc. The second step is to determine what tool, implement or equipment alternatives are available to do the job in the most effective way and efficient manner and to make a choice accordingly (FAO, 1990). The final step is to select the source of power for the tools, equipment or implements chosen in step two. In practice, for a large proportion of small farmers, the theoretical steps are reversed. The power sources and access to tools are fixed, and cash or credits are not often available for them to purchase improved equipment, tools, etc. even if they may be relatively inexpensive.

In addition to the above points there are two other considerations which often become prominent: (a) what levels and types of mechanisation are appropriate; and (b) how can the advantages that mechanisation provides best be made available to the small farmers. These need careful examinations of the socio-economic conditions and cultural practices existing in the community. Positive and negative aspects of selecting technology must be balanced. In all cases criteria for the selection of technology must include technical factors (operational suitability); managerial suitability; financial and economic benefits; social aspects like income, employment, equity and poverty; environmental aspects of stability and degradation; and cultural and political objectives (Morris and Bishop, 1992). Technology selection based on the above criteria would match farmers' goals, practices and circumstances. In this paper attempt for the selection and transfer of appropriate farm power technology for land preparation in Bangladesh has been made following the above criteria and based on available information.

Farm power availability

The situation regarding the draught power availability or DP constraint in the country has been described in the previous sections. As land preparation traditionally is done by DAP, the manual labour or hand technology will not be considered in the estimation of power availability. Only DAP and mechanical power systems are examined to assess the power status.

DAP systems According to the latest livestock census (BBS, 1983/84) there are about 11.2 millions DAs of which 7.6 millions are bullocks, 3.3 millions are cows and 0.3 million are buffaloes (see Table 8.5). As mentioned earlier a shortage of 5 millions (2.5 million pairs) DAs exist in the country on the basis of 2 ha per pair capacity. Sarkar (1981) reported an average draught outputs of 0.25 to 0.35 Kw per pair. On this basis the present availability of DAP is about 2038 MW and the availability per ha of cropped area stands at 0.133 KW. The total DAP requirement of the country on 2 ha per pair basis is about 2795 MW. Thus a shortage of 757 MW exists already.

Mechanical power system Total number of PTs in the country is currently about 120,000 and they supply about 960 MW on the basis of 8 KW per PT. Similarly about 5,200 tractors of 30 KW capacity make available 156 MW in the farms of Bangladesh. The total availability of mechanical power is about 1116 MW. Considering 35 man-days per ha. per year for land preparation, the country needs 336 million man-days supplying 2590 MW at the rate of 0.074 KW/mandays on average. Thus total availability of farm power from all the sources stands at 5744 MW and is shown in Table 8.7. This gives per ha cropped area power availability of about 0.374 KW.

Comparative costs of mechanisation technology

Direct comparison between the costs of alternative farm power systems for cultivation is difficult as they involve different methods, qualities of operation and other variables. Nevertheless a comparison is useful for determining the financial feasibility of alternative systems. Table 8.7 shows cost per ha for cultivation over the relevant range of farm sizes. It has been mentioned earlier that over 90 percent small holders have holdings less than 2 ha and over 95 percent of the total farm holdings are below 3 ha. It is evident from Table 8.7 that the least cost systems are owned oxen followed by hired oxen, hired tiller and manual methods for farm sizes upto 2 ha. Thus economically, for most small farmers, animal power technology are more relevant. By considering higher cropping intensity and timeliness of operation as critical to the existing systems, use of hired PTs show lowest costs for holdings less than 4 ha. PT's ownership are not economic below 5 ha even for intensive tillage. Tractor power is too expensive for less than 50 ha. The need for mechanical power in the marginal farmers category is limited as farm labour is adequate and DAP is cheaper.

Table 8.7
Power available in agriculture

Source	No of units (million)	Power rating of each units kw	Total Power kw * 10^6	Total Power kw/ha of cropped area
Animal:			**2.038**	**0.133**
Buffaloes	0.3	0.746	0.224	
Bullocks	7.6	0.18	1.368	
Cows	3.3	0.135	0.446	
Human	35	0.074	2.59	**0.169**
Mechanical:				**0.062**
Tractors	0.0052	30	0.156	
Power Tiller	0.1	8	0.8	
Total			5.584	**0.364**

Appropriate mechanisation technology

The analysis of the present data shows that it is financially beneficial to own PTs over owned or hired DAP for farms over 5 ha. Where timeliness of field operation is critical, hiring of PTs for farm less than 5 ha can be beneficial and save yield losses due to timeliness. A 2.5 percent extra yield (or 100 KGs equivalent of rice crop) is sufficient to recover the extra costs for hiring PTs. These yield increases are feasible, particularly for HYV crops which are more sensitive to timing of transplanting or crop establishment. The use of PTs would reduce labour per ha by 25 man-days in HYV rice production. Power tiller requires about 6 man-days/ha whereas DAP uses on average 40 man-days/ha for land preparation. Anon (1991) reported that hiring of animal was 20 percent more expensive than PT hiring and also supported that cash flow and benefits are higher in multiple use of PTs. Thus under the present DP constraint PTs would appear best suited to overcome farm power shortages.

Training and transfer of technology

Before the introduction of mechanical power systems to land preparation considerations on service, maintenance and repair, reliability, and training of operators, mechanics and extension workers must be in place. Training of rural labour force through various vocational and informal training institutions would open the scope for increased labour employment in the farming activities. These skilled labours can have a better life by improving labour productivity. However, introduction of further mechanisation for other operations would require more training and skill development for all concerned and technology transfer training for extension people. Besides without the transfer of needed skill it is unlikely that agricultural productivity will increase to the expected level.

Conclusions

Bangladesh needs to increase food grain production to a substantial extent. This then necessitates an increase per ha agricultural productivity through intensification of cropping and use of modern inputs including mechanical power in the farming systems. The choice of inputs is sometimes confounded with considerable controversy about their relative impact employment and other socio-economic factors. The following are the concluding statements and suggestions for successful adaptation of farm power technology in the small farm systems of Bangladesh.

Increased agricultural production will be needed to meet the food shortage for some time to come. This can be achieved through the intensification of cropping and use of biological, chemical and mechanical inputs.

Past agricultural development policies and strategies were not conducive to infra-structure development needs for agriculture, market stabilisation and access to inputs by small and marginal farmers where family labour employment is very high.

Efforts to remove farm power supply constraints are inadequate. Draught power shortage is acute and increased demands at peak period can not be met by DAP systems alone.

Draught animals be slowly replaced to keep the farm power shortage at a minimum and make the new system workable.

Selective mechanisation of agricultural operations is needed to meet the farm power gaps as well as to keep the employment of farm and family members within the sector.

Land preparation operation requires most of the power in agriculture and hence it needs to be mechanised with appropriate systems. Introduction of power tiller for the small farm systems of Bangladesh is recommended.

Studies showed that ownership of power tiller (two wheeler) for farm sizes over 5 ha is economically viable and holding sizes between 2-5 ha are likely to be benefited by custom hire services.

Training for service, maintenance and repair are essential to enhance skills and to sustain the mechanised system.

Government must establish more training centres and workshops for human resource development and appropriate means to transfer the learnt skills for the benefit of farmers be established for sustaining the mechanisation policy.

The present trend of employment in agriculture should be maintained and increased through a balanced policy/strategy and the skill development programme at the rural level should be enhanced.

In selecting mechanisation technology the aim of the planners should be to choose/select technology that will provide maximum employment at an economic level to the labourers as well as farmers and it must suit country's infra-structure and the production processes.

References

Anon (1991), *Experience from FIVDB on multiple use of power tiller*, pp.1-16.

BBS (1983-84), The Bangladesh Census of Agriculture and livestock, Bangladesh Bureau of Statistics, Ministry of Planning, Govt. of Bangladesh, Dhaka.

BBS (1995), Statistical Pocket Book, Bangladesh Bureau of Statistics, Ministry of Planning, Government of Bangladesh, Dhaka.

F.A.O.(1990), Agricultural Engineering in Development: Selection of Mechanisation Inputs. *FAO Agric*, No. 84, Rome, Italy.

Gill, J.G. (1981), 'Farm Power in Bangladesh', Vol. 1, *Development Study* No. 19.

Hussain, A.A.M (1977), Draught power requirements in Bangladesh, in Pro. Maximum Livestock production from Minimum Land, BAU, Mymensingh, Bangladesh.

Khan, A.R. (1980), *Increasing productive employment in Bangladesh agriculture: Problems and policies Employment Expansion in Asian Agriculture, Asian Employment Programme*, ILO, Bangkok, pp.59-98.

Khan, M.H. (1990), Summary of Reports-Agril. Mechanisation Strategy Guide-lines for Bangladesh and the Islamic Republic of Iran, RNAM, ESCAP.

Morris, J. and Bishop, C. (1992), Agricultural Mechanisation Strategy for Malawi Interim Report, Silsoe College, UK.

McColly (1971), 'Proposal of Agricultural Mechanisation in the Developing Countries of South East Asia', *Agric. Mech. Asia*, Spring, pp.21-25.

Sarkar, R.I. (1981), 'Improved Utilisation of Animal Draught Power in Bangladesh', in *Procedure Maximum Livestock Production from Minimum Land*, BAU, Mymensingh.

Sims, B.G. (1994), Bangladesh: Farm Power and Tillage in Small Farm Systems, Silsoe Res. Inst., Overseas Div. Report No. OD/94/12, UK

Sutton, D.H. (1993), Farm Power and Mechanisation, SRI Overseas division, Report No. OD/93/4, Silsoe, UK

9 Training and transfer

Cleofa Assey

Introduction

In work organisation's employees are among the most important and valuable assets and their skills are essential for its success. Despite this fact, in many organisations there is wide spread ignorance among the top management of the need for adequate training investment (Kenny and Reid, 1986). Training in some companies is not seen as a key element in their corporate strategy and the link between training and profits is not always recognised (Analoui, 1993). Frequently it is observed that training, especially at the management level is not based on a systematic assessment of training needs. A thorough needs analysis is required for a training programme to become successful, simply because it focuses the attention of trainees on the needs of the organisation from which the objective of training can be formed. This chapter attempts to explain the main stages of training, and how the improved transfer of learnt knowledge, skills values and beliefs to the work place situation can take place.

Definition of training

In 1981 the Manpower Services Commission defined training and later on Amstrong (1996) redefined training as;

A planned process to modify attitude, knowledge, or skill behaviour through learning experience to achieve effective performance in activity or range of activities. Its purpose in work situation, is to develop the abilities of the individual and satisfy the current and future manpower needs of the organisation (p.529).

Training (now translated into development of human resources in many companies) dimension of human resource management is receiving particular attention at the moment with an increasing interest in certain aspects of training. This is mainly in the field of management development which aims at improving managerial performance. It needs to be contingent, or dependent upon an assessment of prevailing needs experienced by management at a particular time and within particular divisions of an organisation (Legge, 1988). In addition, there is an increased emphasis on training in social skills. It does not require the making of a value judgement nor any kind of rating or measurement of individuals. Instead, it depends on the skills of managers to diagnose what is required next to add on the capacity and inclination of the staff to perform their jobs and then to discuss this skilfully with their staff so that the practical implications of the agreed diagnosis are accepted and acted upon in a committed way both by individual and organisation (Randell, 1981).

The above illustrates the main approach to defining management development. It is worthwhile to note here that an understanding of the concept is necessary but is not sufficient, to be able to put into action the practical implication of knowledge. Consideration of skill is necessary to bridge the 'gap' between complex concepts and appropriate purposeful behaviour. In order to do it, the managers need to start their analysis at the micro level. The activities of the manager is to get the work needed by the organisation done through people who work for and with the organisation and at the same time meet the needs of the people who are involved in its activities. The starting point, therefore, from 'skills' approach to 'management' approach is to undergo an active staff development programme so that the behaviour of an effective manager can stem from a set of interlocking information gathering and using activities (Randell, 1981). This includes first, diagnosis of what subordinates have to do next to achieve an improved performance standard (use or add ability) and second, the diagnosis of what the manager has to do next to maintain or add to subordinate motivation to work and the main issue is to reach an agreement of action plans that bring about the desired outcomes to which both subordinate and manager are committed (Randell, 1978).

Purpose of training

There are three main reasons for having human resource development. Firstly, the assumption that training can increase the effectiveness of managers by reducing learning time to achieve specified performance levels. Secondly, that training can improve job performance levels of present managers which will increase the job satisfaction. Thirdly, training is to ensure future succession of the needs of skilled manpower. Thus, an effective management development effort needs to be a part of the personnel strategy - a conscious and systematic process which has the clear purpose of helping managers meet organisational goals.

In general, management development activities can be focused at one of three levels; individual, group and organisation. The manner in which these activities are introduced according to Molander (1986) can be either prescriptive or consultative, see the figure below which shows the types of management development activities.

Table 9.1
Management development activities

	Individual	Group	Organisation
Prescriptive	• General management course • General qualification course • Some form of appraisal	• Team building • Project based learning • Management by objective	• Management of objectives • Organisational development
Consultative	Counselling Coaching Need analysis Career planning	Problem analysis Role negotiation Action learning	Organisation Analysis and feed back

Source: Molander (1986, p.6)

Any system of management development which is introduced without taking into account the expressed needs of user or client may be said to be prescriptive. In contrast the consultative approach may have more to offer. Appraisal system, counselling, job rotation and career planning, for example, require the active involvement of managers in their process of development. In consultative approach both the manager and the subordinate share information, identify problems and aspirations and

155

mutually agree on a planned development programme that is more likely to be implemented by the subordinate.

Systematic approach to training

Like any other business process, training can be very wasteful if it is not carefully planned and supervised. Without a logical systematic approach, some training may be provided which is not necessary and vice versa, or the extent of training may be too small or too great. Systematic training is one which is specifically designed to meet defined needs. It is planned and provided by people who know how to train and the impact of training is carefully evaluated. It is based on a simple four stage model expressed as follows:

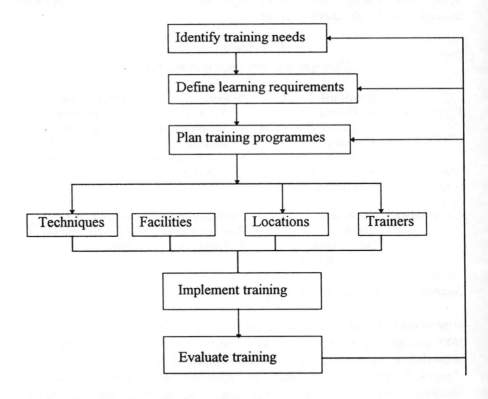

Figure 9.1 Process of planned training
Source: Amstrong (1996, p.536) Process of Planning

156

- define training needs
- decide what sort of training is required to satisfy these needs
- use experienced and trained trainers to plan and implement training
- follow up and evaluate training to ensure that it is effective.

According to Amstrong (1996) the process of planned training involves the following steps shown in Figure 9.1.

Amstrong (1996) explains that the first step in regard to training are:

Identify and define training needs This involves analysing corporate team, occupational and individual needs to acquire new skills or knowledge or to improve existing competence. The analysis covers problems to be solved as well as future demands. Decisions are made at this stage on the extent to which training is the best and most cost effective way to solve the problems.

Define the learning required It is necessary to specify as clearly as possible what skills and knowledge have to be learnt, what competence need to be developed and what attitude need to be changed.

Define objectives of training Learning objectives are set which define not only what is to be learnt but also what learners must be able to do after their training programme.

Plan training programmes These must be developed to meet the needs and objectives by using the right combination of training techniques and locations.

Decide who provides the training The extent to which training is provided from within or outside of the organisation needs to be decided. At the same time, the division of responsibility between the training department, managers or team leaders and individuals is required.

Implement the training Ensure that the most appropriate methods are used to enable trainees to acquire the skills, knowledge, level of competence and attitudes they need.

Evaluate training The effectiveness of training is monitored during programmes and subsequently the impact of training is assessed to determine the extent to which learning objectives have been achieved.

Amend and extend training as necessary decide on the basis of evaluation, the extent to which the planned training programme needs to be improved and how any residual learning requirement should be satisfied.

Analysing training needs

Training must have a purpose and that purpose can be defined only if the learning needs of the individuals, groups and organizations within which work processes are carried out have been systematically identified and analysed. Training needs analysis is partly concerned with defining the 'gap' between what is happening and what should happen. This is to identify what has to be filled by training as shown by the following figure.

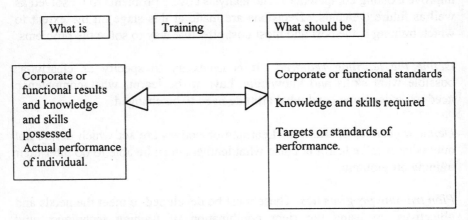

Figure 9.2 Training needs analysis
Source: Armstrong (1996, p.537) The Training Gap

The figure shows the difference between what people know and can do, and what they should know and be able to do. Training should be more concerned with identifying and satisfying development needs - multi-skilling, fitting people to take extra responsibilities, increasing all round competence and preparing people to take on higher levels of responsibility in future (Amstrong, 1996, p.537).

Training needs should be analysed, first for the organisation as a whole - corporate needs; second, for departments, teams' functions or occupations within the organisation - group needs and thirdly for individual employees - individual needs. This can be represented in the following figure.

The analysis of corporate needs will lead to the identification of training needs in different departments or occupations while these in turn will indicate the training required for individual employees. The process operates in reverse. As the needs of individual employees are analysed separately, common needs emerge which can be dealt with on a group basis. The sum of group and individual needs will help to define corporate needs.

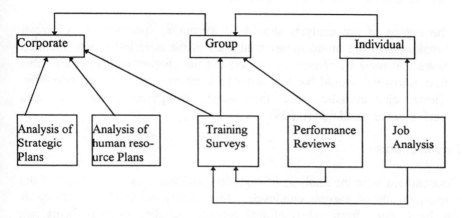

Figure 9.3
Source: Armstrong (1996, p.537) Training needs analysis area and methods

Methods of analysing training needs

Beardwell and Holden (1994, p.242) identified the two elements needed for carrying out a training needs analysis - the job requirements and the person requirements.

Job analysis for training purposes means examining in detail the content of jobs, the performance standards required in terms of quality and output and knowledge skills and competence needed to perform the job completely and thus meet the performance standards. The information obtained from the analysis should specify:

- any problems faced by job holders in learning the basic skills and applying them successfully,
- any weaknesses in the performance of existing job holders arising from gaps in knowledge, lack of skills or post motivation which need to be rectified by training,
- any areas where competence levels are clearly not up to standard required,

- any areas where future changes in work processes methods or job responsibilities indicate a learning needs,
- how training is carried out at present.

Where Amstrong (1996) recommends that;

> the output of job analysis should be a training specification, where it breaks down the broad duties contained in the description into detailed tasks that must be carried out, it sets out the characteristics or attributes that individual should have in order to perform these tasks successfully. These characteristics are knowledge, competence, attitudes and performance standards (p.539).

Person analysis

Concomitant with the analysis of organisational needs is the analysis of the training needs of current employees. Much information about employees can be gleaned from organisational records including original forms and other biodata bases, that is personal profiles, performance appraisal, assessment centre techniques, global review and training audits and relating resources to the training objectives (Beardwell and Holden, 1994, p.344).

Planning training programmes

Every training programme ought to be designed individually, and the design will continually evolve as new learning needs emerge, or when feedback indicates that changes are required. Amstrong (1996, p.540) argues that it is essential to consider carefully the objectives of a training programme. Objectives can be defined as criterion behaviour; for example, the standards or changes of behaviour on the job to be achieved if training is to be regarded as successful. This should be a definition of what the trainee will be able to do when he/she goes back to work on completing the course. Transfer of learning is what counts; behaviour on the job is what matters (Analoui, 1993).

Where should training take place

Amstrong (1996) identifies three places where training can take place - in company, on-the-job, off-the-job and external locations. Where Analoui (1989) argues that the most useful classification, belongs to Minor (1961) and McGhee and Thayer (1961). They have used the proximity of training location to the actual work place as the major criterion and suggest that there are two basic categories, namely on-the-job and off-the-job training. By supporting their point, it is argued that 'Essentially we have a continuum, on one end is the on-the-job and the other is the off-the-job training. Intermediate between these two extremes are the training methods called vestibule, apprenticeship and similar methods' (McGhee and Thayer, 1961, p.186). Each category of training will be discussed briefly below.

On-the-job training

Is one of the widely used methods of training. The trainee is in both the physical and social environment of the work place - simultaneously involved in the process of acquiring both the technical and social requirements of the job. This method is commonly known in industries as 'sitting with Nelly'. The method is very popular in organisations and with management because the trainee requires little specialised attention in terms of extra equipment and manpower. It is the only way to develop and practice specific managerial, technical, and administrative skills needed by the organisation. It has the advantage of actuality and immediacy. The individual works, learns and develops expertise and at the same time concepts and theory are put into practice immediately and their relevance is obvious. Much of the learning can take place naturally as part of the performance management process and through day to day contacts this method is very effective as long as specific learning objectives have been articulated (Amstrong, 1996, p.541). In supporting this view, Analoui (1989, p.14) stresses that if on-the-job training programmes are properly utilised they can be of great value to industry because it provides the individual with the opportunity to become involved in the social system and culture of the organisation while at the same time going through a process of familiarisation with the technical aspects of the job.

Off-the-job training

This can take place on special courses or in training areas or centres, which have been specially equipped and staffed for training. It is the best way to acquire the advanced manual, office, customer service or selling skills and to learn about company procedures and products. It helps to increase the identification of the trainee with the company as a whole and the use of systematic training techniques, special equipment and trained trainers. This implies that basic skills and knowledge can be acquired quickly and often economically (Amstrong, 1996, p.541).

External training

This method of training is said to be the most useful for the development of managerial team leader, technical and social knowledge and skills, especially if the courses cover standard theory and practice which can easily be translated from the general to the particular. External training should be able to supply quality of instruction which it might be uneconomic to provide from internal sources. It can be used to implant highly specialised knowledge or advanced skills and has the added advantage of broadening the horizons of those taking part, not least because they will be exposed to their peers from other organisations.

Evaluation of the training

The pre-ultimate stage in training strategy is the evaluation and monitoring of training. It is one of the most important but often the most neglected or least adequately carried out part of training process. A great deal of management development stops when the managers finish their training courses. However the evaluation of training is just as important as training itself. A systematic evaluation process can be achieved with two important purposes. The first one is to find out how far the training programme has achieved its original training objectives for the need of the organisation. Second, to determine the extent to which individual objectives are achieved.

In general evaluation can be divided into four levels - the reaction level, the learning level, the job behaviour level and the organisation level (Molander, 1987). The reaction level refers to the trainees perception, opinions and evaluation of the training content and methods used and their feeling about the training staff - their presentation and behaviour. The information is usually collected by questionnaire although interviews of selected trainees can be used to achieve greater depth. Assessment at the learning level is concerned with measuring the extent to which trainees have learned the contents of training especially its laid down objectives.

It may be related to a change in individual knowledge, skills or attitude. Tests are used to measure the retention of learning which occurs on training courses and how much is transferred to work situations. The job behaviour level will pinpoint the inhibitory factors for poor transfer of knowledge and skills. A poor supportive climate in the organisation may make implementation difficult, e.g. training managers will need feedback so that trainers can rectify the weak points of the training programme. Finally, the evaluation at the organisation level is an attempt to assess the effects of training on the overall functioning of the organisation. This can be demonstrated by increased productivity, improved quality, reducing learning time and therefore costs.

The four levels can be seen to form a hierarchy or continuum of effect. Consequently evaluation should occur at all four levels. However, two major criteria for deciding the extent of evaluation are the cost of the evaluation process and the usefulness of the results. For example, a simple end of the course questionnaire is relatively cheap, but produces only low quality information, where as quantitative data collected at all levels will be of great value in terms of information but will be expensive in both terms of cost and time.

In considering the modes and methods currently employed in training, the assessment of their potential for transfer led to the emergence of an interesting issue. According to Analoui (1989), there appeared to be a correlation between the proximity of the location of the methods employed to the actual work place, and the degree of effective transfer of the material learnt. Analoui (1989, p.39) recommends that, 'In order to successfully implement a socio-technical approach to the working place, the trainers must pay attention to:

- the individual's cognitive ability and potential for learning the technical related aspect of the job as well as the extent to which his or her orientation and desire for social interaction are determined.
- the degree of complexity of the required task performance and the assessment of appropriate training method which may facilitate the learning processes identified above.
- appropriate use of the created cohesive social system within the learning centre to enhance learning
- preparing the individual trainee for the imminent process of the entry or re-entry to the actual work place. This must include efforts on the part of the trainers to increase the trainees' awareness of the various ideologies in operation and the need to recognise and adapt to the dominant value structure of the work place social system.

Also there is a need to develop appropriate means for evaluation and assessment of the participants performance, which may reach beyond the training centre, and thus functions as a realistic medium not only for improving particular training courses offered, but also for maintaining an on going development of the trainers and the training centre as a whole, and the methods and the training material used in particular' (p.59).

In addition to the above, according to Analoui, there is also a need for reinforcement based on the motivational theories which suggest that a combination of practice and reward on producing a desired response will ultimately lead to effective prolonged transfer. Other writers place the emphasis on self sufficiency autonomy and meaningfulness of the task for the learner. The argument being that individuals who are self motivated or find the task meaningful are more likely to transfer the knowledge and skills acquired to the job. The knowledge of the result or systematic feedback which is provided to learners by trainers in the training situation is also considered to result in enhancement of positive transfer.

Conclusion

Training has the potential to bring about benefits of which its actual values depend on how well it is planned and conducted. The benefits are likely to be the most in the organisations in which individuals and groups can express their training needs in terms of the standards of the work performance needed to achieve the organisations' forward plans. Systematic analysis of the need and attention paid to methods and evaluation of end results in context of transfer can transform the training into a valuable and worthwhile activity.

References

Amstrong, M. (1996), *A hand book of personnel management practice*, Clays Ltd, St Ives plc England.

Analoui, F. (1989), *Social organisation of transfer of learning: An exploration of a neglected aspect of training development*, Occasional Paper No. 14 DPPC, Bradford.

Beardwell, I. and Holden, L. (1994), *Human resource management*, Pitman 128 Long Acre London.

Graham, H. and Bennett, R. (1995), *Human resource management*, Longman Group UK Ltd.

Kenny, J. and Reid, M. (1986), *Training intervention*, Institute of Personnel Management, London.

Legge, K. (1988), 'Personnel management on recession and recovery', *Personnel Review*, Vol.17, No.2.

Molander, C (1987), *Personnel management: A practical introduction*, Chartwell Bralt.

Molander, C. (1986), *Management development, Key concepts for managers and trainees*, Chartwell Bralt.

Randell, B (1981), *Active stall development*, University of Bradford, Management Centre Discussion Paper.

Randell, G (1979), *The skills of staff development*, Proceedings from symposium on the analysis of social skills.

10 Making a commitment to HRD: a challenge for protected area authorities

Nancy Bell-Edwards

Introduction

The future of conservation lies in the hands of personnel working in national parks and protected areas. Nations establish terrestrial and marine protected areas to conserve their unique and often endangered flora, fauna, and ecosystems. Conservation will not occur unless Protected Area (PA) Authorities have well-trained personnel to manage these protected areas. The jobs of Protected area personnel have become increasingly complex and conflicting because they must protect the environment while working together with neighboring local communities and tourists. Protected area personnel require on-going Human Resource Development (HRD) interventions to provide them with the knowledge, skills, and attitudes to meet the changing demands of their jobs. Although the conservation community acknowledges the need for training in documents such as Agenda 21,[1] there are many lessons that conservationists can learn from the professional field of HRD. Protected Area Authorities, Non-Governmental Organisations (NGOs), and donor agencies can greatly benefit from the use of systematic strategies for HRD. This chapter discusses the need for PA Authorities to make a commitment to systematic approaches to HRD. It explains past and current HRD interventions for PA personnel in the Central America, Africa, and Asia and Pacific regions. It also provides a case study of research on a training needs assessment of PA personnel in the Central Volcanic Cordillera Conservation Area of Costa Rica.

Background on protected area training

Conservationists agree that one of the most urgent conservation needs worldwide is to develop nationally trained humanpower with in-country expertise to implement protected area management (Pitkin, 1995; Rabinowitz, 1990; MacKinnon et. al., 1984; Beeton in McNeely, 1993; Rudran et. al., 1993; Duryat and van Lavieren, 1984). The World Conservation Strategy (IUCN, 1980) stated, 'A major constraint to the implementation of conservation measures is a lack of trained personnel' (p.12). It is suggested that ideally all protected area personnel should be offered the opportunity to improve their skills and abilities through training (Miller, 1989). Many conservationists emphasize that without trained personnel, efforts to protect natural habitats are rarely implemented (Wemmer, 1993; Beeton in McNeely, 1993).

Protected area personnel must be trained in the multi-faceted aspects of PA management (Rabinowitz, 1993; Duryat and van Lavieren, 1984; CATIE, 1994). They must handle a range of activities including community relations, extension, environmental education, conflict resolution, as well as ecological research and monitoring, management, patrolling, visitor attention, and law enforcement (MacKinnon, 1984). However, many personnel working in protected areas have received little training, and have limited educational background (primary school, secondary school, or diploma courses only). If they have received further education or training, it is typically in a basic science such as zoology or ecology, or a traditional forestry education which focused on forestry production not conservation and PA management (Duryat and van Lavieren 1984; CATIE 1994). Rabinowitz (1993) said that;

a lack of planning, a lack of knowledge in proper field techniques, and a lack of research data leads to wasted efforts and poor management. In extreme cases such deficiencies can result in actions that are detrimental to wildlife management and conservation. Some examples include the misidentification of species, incorrectly marked PA boundaries, poorly done wildlife surveys, and unrecognized potential of a natural area's value to both wildlife and the surrounding human community, with better training, leadership, and planning, these incidents could be avoided.

Pitkin (1995) stated,

As always, protected area managers need a whole range of scientific and technical skills that enable them to manage their staffs, enforce laws, provide input on plans and policies, and help implement those plans and policies. Now more than ever, however, they need to be spokespersons for protected areas (p.vi).

The Tropical Agricultural Research and Higher Education Center for Central America (Centro Agronomico Tropical de Investigacion y Enseñanza) (CATIE) agreed that the challenges facing PA personnel in Central America are increasingly complex and require highly motivated and well trained staff (CATIE, 1993). McNeely (1993) of IUCN stated that,

> One of the biggest shortcomings in all conservation efforts is the lack of skilled people, at all levels...The challenges of conservation in the modern world require that the protected area manager draws on a greater range of technologies than ever before (p.7).

He emphasized the need to build professionalism for resource managers who require job standards, and training on skills to tackle the different problems on a regional (country-wide) or thematic (fresh water, terrestrial or marine ecosystem) basis. It is argued that without trained conservation personnel and heightened public awareness in tropical countries, efforts to protect natural habitats rarely get beyond the planning stage (Rudran et. al., 1990; Wemmer, 1993).

Training is rarely systematically planned by PA Authorities. Funding and opportunities are usually dependent on NGOs and donor agencies (Pitkin, 1995). Human Resource Development (HRD) Strategies which outline training policies, plans, funding and implementation are urgently needed to ensure that Training and Development (T&D), Organisational Development (OD), and Career Development (CD) occur according to an integrated and systematic plan of action.

Many factors influence how well existing protected area personnel perform their jobs such as: 1) their age; 2) their gender; 3) whether or not they are from the local community near the protected areas; 4) whether or not they live with their families in the park or local communities; 5) how many years they worked for PA Authorities; 6) how many years they worked in their current protected area; and 7) their personality types. However, since many of these factors such as age, gender, and where a person is from can not be changed, it is therefore necessary to focus on attitudes that can be changed. Training and HRD will result in the planned change in knowledge, skills, and attitudes of PA personnel. It will enable them to fulfill their job requirements to effectively manage protected areas.

Definitions of training by conservationists

Most Protected Area Authorities and conservation NGOs usually define training in three ways: 1) Pre-service training; 2) In-service training; and 3) On-the-job training. Pre-service training applies to formal training or courses that occur prior to a candidate beginning their full-time job. This training is often received at a training institute or university which grants diplomas and certificates. Pitkin (1995) described in-service training as 'Training organized by an employer, such as a governmental protected area authority, provided during an individual's term of service, and lasting less than six consecutive months (p.iv)'. On-the-job training is informal training received through the normal course of work through mentoring by supervisors and colleagues, or individual study (Pitkin, 1995).

Background on human resource development

Although the term 'training' is popular among conservationist, few are familiar with the term 'Human Resource Development (HRD). Training is just one component in the professional field of HRD. McLagan (1989) defined HRD as the process of increasing the capacity of the human resource through development. Few Protected Area Authorities use a well-organised, methodical, and businesslike HRD approach to develop the skills, knowledge, and attitudes of their park personnel to effectively manage protected areas. According to the American Society for Training and Development (ASTD), HRD is the integrated use of Training and Development, Organisation Development, and Career Development to improve individual, group, and organisational effectiveness (Rothwell and Sredl, 1992). ASTD further defines the three elements of HRD in the following ways:

Training and development (T&D) Training and Development (T&D) is the process of identifying, assuring and through planned learning helping develop the key competencies that enable individuals to perform current or future jobs (Gilley and Eggland, 1989). The primary emphasis of T&D is on individuals in their work roles. T&D is also described as a short-term learning intervention intended to establish or improve a match between present job requirements and individual knowledge, skills and attitudes (Rothwell and Sredl, 1992). T&D contributes 'to improving organisational competitiveness, supporting product/service quality, fostering effective customer service, enriching the quality of work life and helping individuals achieve their career goals' (Rothwell and Sredl, 1992, p. 480).

Training is the most commonly used and best known HRD activity among PA Authorities, environmental NGOs, and donor agencies. However, although there are many different types of training, basic training is used most often. However, it is essential that PA Authorities are aware of and take advantage of additional categories of training. These include remedial or basic, orientation, qualify, second chance, cross training, appropriate training (Rothwell and Sredl, 1992).

The steps undertaken are:

- Training needs assessment
- Training objectives
- Determining training content
- Principle of adult learning
- Evaluation (Burrow, 1996).

Rabinowitz (1993) suggests the following components for successful training programs:

1. Separate training curricula for senior wildlife officers or administrative staff, and for junior wildlife staff.
2. Instruction in the native language. If this is not possible, at least the outline and handouts should be translated into the native language, and there should be a skilled translator present throughout the course.
3. Instruction geared to the country or region's particular needs and problems regarding wildlife.
4. Assignments, exam questions, and in-class examples using real situations and problems from the region.
5. Field assignments that are relevant to the area and produce real data. This helps develop the groundwork for more comprehensive research projects and for on-going monitoring programs (p.12).
6. Promoting an open atmosphere for the training courses where the participants feel free to discuss issues and interact with each other.

Organisational development (OD) Organisational Development (OD) assures healthy inter- and intra- unit relationships, and helps groups initiate and manage change (Rothwell and Sredl, 1992). The primary emphasis of OD is on the relationships and processes between and among individuals and groups. Rothwell and Sredl (1992) describe OD as a long-term change effort directed toward individuals, groups, and organisations that are designed to improve decision making, problem solving, and group organisational culture. OD interventions are concerned with enhancing organisational effectiveness, efficiency, and the quality of work life of employees. Examples of OD interventions include Total Quality Management, Strategic Planning, and Team Building. French and Bell (1990) provide a detailed definition of OD. They stated that OD is:

> A top management-supported long-range effort to improve an organisation's problem-solving and renewal process, particularly through a more effective and collaborative diagnosis and management of organisational culture-with special emphasis on the culture of formal work teams, temporary teams, and inter-group culture with the assistance of a change agency, including action research (p.1).

In the early 1990's, organisations such as World Wildlife Fund-US began new initiatives on OD. They conducted Strategic Planning exercises with national conservation NGOs, and offered workshops and produced workbooks on topics such as Proposal Writing and Financial Management. The U.S. National Park Service uses many OD interventions such as team building and open system management for their personnel (Bob Krumenaker, 1996).

OD is another important part of HRD that must be addressed by Protected Area Authorities. Protected areas face a variety of problems from biological and social threats such as invasion by exotic species of flora and fauna, encroachment on park land by local people, poaching by tourists and local people, etc. PA personnel (individuals), conservation areas (groups), and PA Authorities (organisation) must develop the capacity to improve decision-making, problem solving, and group organisational culture to address the changing problems facing PAs. If PA Authorities participate in collaborative diagnosis, PA personnel could contribute to the effectiveness, efficiency, and quality of their work. OD interventions supported by top management could strengthen the institutional capabilities of PA government agencies. OD is especially important for effective management and group decision-making.

Career development (CD) Career Development (CD) seeks to align individual career planning with organisation career-management process in order to achieve an optimal match of individual and organisational needs (Rothwell and Sredl, 1992). The primary emphasis of CD is on the person as an individual who performs and shapes his/her various work roles. CD provides direction and purpose for an individual's career. At the same time, it ensures that the Organisation has the human resources to meet present and future demands (Rothwell and Sredl, 1992). CD often involves educational activities such as university degrees, certifications, and continuing education which encourage individual development and professional strengthening.

Career Development has not received much attention by PA Authorities, NGOs, or donor agencies. Many PA personnel desire to better themselves, and would actively pursue career development options such as further university studies, continuing education, and certification programs. They would be especially eager to participate in CD, if opportunities were available and supported by the PA Authorities (through financial and professional advancement incentives, and institutional commitment for CD). These interventions would provide opportunities for individuals to further their career plans while matching the career-management process of the PA Authorities. CD would help to ensure that these personnel remain with the agencies, and grow with the challenges faced in conservation and PA management. In developing nations, it is common to have 'brain drain' in PA government agencies where the best and brightest staff leave to take higher paying career advancing jobs with NGOs, donor agencies, and universities (Barzetti, 1993). CD is a way for government agencies to keep personnel by providing opportunities for personal achievement and development. Career Development does not have to be limited to formal education, it could also include supporting general learning. With the use of new technologies such as instructional telecommunications and distance learning, protected area personnel in even remote areas can benefit from CD opportunities.

Regional training needs

Protected Area Authorities in Central America, Africa, and Asia and the Pacific are progressing with training for PA personnel in different ways. Donor agencies and NGOs play a strong role in determining how training is funded, addressed, and evaluated. Likewise, regional training institutes and universities play an important role in conducting research to determine and fulfill national and regional training needs. These institutes require stable and consistent long-term funding to ensure the quality of their faculty, curricula, materials, and facilities, especially as these centres are often the major sources of pre-service and in-service training for the region. Regional level training enables PA personnel from different nations to interact and network together as well as discuss common conservation problems and solutions. Since plants, wildlife and ecosystems do not observe political boundaries, it is essential to have regional dialogue which can begin in the academic and training forum.

In 1992 and 1994, the Protected Areas Program of the Tropical Agricultural Research and Higher Education for Central America (Centro Agronomico Tropical de Investigacion y Ensenanza (CATIE)) located in Costa Rica, conducted a regional survey in Central America to assess the training needs for PA personnel (Barzetti, 1993). The survey revealed that current training activities are not usually based on objective analyses of training needs. The 1992 survey conducted in Panama, Costa Rica, Nicaragua, El Salvador and Guatemala reported a total field staff of over 15,000 persons, including park guards, technicians and directors. Main conclusions are:

1. New personnel at all levels have little experience or preparation prior to working in protected areas. Training is needed to provide them with the necessary knowledge, skills, and attitudes to perform their jobs as well as to develop a common institutional culture.
2. Conservation NGOs have arranged a surprising high number of training interventions in the Central America region, however, there is no coordination of these events and between trainers, trainees and supervisors. A HRD strategy is needed in each country to plan and coordinate all protected area training activities.
3. All countries indicated PA Authorities assume a wide range of responsibilities and correspondingly require training on a wide range of topics.
4. There are only limited incentives for trainees and trainers to participate in training events.
5. Most Central American nations have sufficient technical expertise for basic training at the park guard, technician, and professional levels. However, problems exist for providing advanced training courses, and in arranging the logistical and technical support for training.
6. Strategic topics identified for training include: Operational Planning, Buffer Zone Management and Biological Corridors, Visitor Management and Ecotourism, Participatory Planning Techniques, and Strategic Management Planning (CATIE, 1993).

Barzetti (1993) explained that one of the problems in securing qualified personnel is the lack of adequate training programs to educate them. She stated that although many nations in the Central American region have organized some training for their PA personnel (through universities, ministries and private institutions), training needs are far greater than their capacity to respond. There is a broad spectrum of training levels in PA personnel. In many cases, issues of literacy such as reading and writing must be addressed before basic environmental subjects at both the practical and operational levels. At the other end of the spectrum, there are also PA personnel who require advanced training at the postgraduate education level. Barzetti also found that training was sporadic and opportunistic. There was little recognition of accomplishments, low salaries and benefits, and difficult working conditions. As a result, she concluded that PA management did not always attract a nation's best talent (Barzetti, 1993).

The issue of training for protected area personnel continues to receive attention in Central America. A regional workshop on training was held in May 1997 at the First Latin American Congress on Protected and Other Areas. The workshop provided a forum for representatives from universities, training institutions, NGOs, donors, and PA Authorities to discuss how to address training and capacity building in Central and South America. In addition, WWF has a new regional initiative on training (Carvalho, 1997).

Protected area training in Africa

There are currently new initiatives in Africa to systematically address training needs. The Biodiversity Support Program in collaboration with other international NGOs conducted an assessment of training needs and opportunities among protected area managers in Eastern, Central, and Southern Africa called the 'Protected Area Conservation Strategy (PARCS)' (Pitkin, 1995, p.vii). Funded by the US Agency for International Development (USAID), PARCS found that most training for PA managers occurred before they began their jobs. Most PA managers received pre-service training at the two leading training institutions in Africa: the College of African Wildlife Management in Mweka, Tanzania, and the Ecole des Specialistes de la Faune in Garoua, Cameroon. Yet once on-the-job, few in-service training or career development opportunities were available to PA managers. However to address these issues, one of the outcomes of PARCS was to work on institutionalizing in-service training programs for PA managers (Feral, 1997).

Southern Africa has a Wildlife Management Training Project (WMTP) to strengthen the capacity of wildlife and protected area personnel working in the Southern Africa Development Community (SADC). Funded by the European Commission, WMTP focuses on training for middle- and senior-level personnel by increasing the availability of high quality regional training opportunities at the College of African Wildlife Management in Tanzania, and the University of Zimbabwe. The project provides institutional strengthening through staff exchanges with British universities, and sponsorship of overseas education and training for faculty. WMTP also addresses training for lower-level staff by improving in-house training at the PA Authorities themselves (Banham, 1997).

Protected area training in Asia and the Pacific

In the early 1990s, WWF-US and the UN Economic and Social Commission for Asia and the Pacific (ESCAP) conducted workshops to discuss regional training needs on terrestrial protected area management. They found that the region lacked a regional training centre for protected area management at lower and mid-levels. However, because of the diversity of languages and cultures in Asia and the Pacific, a regional initiative would be best at the post-graduate education level (WWF, 1992). Numerous national training centres exist in the region such as the Wildlife Institute of India, and the School of Environmental Conservation Management in Indonesia. There are also many new national training initiatives in Asia and the Pacific, many of which have received funding through the Global Environmental Facility (GEF). The GEF is an international funding authority managed by the World Bank, United Nations Environment Programme, and the United Nations Development Programme. It was institutionalized and funding was arranged by developed and developing nations at the Earth Summit. For example, the GEF Nature Reserve Management Project for the People's Republic of China has a component to design training curricula for all levels of protected area personnel working in nature reserves including park guards, managers, researchers, and directors. A team of nature reserve trainers have recently designed training curricula and training courses are being held at five pilot nature reserves throughout the country (Liu, 1997). Another initiative, the GEF Conservation Training and Biodiversity Action Plan for Vietnam provides training for the personnel of the Vietnamese Ministry of Science, Technology, and the Environment and the Ministry of Forestry on protected area management. Bhutan, Laos and the Philippines also have training initiatives supported through the GEF (GEF, 1996).

Case study on training for PA personnel in the central volcanic cordillera conservation area in Costa Rica

During the summer of 1994, a training needs assessment was conducted for personnel working for the Costa Rican National Park Service (Servicio de

Parques Nacionales (SPN)) in the Central Volcanic Cordillera Conservation Area (Area de Conservación Cordillera Volcanica Central (ACCVC)) in Costa Rica. The purpose was to enquire directly about the training needs and objectives.

The Central Volcanic Cordillera Conservation Area (ACCVC) was selected as the research site after consultation with several conservation experts in Costa Rica. ACCVC is the one of the most important Conservation Areas in Costa Rica as it serves as the watershed for more than fifty percent of the country's population who live in the cities of San José, Heredia, Cartago and Alajuela (Padilla, 1994; Acuña and Araya, 1993). ACCVC is located in the center of Costa Rica, and contains 135,500 hectares of land. Special characteristics of the ACCVC protected areas include numerous migratory species, endemic species, unique geology, and watershed protection (Vaughan in Meffe and Carroll, 1994.) ACCVC is also one of most developed conservation areas in Costa Rica. In 1993, it received approximately 370,000 visitors. Approximately half of all visitors were nationals, while the others were foreign (Rojas, 1994).

The study focused on the four national parks, one national monument, and one forest reserve in ACCVC which contained permanent field personnel of SPN:

1. Volcano Irazú National Park (Parque Nacional Volcán Irazú);
2. Volcano Poás National Park (Parque Nacional Volcán Poás);
3. Braulio Carrillo National Park (Parque Nacional Braulio Carrillo);
4. Juan Castro Blanco National Park (Parque Nacional Juan Castro Blanco);
5. Guayabo National Monument (Monumento Nacional Guayabo); and Bosque del Niños Forest Reserve (Reserva Forestal Bosque del Niños) located within the Grecia Forest Reserve.

Sample of personnel

The study sample included all of the available field park personnel working for ACCVC during June and July 1994. This included program heads (2), operative center directors (6), subdirectors (2), heads of patrol units (3), park guards, and cooks. Based on observation and interviews with park personnel and their superiors (38), park personnel were classified into the following four categories.

Park guards (*Guardaparques*) The park guards category also included heads of patrol units, and subdirectors. These categories were further broken down according to their function:

Environmental education Environmental education park guards were responsible for collecting entrance fees from tourists, collecting basic tourist data such as nationality and number of visitors, overseeing the safety of tourists, providing lectures and tours to school groups about the protected areas, general maintenance of facilities and trails, preventing poaching of flora, fauna, and rocks by tourists, preventing vandalism, etc.

Protection/patrolling Protection/Patrolling park guards were responsible for demarcating the boundaries of the protected area, patrolling these boundaries, catching poachers, confiscating poached wildlife, plants, and timber, handling legal implications when national park laws are violated, enforcing protection, etc.

Cooks (*Cocin/oras*) Cooks were responsible for preparing hot meals for the other park personnel, purchasing food and living supplies, maintaining the headquarters facility, responding to radio calls, and in some cases collecting entrance fees, filling in for environmental education park guards, etc.

Medium command (*Mandos/Medios*) Medium Command positions included operative center directors (formerly called Directors of National Parks) for the core protected areas.

Management level (*Nivel Gerencial*) Management Level positions included heads of programs and the conservation area directors.

To gather information about the training of park personnel, the researcher and counterpart traveled to the six ACCVC protected areas to conduct interviews with PA personnel. Semi-structured interviews were held with administrative and management positions (program heads and operative center directors). The semi-structured technique was used to allow for two-way communication to obtain general information and gain insights on specific issues (D'Arcy Davis-Case, 1989). For field level staff including subdirectors, heads of patrol units, park guards and cooks, in-depth interviewing techniques were used. The in-depth interviews utilized a pre-determined list of questions to guide the interview in order to gain the perceptions and knowledge of people through intensive discussion (Patton, 1990). The topics included:
- What the job entails;

- Education level of PA personnel;
- Training received by PA personnel;
- Training needs;
- Threats to the protected areas; and
- The role of training in improving PA management and relationships with local communities.

Background information on training for PA personnel was also provided through discussions with the ACCVC Director, the Head of Training for the Costa Rican National Park Service (SPN), Central American University faculty, staff of NGOs, and municipal and community representatives. Secondary data from official publications, unpublished reports, and internal SPN documentation also served as sources of information on the parks. Informal interviews were also held with park volunteers, local shopkeepers, taxi drivers, and school teachers to determine their views on the status and threats to the protected areas. These people were selected through a convenience sample as the participants were available, and willing to be interviewed.

Training

Of the 65 field personnel working in ACCVC, 56 (86 percent) were interviewed in this study. Nine staff were not interviewed as they were not available to be interviewed due to sick leave, time off, scheduling conflicts or refusal to participate. Of the 56 personnel, 43 (77 percent) participated in one or more in-service training courses (see Figure 10.1) The number of in-service training courses participated in by individual PA personnel ranged from no courses to more than five courses. Those who attended with a higher number of in-service training courses were working on special issues such as parataxonomy or land tenure. PA personnel attended in-service training courses from 1978 to the time of this study. The length of the training courses ranged from 1 day to six months. Most courses lasted from two weeks to one month. The sponsors of training ranged from the national government of Costa Rica, training centres and universities, NGOs, a UN Organisation, and U.S. institutions. The location of the training included the SPN office and other locations in San Jose. Many training courses were held in Costa Rican National Parks such as Braulio Carrillo, Poás, and La Amistad.

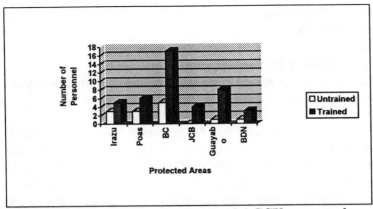

Figure 10.1 Trained versus untrained ACCV personnel
Source: Padilla (1994).

Additional training courses were held in Latin American countries such as Mexico and Columbia and in the United States. The majority of ACCVC personnel (36 percent) received SPN training in protection topics including basic operations. Other topics included administration, science, environmental law, environmental education, tourism, and other topics (see Figure 10.2).

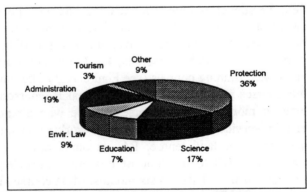

Figure 10.2 Topics of courses received by ACCVC personnel
Source: Padilla (1994).

Threats and problems to the protected areas

In order to understand the training needs of ACCVC personnel, it is essential to understand the threats and problems facing the protected areas.

180

The need for more personnel was the problem most commonly identified by ACCVC personnel (12.9 percent). This was followed by hunting at 11.7 percent, logging at 6.1 percent, garbage at 4.3 percent and too many tourists at 3.7 percent. The threats and problems described by protected area personnel can be categorized as follows:

Conservation-related

Logging, hunting, plant extraction, conflicts over logging and hunting permits, need for protection of nature, large area to patrol, and deforestation.

Nature-related

Volcanic activity, lack of water, environmental impact, chemical contamination, and erosion.

Tourism-related

Too many tourists, destruction and vandalism, misuse and bad attitudes of tourists (e.g. 'they don't listen to the park guards'), tourists complain about the cost of entrance fee, security of tourists, lack of language skills (e.g. 'English to deal with tourists'), unprepared tourists, and poaching by tourists.

Community-related

Negative or lack of interaction with local communities, cultural and economic issues, changing land uses, bad image of park guards, squatters on land, and spread of cattle fincas (ranches).

SPN 'policy'-related

Not enough money for the park, lack of information for PA personnel and tourists, lack of training for personnel, need for more personnel, lack of equipment, lack of environmental education, government doesn't own land for protected area, only can use the PA vehicle until 6 pm, lack of transportation, different agendas for different government agencies that affect the protected area such as the Costa Rican Forestry Directorate, scheduling and management, no money for extension, have to work alone,

ACCVC's role with the community not clear, and political problems between conservation and local communities.

Infrastructure-related

Bad road conditions, no communication such as a working radio, no exhibits for tourists in case they visit on rainy days, and lack of infrastructure for the public.

Other

Rubbish, litter from highway, and highway through Braulio Carrillo.

Training needs for ACCVC

According to the American Society for Training and Development (ASTD), a training needs assessment has three levels: 1) learner analysis, 2) job analysis, and 3) Organisational analysis (Rothwell and Sredl, 1992).

Learner analysis

Of the fifty-six personnel interviewed, 50 responded 'yes' that they wanted additional training, and 6 responded 'no' that they did not want additional training, 89.3 percent and 10.7 percent respectively. Those responding 'no' were generally older and had less formal education. The training needs in order of frequency of responses were described as: 1) English; 2) biodiversity/ biology studies (including natural history, flora and fauna); 3) public attention, environmental education, volcanology, computers and geology. The general topics of desired training as identified by the ACCVC personnel can be categorized into technical and behavioral areas:

Technical

The technical training areas included:

Management-related Basic operations, protection, mountaineering/survival skills, forest fires, wildlands, protected area management, trail interpretation, scuba diving, mechanics, and use of equipment.

Conservation-related Biodiversity studies, natural history, conservation, botany, entomology, geology, volcanology, parataxonomy, archaeology, wildlife monitoring, research, forestry, and biology.

Cooking-related Cooking.

Behavioural

The behavioural areas of training included:

Communications and education-related Languages (i.e. English), environmental education, and general education.

Social-related Leadership, human relations, communications, and public speaking.

Tourism-related Tourist relations, public attention, and first aid.

Enforcement-related Laws, police skills, weapons, and tacticals.

Community-related Community relations.

Administration-related Administration, human resources, personnel management, and computers.

Job Level

The most frequent response from the directors and program heads about the needs of their staff at the job level were training in human relations and English. This was followed by training needs in community relations, environmental education, public attention (tourism), volcanology, botany, geology, entomology, and writing skills. The job skills identified by directors and program heads as needed at each protected area are listed in the following Table 10.1.

Organisational level

Adalberto Gorbitz Padilla, Director of ACCVC in 1994, stated that one problem for SPN in general was the low education level of the staff. Most park personnel did not have high school or university education. He also felt that ACCVC was weak in environmental education, and he wanted this area strengthened for the park guards. He planned to focus on three types of training: 1) Short courses of less than two weeks in specific topics such as computers, volcanology, protection; 2) Mid-term training for staff to professional courses such as the month-long Tourism course at Thunderbird University in Arizona and protected area courses at Colorado State University; and 3) Professional education programs. He said that in the Spring of 1995, SPN would focus on career development (CD) by arranging staff to obtain high school diplomas, and university degrees. Director Padilla stated that training was a component of the five-year plan for SPN.

Table 10.1
Training needs for park personnel as identified by their directors

Training Needs for Park Personnel	Number of Responses (n=9)
Human Relations	3 (Guayabo, Barva, Q. Gonzalez)
English	3 (Irazú, Zurqui, Q. Gonzalez)
Community Relations	2 (Poás, Barva)
Environmental Education	2 (Poás, Q. Gonzalez)
Public Attention (Tourism)	2 (Poás, Barva)
Volcanology	2 (Irazú, Zurqui)
Botany	2 (Zurqui, Barva)
Geology	2 (Irazú, Zurqui)
Entomology	2 (Zurqui, Barva)
Writing Skills	2 (Q. Gonzalez, Bosque)
Administration	1 (Guayabo)
Leadership	1 (Guayabo)
Research	1 (Zurqui)
Biodiversity studies	1 (Irazú)
Wildlife	1 (Irazú)
Ecology	1 (Bosque)
Computers	1 (Bosque)
Discipline	1 (Q. Gonzalez)
Audiovisual	1 (Q. Gonzalez)

He also mentioned that ACCVC was working with the Organisation for Tropical Studies (OTS) on training park guards on how to initiate environmental education activities with local communities near protected areas. Padilla said that SPN did not have all the employees they need. He would like to have had a staff of 150 for ACCVC.

Luisa Alfaro, the head of the Training Office for SPN in 1994, was conducting a training needs assessment for all of SPN during the time of this study. Her draft paper entitled, 'Strategy for Training for the National System of Conservation Areas' (Estrategia para la Capacitacion en el

SINAC) (1994), stated that since its creation, SPN has considered the training of its personnel to be a priority. During the first eight years of its existence, SPN carried out isolated in-service training activities for its employees. In 1978, SPN created the Section of Training to attend to the needs of training for its personnel. In 1982, SPN made its first formal training program with the specific objectives of analyzing source materials, and providing technical and human resource training. In 1992, a new training program was initiated consisting of 37 courses for 562 employees and funding for 30 SPN employees to attend 19 international training events outside of Costa Rica. In 1993, SPN's Central Office and each Conservation Area put in a budget for training courses based on the necessities of each area. The training provided through this program were (see Table 10.2).

Under Luisa Alfaro's direction, SPN was planning a systematic training program that permits all of the employees of SPN to understand the principles and politics of the system. SPN was also working on the plans for a program of professional career development.

Table 10.2
Courses offered by SPN in 1993

Topics	Number of Courses
Computers (including Windows, WP51, Advanced Lotus, Basic Lotus, Red, and Dbase)	6
Environmental Education	2
Forest Fires (USAID and US Forest Service also conducted forest fire courses)	1
Human Relations	1
Labor Relations	1
Human Resources	1
Accounting and Filing	1

Source: (Alfaro, 1994)

Training for protected area personnel in ACCVC

In 1993, SPN hired a HRD consulting group of CATIE and Price Waterhouse staff to draft a training strategy for ACCVC entitled, 'Emerging

Plan for Training for the Core Zones of the Central Volcanic Cordillera Conservation Area' (CATIE/Price Waterhouse, 1993). The Plan provided specific details on the types of training needed, and where to obtain the training for the PAs personnel. It recommended the establishment of a human resources and training unit to facilitate the training. The preliminary plan identified 39 priorities for training, plans to train 1800 participants, 100 events over four years, and a budget of US $55,600. Events range from in-service training, formal courses, job workshops, to public seminars.

The Plan stated that the difference in the education of the three levels of management reflected differences in protected area personnel's capacity to perform skills. To address training needs CATIE/Price Waterhouse recommended mobile seminars, workshops, and courses held on topics such as research and monitoring, conservation of natural and cultural resources, public use and tourism, options for sustainable development, local participation, extension, environmental education, legislation, land tenure, planning of PAs, administration and management, English, and economical evaluation of biodiversity to address ACCVC personnel's training needs (CATIE, 1993). CATIE/Price Waterhouse found that personnel training was weak in the past, however, ACCVC knows that this weakness exists. The CATIE/Price Waterhouse strategy focused on the need for HRD interventions, and necessities and priorities for training and development, organisational development and career development. The strategy stated that training is seen as an instrument to improve the workforce capacity. Training should facilitate organisational changes necessary to permit ACCVC the potential to become the most important PA in Central America. It must create organisational capacity in human resource to design, execute, and evaluate programs of training (CATIE/Price Waterhouse, 1993).

The strategy concurs with the SPN Office by recommending that ACCVC establish their own human resources and training initiatives to do these tasks. However, even with creating a human resource coordinator or unit, ACCVC must commit more to all employees and develop effective programs particularly to support organisations in technical aspects, logistics and emphasis on analysis discussion of results and evaluation (Price Waterhouse/CATIE, 1993). The consultants' methods of reviewing HRD activities within ACCVC included completing a brief analysis of ages of SPN employee, formal education levels, years working for SPN, and looking at current options for domestic and international training.

Recommendations for training park personnel in ACCVC

Based on the interviews with ACCVC personnel at the learner, job, and organisational levels, and on the examination of other training analyses including the training needs assessment by the SPN Office and Price Waterhouse/CATIE, the following points are clear. SPN and ACCVC, in particular, must make a commitment to institutionalizing HRD. The various analyses on training must be set forth into a comprehensive HRD Strategy. The HRD Strategy should adopt a formal policy on Training and Development (T&D), Organisational Development (OD), and Career Development (CD). It must include long-term training plans which outline the types of training needed, where the training should be held, the length of the training, dates for training, who should attend, and how it will be funded. These plans must link training to job descriptions. Written job descriptions are essential so PA personnel and their supervisors clearly understand their job requirements. Training objectives must also be based on these job descriptions. Protected Area Authorities must work with NGOs and donor agencies to coordinate training efforts in order to systematically meet training needs and ensure effective use of funding for training. Coordination will also help to avoid duplication in efforts. Training must be systematic. Every member of the Protected Area Authority will benefit from training including cooks.

The training for ACCVC personnel was not systematic, and there did not appear to be a pattern. Personnel with the same age, education level, and number of years with SPN attended different numbers of training courses. In one case, two personnel with the same qualifications had different experiences with training, one guard attended more than five courses while his counterpart had not participated in any training activities. Training should not be a perk for favorites, but instead a long-term mechanism for causing planned change across the entire organisation. HRD is not just a benefit for a few, but a necessity for all. Long-term funding mechanisms such as Trust Funds could be used to provide continuous funding for the institutionalisation of HRD interventions such as in-service training courses. Records of training implementation must also be kept and maintained. Implementation is the most important part of HRD. Each HRD activity should be evaluated, and future experiences should build upon past interventions.

Future training and HRD interventions for ACCVC

Based on the research in the summer of 1994, the author makes the following suggestions to SPN for the future training of park personnel in ACCVC. The first suggestion is that SPN conduct a strategic plan for training of ACCVC staff for the next ten years. The second suggestion is on training and career development for ACCVC park guards, patrol unit heads, subdirectors, and cooks. Selected leaders from the neighboring local communities should also be invited to participate in these courses. The third suggestion is on HRD interventions for operative center directors and program heads.

Training for park guards, patrol unit heads, subdirectors, and cooks

Park Guards, Patrol Unit Heads, Subdirectors, and Cooks overwhelmingly expressed their interest in increasing their understanding of natural history and biodiversity conservation. They expressed the need to work with local communities on environmental education so the communities understood the benefits they received from the parks. These PA personnel also suggested skills like community relations to help address the needs of the locals by establishing dialogues and joint projects. Based on the interviews and observations, the author recommends the following three courses be given to all of the park guards, patrol unit heads, subdirectors and cooks of ACCVC. These courses would be supplemented by special courses on topics such as forest fire control, wildlife research, archaeology and cultural resource management, volcanology, etc. Untrained park personnel would be the first individuals to attend these courses:

- A ten-day course on biodiversity conservation.
- A ten-day course on environmental education and extension to local communities.
- A week-long course on tourism.

Organisational development for operative center directors and program heads

Operative Center Directors and Program Heads can not spare long periods of time for training. Also, most of them have strong backgrounds in conservation. Therefore instead of training for one week to ten days, they would benefit more from short workshops on specific Organisational Development (OD) topics, as described below.

- Workshop series on organisational development topics

Operative Center Directors and Program Heads could meet for two days every month to participate in workshops on organisational development topics including group dynamics (Month 1), communication skills (Month 2), facilitation skills (Month 3), conflict resolution (Month 4), negotiation skills (Month 5), and developing Integrated Conservation and Development Projects (ICDPs) with local communities (Months 6, 7, and 8).

Career development for SPN personnel

All ACCVC park personnel would benefit from opportunities for continuing education. These opportunities could include certification programs and further education towards high school or university diplomas. Because many of the parks have TVs and VCRs, park personnel could participate in long distance learning and instructional opportunities such as videotape courses, correspondence courses, as well as evening courses at nearby schools. Career Development (CD) opportunities would provide motivation, incentives and encourage employees to continue their career with SPN.

Conclusion

PA Authorities like SPN must recognize the importance of their human resources, and give them incentives for participating in training and career development. PA Authorities must also recognize the need for a long-term commitment to Human Resource Development, and the need to formulate and implement a comprehensive HRD Strategy. They must realize that conservation is continually changing especially as there is more pressure within national parks and protected areas from tourism, and more pressure outside the parks from growing human populations, agriculture, and pollution. Protected area personnel need training to improve their knowledge of ecology and biological diversity conservation, their skills in environmental education and sustainable development extension with local communities, and their attitudes about the needs of local communities and how to help them recognize the benefits they receive from the PAs. Personnel need motivation and incentives for Training and Development (T&D) and Career Development (CD), such as financial benefits, career advancement, or special acknowledgment. The entire PA Authority will benefit from the use of Organisational Development (OD) interventions which enable them to meet their organisational goal of conservation and protected area management.

Note

1. The proceedings from the United Nations (UN) Conference on Environment and Development held in 1992, also called the Earth Summit.

References

Acuña, Fernando Bermudez y Yadira Mena Aray (1993), *Parques Nacionales de Costa Rica*, Ministerio de Recursos Naturales, Energia y Minas, Servicio de Parques Nacionales, Departmento de Planificacion y Servicios Tecnicos, Seccion de Turismo, San Jose, Costa Rica.

Alfaro, Luisa (1993), '*Nuevos Enfoques: El Sistema de Areas Protegidas de Costa Rica*', Paper presented at the XV Curso Internacional de Areas Protegidas, Turrialba, Costa Rica: 23 de Marzo al 27 de Abril.

Alfaro, Luisa. (1994), *Estrategia para la Capacitacion en el SINAC (Draft)* San Jose, Costa Rica.

Banham, Will (1997), Personal Communication, Bradford, England, June.

Barzetti, Valerie (ed.) (1993), *Parks and Progress: Protected Areas and Economic Development in Latin America and the Caribbean*, IUCN-The World Conservation Union in collaboration with the Inter-American Development Bank, Washington, DC.

Beeton, Bob (1993), 'Training Protected Area Managers: Building the Capacity to Conserve', in McNeely, Jeffrey A. (ed.) *Parks for Life: Report of the IVth World Congress on National Parks and Protected Areas*, IUCN-The World Conservation Union. Gland, Switzerland. pp.165-168.

Carvalho, Cristina Aires Ribero de (1997), Personal Communication, Bradford, England. June.

Centro Agronomico Tropical de Investigacion y Ensenanze (CATIE) and Price Waterhouse (1993), *Plan Emergente de Capacitacion Para Las Zonas Nucleo de Area de Conservacion Cordillera Volcanica Central*, Turrialba, Costa Rica.

Centro Agronomico Tropical de Investigacion y Enseñanza (CATIE) (1993), 'Regional Project for Protected Areas Training in Central America and Other CATIE Member Countries', CATIE: 29 September.

190

D'Arcy Davis-Case (1989), *Community Forestry: Participatory Assessment, Monitoring, and Evaluation*, FAO Rome: pp.87.

Duryat, H.M. and L.P. van Lavieren (1984), 'Indonesia's Experience in Training Protected Areas Personnel', in *National Parks, Conservation, and Development*, (eds) J. A. McNeely and K. R. Miller, Smithsonian Institution Press, Washington, DC. A Paper presented at the 1982 World Congress on National Parks. pp.228-232.

Feral, Chris (1997), Personal Communication, Biodiversity Support Program, Washington, DC. Summer.

French, Wendell L. and Cecil H. Bell (1990), *Organization Development: Behavioral Science Interventions for Organization Improvement* (4th ed.), Prentice-Hall International Edition. NJ.

GEF Quarterly Report (1996), World Bank, Washington, DC: July.

Herrera, Carlos (1993), *'Organisation y Estructura del Area de Conservacion Cordillera Volcanica Central'*, Paper presented at the XV Curso Internacional de Areas Protegidas, Turrialba, Costa Rica: 23 de Marzo al 27 de Abril.

IUCN-The World Conservation Union (1992), *Protected Areas of the World: A Review of National Systems*, Vol.4, Nearctic and Neotropical. Gland, Switzerland.

Krumenaker, Bob (1996), Personal Communication, Shenandoah National Park, Virginia, March.

Liu, Shirong (1997), Personal Communication, Summer.

McNeely, Jeffrey A. (ed.) (1993), *Parks for Life: Report of the IVth World Congress on National Parks and Protected Areas*, IUCN-The World Conservation Union, Gland, Switzerland.

MacFarland, Craig, Roger Morales, and James R. Barborak (1984), 'Establishment, Planning, and Implementation of a National Wildlands System in Costa Rica' in *National Parks, Conservation, and Development*, (eds) J. A. McNeely and K. R. Miller. Smithsonian Institution Press, Washington, D.C. A Paper presented at the 1982 World Congress on National Parks. pp.592-599.

MacKinnon, John and Kathy, Graham Child and Jim Thorsell (1986), *Managing Protected Areas in the Tropics*, IUCN-The World Conservation Union, Gland, Switzerland.

Miller, Kenton R (1989), *Planning National Parks for Ecodevelopment: Methods and Cases from Latin America*, Volumes I & II, Peace Corps Information, Collection and Exchange, Reprint R0073, Washington, D.C. March.

Padilla, Adalberto Gorbitz (1994), Personal Communication with the Director of ACCVC, San Pedro, Costa Rica, Summer.

Patton, Michael Quinn (1990), *Qualitative Evaluation and Research Methods*, Sage Publications, 2nd Edition, London.

Pitkin, Barbara (1995), *Protected Areas Conservation Strategy: Training Needs and Opportunities Among Protected Area Managers in Eastern, Central, and Southern Africa*, Biodiversity Support Program. Washington, DC.

Rabinowitz, Alan (1993), *Wildlife Field Research and Conservation Training Manual*, Paul-Art Press, Inc. New York.

Rojas, Amancio (1994), '*Autofinanciamiento del Area de Conservacion Cordillera Volcanica Central*', Universidad Estatal a Distancia Escuela de Ciencias de la Administracion (unpublished paper).

Rothwell, William J. and Henry J. Sredl (1992), *Professional Human Resources Development: Roles and Competencies*, 2nd Edition, Vol II, HRD Press Inc, Amherst, Massachusetts.

Rudran, Asanayagam, Chris M. Wemmer and Mewa Singh (1990), 'Teaching Applied Ecology to Nationals of Developing Countries', in *Race to Save the Tropics*, Goodland, Robert (ed.) Island Press, Washington, DC pp.125-140.

Stone, Roger D. (1991), *Wildlands and Human Needs: Reports from the Field.* World Wildlife Fund: Washington, DC.

Tenorio, Rodolfo J. (1992), '*Area de Conservacion Cordillera Volcanica Central Diagnostico Sobre Su Estructura Organizativa, Politicas y Procedimientos*', Fundacion para el Desarrollo de la Cordillera Volcanica Central (FUNDECOR) October.

Vaughan, Christopher (1994), 'Management of Conservation Units: The Costa Rican National System of Conservation Areas', in *Principles of Conservation Biology*, (Meffe, Gary K. and C. Ronald Carrol) Sinauer Associates, Inc, Sunderland, Massachusetts, pp.395-404.

Wemmer, Chris, Rasanayagam (Rudy) Rudran, Francisco Dallmeier, and Don E. Wilson. (1993), 'Training Developing-Country Nationals is the Critical Ingredient to Conserving Global Biodiversity', in December *BioScience*, Vol. 43, No. 11, pp.762-767.

World Wildlife Fund (1992), 'Final Report on the World Bank/United National Development Programme Project on Strengthening the Conservation and Management of Terrestrial Protected Areas in Asia and the Pacific.

11 Effective total quality management

Abdullah Kisuju and Dr Farhad Analoui

Introduction

Total Quality Management (TQM) system of any firm encompasses all its policies, operational methods and organisational structures concerned with quality management and continuous improvement of quality of its output. It focuses on the totality of the system rather than individual parts, seeking to identify the causes of failure rather than the simple fact that failures have occurred. TQM has implications for human resources management because it demands a management style that involves full committed co-operation from employees. It assumes that quality is the outcome of all the activities that take place within the organisation, and therefore one would expect that all functions and all employees have to participate in the improvement process. Improvement of total quality management in any organisation needs both quality system and quality culture.

Wilkinson and Willmot (1995, p.36) and Lock (1994, p.12) argue that many quality problems originate not only in the manufacturing or operations areas of companies, but also in the marketing service, finance, personnel, and administrative function. Quality can not be inspected in as a final, isolated function at the end of the process or sequence of processes. Quality, the quest for customer satisfaction must be designed into all the organisation systems and instilled into all its employees.

This chapter is aimed at explaining the elements of TQM and discussing the importance of training and team building towards achieving TQM in the organisation.

Definition of TQM

Mullins (1996, p.774) defines Total Quality Management as a way of life for an organisation as a whole, committed to total customer satisfaction through a continuous process of improvement and the contribution and involvement of the people. Mullins argues that organisations should have policies which seek opportunities to improve the qualities of its products and/or services and processes, if they are to be successful. These policies of course should go hand in hand with the required level of productivity. Mullins' argument is supported by Lock (1994) who argues that 'TQM is a way of managing, to improve the effectiveness, efficiency, flexibility and competitiveness of the business as a whole' (p.12). TQM according to him is a complete departure from the traditional trap of concentrating solely on inspection and testing to find and eliminate failures. Lock continues to argue that TQM involves the whole company getting organised and committed to quality in each department, each activity and each person at each level. It is believed that TQM recognises the fact that for an organisation to be truly effective each of its parts must work smoothly with the others because every person and every activity affects and is affected by one another (Analoui, 1997).

Amstrong (1996, p.113) defines TQM as a process which involves everyone in the organization with a singular aim of satisfying both the external and internal needs of customers. He argues that quality should be a way of life, deeply rooted in the culture and values of business and dependent on attitudes, behaviours and competencies of people as individuals or teams. Lock (1994) also supports this argument by explaining TQM as a method of removing waste by involving everyone in improving the ways in which things are done. The techniques of TQM can be applied throughout the company so that people from different departments with different methods are equally useful in finance, sales, marketing, design, accounts, research development, purchasing personnel, distribution, stores and production.

The elements of the TQM therefore have been identified by Pentecost (1991) as follows:

- A 'total process' involving all operations and management units in organisations, and led from the top;
- The 'customer as king' with every strategy, process and action directly related to satisfying customers needs;
- A greater emphasis on 'national information collection and analysis' using modern technology where appropriate;

- An emphasis on a different approach to looking at the 'costs of poor quality' by examining all processes in the organisation which add to costs;
- A greater involvement of people recognising that they are a great untapped resource in most companies;
- 'Team work' as critically important, involving multi-discipline and multi level working to solve problems and to meet customers' needs; and
- Requirement for 'creative thinking' and the ability to think beyond the immediate job or work environment (pp.8-10).

It is also argued that most companies adopt TQM not for its elegance but because it helps the management to:

- focus clearly on the need of their markets,
- achieve a top quality performance in all areas not just in product or service quality,
- operate the simple procedures necessary for the achievement of quality performance,
- critically and continually examine all processes to remove non-productive activities and waste,
- see the improvements required and develop measures of performance,
- understanding fully and in detail its competition and develop an active competitive strategy,
- develop the team approach to solving the problems, develop good procedures for communication and acknowledgement of good work,
- review continually the processes to develop the strategies of never ending improvement.

Total quality control (TQC)

Whenever, quality is discussed, its believed that quality improvement can relate to the physical attributes of a product, or to the information on a document which enables subsequent operation to be performed correctly the first time. However, production requires a system which reproduces quality and by definition this is what is termed Total Quality Control (TQC) or Company-Wide Quality Control (CWQC) (Prokopenko, 1987).

TQC, it is argued, ensures that the product meets customers' needs, ranging from physical use of product to its aesthetic characteristics. Products life cycle assurance procedures are necessary within the TQC policy and programme which generally consist of the following components, according to Prokopenko (1987, p.181):

- identification of customers' needs
- quality assurance
- reliability
- quality assurance procedures in the market.

The following (see Figure 11.1) demonstrates the analysis of the results of market research and therefore accommodates the above mentioned points;

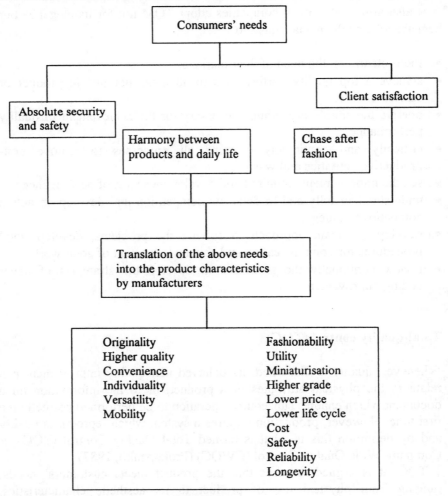

Figure 11.1 Customers' need identification
Source: Prokopenko (1987, p.182)

After identifying the customers' need the producer should integrate them into the products using TQC system to ensure that they are all met during production process. In most industries reliability, is the most critical customer need. In most companies, the requirements to satisfy this need are implemented at the stage of production design and are met by specific tests. Testing is aimed at improvement of quality design in order to meet the customers' needs and to ensure quality by consistent feedback during testing:

- Identification of possible causes of failure while in use,
- Assessment of the standard of manufactured product and the implementation of better quality manufacturing process (Prokopenko, 1987, p.183).

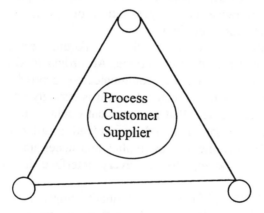

Figure 11.2 The Foundation for TQM
Source: Oakland and Porter (1994, p.3)

According to Oakland and Porter (1994 p.viii) the reputation enjoyed by an organisation is built on quality, reliability, delivery and price. The quality is therefore argued to be the most important of these competitive weapon, as it meets the customers' requirements and it is not restricted to the functional characteristics of product or service. And by definition reliability is the ability of the product or service to continue to meet the customers' requirements over time. It is also conceived that throughout the organisation there exists a series of internal suppliers and customers. These form the so-called quality chains, and this is the basis of the core of company-wide quality improvement. The internal customer-supplier relationships must be managed by interrogation using a set of questions at every interface.

According to Oakland and Porter quality has two distinct but inter-related aspect of quality namely design and conformance to design. They argue that quality design is a measure of how well the product or service is designed to achieve the agreed requirements. Quality conformance to design is the extent to which the product or service achieves the design. It is emphasised that organisations should assess how much time they spend doing the right things right. It is further reiterated that Quality Control is the employment of activities and techniques to achieve and maintain the quality of the product, process or service. And quality includes innovation which is a search for more effective ways of meeting customers' requirements as well as improving the efficiency of existing operations.

Oakland and Porter contend that top management determines quality priorities, establishes the systems of quality management and the procedures to be followed, provides resources and leads by example. It is also argued that Quality Assurance is the prevention of quality problems through planned and systematic activities.

There is also an argument that marketing establishes the true requirements for the product or service. According to Oakland and Porter (1994, p.viii) these must be communicated properly throughout the organisation in the form of specifications. It is strongly advised, and indeed, it is seen as a requirement that management ought to make sure that each member of the organisation should be involved in order to attain Company Wide Quality Improvement. This implies and necessitates every one in an organisation to work together at every interface in order to achieve perfection.

Wilkinson (1995, p.36) notes that quality improvement occurs in two places; one is the existing vertical structure, where improvement activity takes place within naturally occurring organisational units such as department, section and work teams rather than outside. He contends, that one principle of horizontal activity is an idea of the internal customers: Organisational units discuss the quality of their performance with those who receive their output in order to improve the service they provide to these customers. And interdepartmental project team is the second way of organising across the vertical lines.

Oakland and Porter (1994, p.x) even suggest that TQM is a comprehensive approach to improving competitiveness, effectiveness and flexibility through planning, organising and understanding each activity and involving each individual at each level. They argue that TQM ensures that management adopt a strategic overview of the quality and focus on prevention not detection of problems. They assert that TQM must start at the top where serious commitment to quality must be demonstrated. They also insist that middle management have a key role to play in communicating the message. Mullins (1996) on the other hand believes that 'a total process involving all operations and management units in the organisation must be led from the top' (p.774). Every chief executive must accept the responsibility for commitment to a quality policy which deals with the organisation for quality, customer needs, the ability of the organisation, supplied materials and services, education and training and review of the management systems for never ending improvement.

Mullins (1996, p.774) identifies the second element of TQM as the customer being treated as a king. This simply means in an organisation every strategy, process and action should directly be related to satisfying customers' needs. Oakland and Porter (1994, p.XI) support the ideas of Mullins by arguing that the core of TQM is the customer - supplier relationship where the process must be managed. They argued that the soft outcomes of TQM - the culture, communications and commitment - provide the foundations for the TQM model. The process core must be surrounded by 'hard' management necessities of the systems, tools and teams (please see the previous figure).

According to Mullins (1996, p.774) the third element of TQM is team working as a crucially important. This involves multi-disciplines and multi-level working to solve problems and to meet customers' needs. In expanding this point, Beardwell and Holden (1994 p.568) note that team working is one of the most recent initiatives in employee involvement and like quality circles originated in Japan. It emphasises problem solving in team working situations and in order to function effectively it must be bound up with policies of task flexibility and job rotation.

Teams vary in size from seven to ten people or even more, and large elements of training are necessary to ensure that workers, team leaders/ supervisors and managers have the requisite skills to enable the team to function effectively and efficiently. A large part of such training is of a managerial or inter-personal skill and communicational nature as well as of a technical nature. It is argued that within a team, individuals are encouraged to improve personal performance and that innovations are made in order to improve productivity and product quality. And team meetings provide the forums where such issues are debated and information shared.

Wilkinson and Willmot (1995) explain that the improvement process both creates and depends on cultural change. And that:

> the appropriate culture has many elements which include: the internalisation of quality and continuous improvement as a goal of all activities; the absolute priority of customer satisfaction; a systematic and

rational approach to quality improvement issues; more open communications, so that those further down are listened to by those further up; the greater involvement creation of high-trust social relationship (p.38).

Training and TQM

Lock (1994) argues that quality is concerned with delivering on time and at a competitive price, the goods or services that exactly satisfy the customer. Therefore it is argued that any training which helps an organisation to achieve these results is in effect an investment for quality. To achieve the highest quality everyone who works in an organisation will know precisely what to do, use correct methods and procedures, and be able to perform their task well and right first time. This according to Lock, 'demands the provision of planned and methodical training' (p.727). Salaman (1992) also concurs with Lock and suggests that increased competition has led some organisations to adopt a strategy of attempting to compete in terms of quality rather than price, and in such cases training has been closely associated with attempts to improve product quality. In manufacturing for instance, quality has meant not just the introduction of quality circles and statistical process control methods, but also various initiatives to build a quality approach into the production process through major improvements in the motivation and competence of the work force at all levels. For example, British Steel Company introduced a package of measures, originally promoted under the title Total Quality Performance (TQP) aimed at securing competitive advantage through a higher quality product (Salaman, 1992, p.326). He argues that the most important training element within TQP has been the decision to identify required standards of competence for every level of activity and to undertake training and development needs assessments of the corporation's entire workforce against criteria. While in service oriented sector, he continues to argue, the drive for quality has most often been seen in attempts to improve the level of customer care services such as the case of British Railways/Airways.

Lock (1994) explains the aim of training in organisations as that of making those organisations measurably more successful and prosperous than they could ever be without training. According to him training achieves this improvement by increasing the job performance of individuals which results in;

- Improved efficiency and productivity of sections and departments;
- Improvement in the quality of work produced;

- A more competitive organisation; and
- A more successful and prosperous organisation (p.727).

In order to improve the TQM in an organisation, Lock (1994) recommends that there must be on-the-job training which is conducted in precisely the same environment in which the employee does his/her job. This includes not only the same physical location, but also the same conditions and surroundings, the same tools and equipment, materials, standards and facilities that are used when doing the actual job. He insists that on-the-job training is so effective because unlike off-the-job it can not fail to be;

Relevant Learning by doing the actual job makes the training automatically 100 per cent relevant.

Effective Learning by actually doing the job, with a great deal of practice and constant feedback about progress produces by far the most effective conditions of learning.

Applied on-the-job Upon completion of training the learner continues doing the job, without interruption at the place where he or she was trained. The trainee is thus not disadvantaged by difficulties of having to transfer the learning from one environment and set of conditions to another.

Lock (1994, p.732) concludes that, in practice organisations can not become highly competitive and achieve high standards of efficiency, productivity and quality for their products and services without providing systematic approach to on-the-job training in all their sections and departments.

Team working and people

Most of the processes which are operated in an industry are very complex in a way that they can not be under the control of any one individual. The suggestion is that the only way to tackle problems concerning such processes is through some form of 'team work' (Kakabadse, et. al., 1987). Analoui (1997) sees the process as in inevitable progression from the realm of traditional management with emphasis on isolation of people as individuals to the belief held by proponents of values systems of Human Relation Schools with emphasis on groups. To use the potential of people at work, teams, will have to have been employed as an alternative to unorganised and unstructured ways, to fully utilise the values of human resources at work (Analoui, 1993).

According to Lock (1994) the use of the team approach to problems solving has many advantages over allowing individuals or isolated departments to work separately on problems. The advantages according to Lock are listed here under:

- The problems are exposed to a greater diversity of knowledge, skills and experience.
- The approach is more satisfying to team members and boosts morale.
- The problems at cross departmental or functional boundaries can be dealt with more easily.
- A greater variety of problems can be tackled including those beyond the capability of any one individual or department.
- Recommendation by the team are more likely to be implemented than suggestion by individuals (p.21).

It is further argued that when properly managed, teams improve the process of problem solving, producing results quickly and economically. (Cummings, 1981; Margerison and McCann, 1985). Teamwork throughout an organisation is an essential component of the implementation of TQM, for it builds trust, improves communication and develops interdependence. Lock continues to argue that teamwork is devoted to quality improvement, changes the independence to inter-dependence through improved communications, greater trust and the free exchange of ideas, data and knowledge. The employees will not be motivated towards continued improvement in the absence of:

- commitment to quality from management,
- the organisational quality climate,
- a team approach to quality problems.

All these, according to Lock, are focused essentially on enabling people to feel, accept and discharge responsibility. He asserts thus, TQM organisations have made a part of their quality strategy - to empower people to act. And that encouragement of ideas and suggestions from the workforce, particularly through their involvement in team/group activities, requires investment. At this point the rewards are total involvement both inside the organisation and outside through all the supplier and customer chains. Diagram (Figure 11.3) according to Oakland (1990) helps to illustrate the independence to interdependence through team working.

Oakland (1990, p.237) argues that the use of face to face interaction methods of communication with a common goal develops over time the sense of dependence on each other. According to him this forms a key part of any quality improvement process and provides a methodology for employee recognition and involvement, through active encouragement in-group activities.

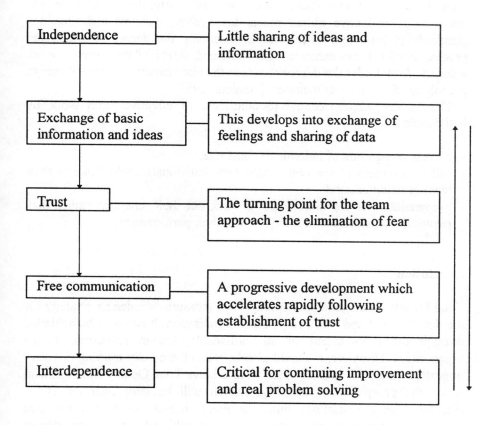

Figure 11.3 Independence to interdependence through team work
Source: Oakland (1990, p.237)

The proponents of team working within the organisation believe that team working is essential for competitive survival, enhances the variety and skills content of the jobs and is consistent with the organisation's long term goal of increasing the level of worker and organisation participation in decision making (Kakabadse, et. al., 1987; Analoui, 1993).

It is further argued that there are three dimensions to the notion of effective team working. These dimensions are, firstly, the degree to which the team's productive output meets the quality, quantity and timelines standards of the users of the output. Secondly the degree to which the process involved has enhanced the continued ability of the team to work together. And thirdly the degree to which the team experience contributes to the job satisfaction of its members (Analoui, 1993).

The factors which seemed to contribute to effective team work by individuals include;

- correct recognition of individuals' best role,
- self - awareness of the best contribution individuals could make to their team or situation, and
- preparedness of the individuals to work out their strengths rather than permitting weaknesses to interfere with their performance.

Conclusion

Total Quality Management is an important measure or indeed a strategy for the development and well being of any organisation. It can only be achieved through the involvement of all individuals, human resources, in an organisation. However, it should also be remembered that training is a very important aspect for any organisation to achieve Total Quality Management. Since the prosperity of any organisation will be dependant on TQM, therefore the organisations ought to invest heavily in human resource development and managerial processes which will lead to the satisfaction of consumer. This can only be realised through acceptance of the human resource and then interaction with client as an essential source as well as quality of information.

References

Amstrong, M. (1996), *A hand book of personnel management practice*, (6th ed.) Kogan Page Ltd, London.

Analoui, F. (1993), 'Skills of management', in J W Cusworth and T F Franks (eds), *Managing projects in developing countries,* Essex, Longman. pp.68-73.

Analoui, F. (1997), *Senior Managers Effectiveness,* Avebury, Ashgate.

Beardwell, I. and Holden, L. (1995*) Human resource management: A contemporary perspective,* Pitman Publishing, London.

Cummings T. G. (1981), 'Designing Effective Work Groups', in Nystrom P C and Starbuck W H (eds), *Handbook of original design,* Vol. 2, Oxford University Press, pp.250-71.

Feigenbaum, A. (1991), *Total Quality Control,* (3rd ed.) McGraw Hill, Inc.

Kakabadse, A. Ludlow R; Vinnicombe C. (1987) *Working in Organization,* Gower, UK.

Lock, D. (1994), *Gower hand book of quality management,* (2nd ed.) Hartnoll Ltd, Bodmin, England.

Margerison, C. and McCann, R. (1985), *How to Lead a Winning Team,* MCB University Press.

Mullins, L. (1996), *Management and organisational behaviour,* (4th ed.) Pitman Publishing.

Oakland, J. and Porter, L. (1994), *Cases in Total quality management,* Clays Ltd. Great Britain.

Pentecost D. (1991), 'Quality Management: the Human Factor', *European participation monitor,* No. 2, pp.8-10.

Prokopenko, J. (1987), *Productivity management: A practical hand book,* International Labour Organisation.

Salaman, G. (1992), *Human resource strategies,* SAGE Publication Ltd. London.

Wilkinson, A. and Willmot, H. (1995), *Making quality critical: New perspectives on organisational change,* Mackays of Chatham PLC, London.

12 The strategic role of human resources in corporate strategy

Dr Mark Hiley

Introduction

The development of Human Resources has been recognised as a challenge, one amongst a number of objectives of long-term economic growth by most developing countries. Since the early 1970s, however, it has moved to the centre stage of development priorities. Far greater attention is now paid to human resource capability, particularly the calibre of management and the structure and culture of the organisation. For corporate strategy to succeed, there has to be a high level of commitment and involvement by employees.

Corporate strategy, as Miller (1983) points out, is a market-led concept affected by product-market considerations and directed at the achievement of competitive advantage. The tendency is for management to react to its environment rather than to anticipate it. The logic of the competitive environment dictates action.

Johnson and Scholes (1988) discounted the corporate strategy as '... the matching of the activities of an organisation to the environment in which it operates' and '... the matching of the organisation's activities to its resource capability' (p.171). Developing a strategy for human resources is concerned with the manner and extent to which the stock of manpower should be varied to match predicted changes in the environment and to matching the demands of the corporate plans of the enterprise for manpower. Corporate strategy is also concerned with examining whether the corporate plans of the enterprise have to be modified because of limitations and costs relevant to the people side of the business (Cowling and Chloe, 1990).

Corporate strategy is not monolithic; neither are there any general rules as to how it should be developed or expressed. Within the same organisation there will be different levels of strategy, and the approach to strategy formulation in diversified companies will vary, making it increasingly difficult to develop an integrated human resource strategy.

The discussions in this chapter will focus on the Corporate Strategy and the role of the Human Resources in order to place the right kind of people in organizational structures. The aim is to high light the need for integrating human resources and corporate strategies. In a separate discussion relevant conclusions are reached.

Corporate strategy

The increasing globalisation of business seemed likely to play to the giant corporation's strengths. They would be able to manufacture their goods wherever they could find the best combination of price and quality, and distribute them wherever they could discover (or create) a demand. Above all, most giant corporations are a product of the doctrine of 'economies of scale' - the idea that producing things in ever larger volumes brings down unit costs, so that the larger companies will do better than small ones (Economist, 1995).

However, economies of scale have been declining. Techniques such as lean manufacturing and just-in-time production have shifted the emphasis from size to timeliness, and computerised production has allowed factories to produce customised goods at mass-produced prices. At the same time, the diseconomies of scale are looming ever larger. Giant companies generate bureaucratic bloat, shop floor alienation and often fail to attract creative workers, or to make good use of those they have.

Since the late 1960s the average size of the workplace has been falling steadily throughout the industrialised world as large organisations try to break themselves into smaller parts. Standardised products are a thing of the past. Customers increasingly want goods tailored to their particular needs, and value conscious customers are less willing to pay a premium price for a global brand (Economist, 1995).

Many corporations are also legacies of an age of high tariffs and high transport costs. This was the classic organisational pattern adopted by many European corporations expanding in the prewar period - the multinational strategy. Because of the enduring influence of family ownership, organisational processes were built on personal relationships and informal contacts rather than formal structures and systems. Such management processes reinforced the tendency to delegate operating independence to expatriate managers.

Corporations pursuing a multinational strategy orient themselves toward achieving maximum responsiveness to the local market and tend to transfer skills and products developed at home to foreign markets. Multinational firms extensively customise both their product offering and their marketing strategy to different national conditions. Consistent with this, they also have a tendency to establish a complete set of value-creation activities (including production, marketing and research and development) in each major national market in which they do business[1]. As a consequence they are generally unable to realise economies of scale. Accordingly many multinational corporations have a high cost structure. Corporations such as Ford and Unilever essentially set up clones of themselves in all the countries where they operated, complete with head offices, engineering and design facilities and production plants. A strategy which was expensive to implement and wasteful at the best of times.

A multinational strategy makes most sense when there are high pressures to respond to local market needs and low pressures for cost reductions. The high cost structure associated with the duplication of production facilities makes this strategy inappropriate in industries where cost pressures are intense. Another weakness associated with this strategy is that many multinational corporations have developed into decentralised business units in which each national subsidiary functions in a largely autonomous manner. As a result, after a time they begin to lack the ability to transfer the skills and products derived from core competencies to their various national subsidiaries around the world.

Not all corporations have pursued this multinational strategy. The Japanese corporations, which appeared on the international scene in the 1950s, when tariff barriers were falling, preferred to produce as much as possible at home for export. But western governments eventually objected to the huge trade surpluses this created, especially when the Japanese seemed so adept at keeping foreigners out of Japanese markets. By the late 1970s and early 1980s Japanese companies began to adopt a more global strategy. Global-scale facilities were built in neighbouring Asian countries to produce standard products which could be shipped worldwide under a tightly controlled central strategy.

Corporations that pursue a global strategy focus on increasing profitability by reaping the cost reductions that come from economies of scale. They are pursuing a low-cost strategy. The production, marketing, and research and development activities of firms pursuing a global strategy are concentrated in a few favourable locations. Global firms tend not to customise their product offering and marketing strategy to local conditions because customisation raises costs (it involves shorter production runs and the duplication of functions). Instead global firms prefer to market a standardised product worldwide so they can reap the maximum benefits from economies of scale. These conditions prevail in many industrial goods industries, such as the semiconductor industry, where global standards have emerged that have created an enormous demand for standardised global products. As the product becomes standardised, and costs continue to fall, corporations tend to use their cost advantage to support aggressive pricing in world markets. Thus, this strategy makes most sense in those cases where there are strong pressures for cost reductions and where demands to respond to local market needs are minimal.

Over time corporations have changed their ideas about where their competitive advantage lies. They used to think their most precious resource was capital, and that the prime task of management was to allocate it in the most productive way. Now corporations have become convinced that their most precious resource is knowledge, and that the prime task of management is to ensure that their knowledge is generated as widely and used as efficiently as possible.

Corporations pursuing an international strategy follow a similar organisational structure to those pursuing a multinational strategy. They try to create value by transferring valuable skills and products to foreign markets where indigenous competitors lack those skills and products. Most international corporations have created value by transferring differentiated offerings developed at home to new markets overseas. Accordingly they tend to centralise product development functions at home research and development. However, they also tend to establish manufacturing and marketing functions in each major country in which they do business. But while they undertake some local customisation of product offering and marketing strategy, this tends to be limited. Ultimately, in most cases the head office retains tight control over marketing and product strategy.

The managerial culture of US-based corporations fits this structure well. These corporations built a reputation for professional management that implied a willingness to delegate responsibility, while retaining overall control through sophisticated management systems and the specialist corporate human resource structures. Holding the managerial reins, top management could control the free-running team of independent subsidiaries and guide the direction in which they were heading (Bartlett and Ghoshal, 1992).

Competitive conditions are so intense that to survive in the global market place corporations must exploit economies of scale, they must transfer distinctive competencies within the corporation, and they must do all of this while paying attention to pressures of responsiveness to local market needs.

This is termed a transnational strategy. In modern corporations distinctive competencies do not just reside in the home country, they can develop in any of the corporation's worldwide operations. Thus, corporations pursuing a transnational strategy maintain that the flow of skills and product offerings should not all be one way, from home firm to foreign subsidiary, as in the case of corporations pursuing an international strategy. Rather the flow should also be from foreign subsidiary to home country, and from foreign subsidiary to foreign subsidiary - a process referred to as global learning (Bartlett and Ghoshal, 1989).

In line with this transnational strategy a number of corporations have been giving subsidiaries responsibility for global products or global functions, partly to disperse decision-making throughout the organisation and partly to capture local expertise. IBM, AT&T and Hewlett Packard have moved the worldwide headquarters for some products from America to Europe. Glaxo, Unilever and Siemens have all created global product groups. Nestle has moved the headquarters of its pasta business to Italy. Johnson and Johnson has given its Belgian subsidiary worldwide responsibility for pharmaceuticals (Economist, 1995).

Table 12.1
Organisational Characteristics of Multinational, Global,
International and Transnational Corporations

Organisational Characteristic	Multinational	Global	International	Transnational
Configuration of assets and capabilities	Decentralised and nationally self-sufficient	Centralised and globally scaled	Sources of core competencies centralised, others decentralised	Dispersed, interdependent, and specialised
Role of overseas operations	Sensing and exploiting local opportunities	Implementing parent company strategies	Adapting and leveraging parent company competencies	Differentiated contributions by national units to integrated worldwide operations
Development and diffusion of knowledge	Knowledge developed and retained within each unit	Knowledge developed and retained at the center	Knowledge developed and retained at the center and transferred to overseas units	Knowledge developed jointly and shared worldwide

Source: Bartlett and Ghoshal, (1992)

A transnational strategy makes sense when a corporation faces high pressures for cost reductions and high pressures to respond to local market needs. Corporations pursuing a transnational strategy are trying to simultaneously achieve lower costs of production and differentiated products. As attractive as this sounds, in practice the strategy is not easy. Pressures to respond to local market needs and achieve cost reductions place conflicting demands on a corporation. Being responsive to respond to local market needs raises costs, which obviously makes cost reductions difficult to achieve (see Table 12.1 above).

The strategic role of human resources

Multinational corporations try to create value by emphasising responsiveness to local markets; global firms, by realising economies of scale; international firms, by transferring core competencies overseas; and transnational firms by doing all these things simultaneously. There are advantages and disadvantages of the four strategies employed (see Table 12.2).

Table 12.2
The Advantages and Disadvantages Involved in Strategic Choice

Strategy	Advantages	Disadvantages
Multinational	Customise product offerings and marketing in accordance with responsiveness to local markets	Inability to realise economies of scale Failure to transfer distinctive competencies to foreign markets
Global	Exploit economies of scale Exploit location economies	Lack of responsiveness to local markets
International	Transfer distinctive competencies to foreign markets	Lack of responsiveness to local markets Inability to realise economies of scale
Transnational	Exploit economies of scale Exploit location economies Customise product offerings and marketing in accordance with responsiveness to local markets Reap benefits of global learning	Difficult to implement due to organisational problems

None of the structures or controls implemented by the corporation mean much if the human resources that support them are not appropriate. Without the right kind of people in place the organisational structure will be ineffective. Both formal and informal structure and controls must be congruent with the corporate strategy in order for it to succeed. Corporations pursuing a transnational strategy need to build a strong corporate culture and an informal management network for transmitting information within the organisation. Through its employee selection, management development, performance appraisal, and compensation policies, the human resource strategy can help develop these things. Creating a structure of international managers with experience in various countries should help to establish an informal management network. In addition management development programmes can build a corporate culture that supports strategic goals. In short human resources has a critical role to play in implementing corporate strategy (Guest, 1989).

The human resource policy of corporations is concerned with the selection of employees for particular jobs. At one level this involves selecting individuals who have the skills required to do particular jobs. At another level the human resource policy can be a tool for developing and promoting corporate culture[2]. Corporations pursuing global and transnational strategies have high needs for a strong unifying culture, whereas for corporations pursuing an international strategy the need is somewhat lower, and lowest of all for corporations pursuing a multinational strategy

Thus corporations pursuing global and transnational strategies would be expected to implement more complex human resource strategies. The human resource strategy should pay significant attention to selecting individuals who not only have the skills required to perform particular jobs but who are also suited to the prevailing culture of the corporation. Not only do global and transnational strategies aim to use human resources efficiently, they also aim to build a strong corporate culture and informal network of management. The belief is that if integration of human resource and corporate strategies can be achieved the corporation will experience fewer problems and performance ambiguity.

In a multinational corporation the need for integration is substantially lower and, as a result, there is less performance ambiguity and not the same need for cultural controls. In theory this means the human resource strategy can pay less attention to building a unified corporate culture. Consequently, in multinational corporations the culture can be allowed to vary from national operation to national operation. This however may not be the best policy to pursue as career mobility may be limited forming a gap between host country managers which could ineffect isolate the corporate headquarters from its subsidiaries.

Integrating human resource and corporate strategies

The different levels at which corporate strategy is formulated and the different styles adopted by organisations may make it difficult to develop a human resource strategy which will fit the overall strategy of the corporation. There are three approaches a corporation can pursue in an attempt to integrate its human resource strategy into its corporate strategy. The three approaches are termed ethnocentric, polycentric and geocentric.

Ethnocentric approach

An ethnocentric human resource policy is one in which all key management positions are filled by parent-country nationals. Corporations pursue an ethnocentric human resource policy for three reasons.

Firstly, the corporation may believe that there is a lack of qualified individuals in the host country to fill senior management positions. This argument is heard most often when the firm has operations in less developed countries.

Secondly, the corporation may see an ethnocentric human resource policy as the best way to maintain a unified corporate culture. Despite the fact that the large Japanese corporations accept that they must learn the art of global management, many Japanese corporations still find it difficult to manage foreigners, particularly above the level of production workers. The main problem lies with exporting their consensus-based approach. This has served them well at home, institutionalising perpetual discussion, obliging managers to gain the enthusiastic support of their workers and encouraging all employees to collaborate across functional boundaries. Such a package does not travel well.

What the Japanese have succeeded in exporting is their unique approach to manufacturing. Workers all over the world are using 'Japanese' methods to produce Toyotas and Nissans for their domestic markets. Many of them regard the Japanese as much better employers than their western counterparts. The whole point of the system is to expose the problems below the surface, and then let the workers solve them in their own way. Both the problems and the favoured solutions differ strikingly from country to country (Economist, 1995).

214

The idea seems to be that Japanese managers should set things rolling and then withdraw gracefully, leaving the field to the locals. But at that point the model stops working as intended. Japanese corporations' foreign subsidiaries depend much more heavily on expatriate managers than do their western counterparts. They also promote far fewer foreigners to senior positions and involve them in fewer important decisions. In many Japanese firms today, such as Toyota and Matsushita, key positions in international operations are still often held by Japanese nationals.

Thirdly, if the corporation is trying to create value by transferring core competencies to a foreign operation, as corporations pursuing an international strategy are, it may believe that the best way to do this is to transfer parent-country nationals who have knowledge of that competency in marketing to a foreign subsidiary without supporting the transfer with a corresponding transfer of home-country marketing management personnel. The transfer would probably fail to produce the anticipated benefits, because the knowledge underlying a core competency cannot easily be articulated and written down as such knowledge is often acquired through experience over time. The need to transfer managers overseas arises primarily because the knowledge that underlies the corporation's core competency resides in the heads of its domestic managers. Thus, if a corporation is to transfer a core competency to a foreign subsidiary, it must also transfer the appropriate managers (Mintzberg, 1987).

Despite this rationale for pursuing an ethnocentric human resource policy, it is now rarely pursued in most international businesses. There are two reasons for this.

1. An ethnocentric human resource policy limits advancement opportunities for host country nationals, which can lead to resentment, lower productivity, and increased turnover of host-country nationals. Resentment can be greater still if, as often occurs, expatriate managers are paid significantly more than host-country nationals.
2. An ethnocentric human resource policy can lead to cultural myopia[3]. The adaptation of expatriate managers to cultural differences can take a long time, during which they may fail to appreciate how product attributes, distribution strategy, communications strategy, and pricing strategy should be adapted to host-country conditions. The result can lead to an increase in value creation as the expatriate managers may make some costly mistakes.

Polycentric approach

A polycentric human resource policy requires host-country nationals to be recruited to manage subsidiaries, while parent-country nationals occupy key positions at corporate headquarters. In many respects a polycentric approach is a response to the shortcomings of an ethnocentric approach. One advantage of adopting a polycentric approach is that the corporation is less likely to suffer from cultural myopia. Host-country managers are unlikely to make the mistakes arising from cultural misunderstandings that expatriate managers are vulnerable to. A second advantage is that a polycentric approach may be less expensive to implement. Expatriate managers can be very expensive to maintain, as host-country nationals do not require the same level of expenditures. Thus, by gearing the strategy towards host-country nationals the costs of value creation can be reduced.

However, a polycentric approach also has its drawbacks. Host-country nationals have limited opportunities to gain experience outside their own country and thus cannot progress beyond senior positions in their own subsidiary. As in the case of an ethnocentric policy, this may cause resentment. Perhaps the major drawback with a polycentric approach, however, is the gap that can form between host-country managers and parent-country managers. Language barriers, national loyalties, and a range of cultural differences may isolate the corporate headquarters staff from the various foreign subsidiaries. The lack of management transfers from home to host countries, and vice versa, can exacerbate this isolation and lead to a lack of integration between corporate headquarters and foreign subsidiaries. The result can lead to the growth of largely independent national business units with only nominal links to the corporate headquarters. Within such a set up, the coordination required to transfer core competencies or to pursue economies of scale and location economies may be difficult to achieve. Thus, although a polycentric approach may be effective for firms pursuing a multinational strategy, it is inappropriate for other corporate strategies.

Geocentric approach

A geocentric human resource policy seeks the best people for key jobs throughout the organisation, regardless of nationality. There are a number of advantages to this policy. Firstly, it enables the corporation to make the best use of its human resources. Secondly, and perhaps more important, a geocentric policy enables the corporation to build and nurture a team of elite international executives who feel at home working in a number of different cultures. The ability to develop international executives is becoming increasingly important as the world's centres of economic activity are becoming more dispersed, and that corporations should therefore put a wider variety of people onto their boards to broaden their perspective and alert them to changes in demand and fashion. Such a policy might also improve their chances of recruiting and motivating able people from the many countries in which they operate.

The creation of a truly 'international executive' may be a critical first step toward building a strong unifying corporate culture and an informal management network, both of which are required for global and transnational strategies. Put another way, corporations pursuing a geocentric human resource policy may be better able to create value from the pursuit of economies of scale and location economies and from the multidirectional transfer of core competencies than corporations pursuing other human resource policies. In addition the international composition of the management team that results from the geocentric approach tends to reduce cultural myopia and enhances the responsiveness to local market needs. Thus, implementing a geocentric human resource policy seems to be the most attractive option for corporations to pursue.

However, as attractive as a geocentric human resource policy might first appear, a number of problems limit the corporation's ability to pursue such a policy. One problem is that many countries want foreign subsidiaries to employ their citizens. To achieve this goal, they use immigration laws in order to give priority to host-country nationals if they are available in adequate numbers and have the necessary skills. A further problem is that a geocentric human resource policy can be very expensive to implement. There are increased training costs, relocation costs involved in transferring managers from country to country, and the need for a compensation structure with a standardised international base pay level that may be higher than national levels in many countries. In addition the higher pay enjoyed by managers selected to become 'international executives' may be a source of resentment.

Conclusion

It is clear that to integrate a human resource strategy into a corporate strategy is a complex process. Human resource strategies may well vary from corporation to corporation irrespective of the corporate strategy they chose to pursue. Broadly speaking, an ethnocentric approach is compatible with an international strategy, a polycentric approach is compatible with a multinational strategy, and a geocentric approach is compatible with both global and transnational strategies. There are advantages and disadvantages for the use of three Human Resource Strategies (see Table 12.3).

Table 12.3
Comparisons of Human Resource Strategies

Human Resource Approach	Strategic Appropriateness	Advantages	Disadvantages
Ethnocentric	International	Overcomes lack of qualified managers in host nation Unified Culture Helps transfer core competencies	Produces resentment in host country Can lead to cultural myopia
Polycentric	Multinational	Alleviates cultural myopia Inexpensive to implement	Limits career mobility Isolates headquarters from foreign subsidiaries
Geocentric	Global and Transnational	Uses human resources efficiently Helps build strong culture and informal management network	National immigration policies may limit implementation Expensive

For the human resource strategist it is important to take pains to understand the levels at which corporate strategies are formed and the style adopted by the corporation in creating strategies and monitoring their implementation. It will then be easier to focus on those corporate or business unit issues which are likely to have human resource implications.

The key business issues which may impact on human resource strategies include:

- intentions concerning growth or retrenchment, acquisitions, mergers, divestments, diversification, product-market development;
- proposals on increasing competitive advantage through productivity, improved quality/customer service, cost reduction;
- the felt need to develop a more positive, performance-oriented culture;
- any other culture management imperatives associated with changes in the philosophies of the organisation.

Corporate strategies in these areas should not be over-influenced by human resource factors. Human resource strategies are, after all, about making corporate strategies work. But the corporate strategy must take into account key human resource opportunities and constraints.

The different levels at which corporate strategy is formulated and the different styles adopted by organisations may make it difficult to develop a coherent view of what sort of human resource strategies will fit the overall strategies and what type of human resource contributions are required during the process of formulation.

It has been aptly argued that to achieve competitive advantage, each business unit in a diversified corporation should tailor its human resource policy to its own product-market conditions, irrespective of the human resource policies being pursued elsewhere in the corporation (Miller, 1983). If this is the case, there may be coherence within a unit, but not across the whole organisation.

Those organisations having a reputation for pursuing successful human resource strategies tend to be well known corporations such as IBM, Hewlett-Packard, Motorola, Nissan, Toyota and Texas Instruments are large, single product-range firms which have a tradition of sophisticated personnel practices and a belief in the importance of treating people as valued assets. Implementing a standardised human resource policy which can be easily replicated from corporation to corporation is less likely to be adopted in a highly diversified conglomerate.

Notes

1. Firms can create value (increase profits) by adding value to a product so consumers are willing to pay more, or by lowering the costs of production.
2. Corporate culture is the organisation's norms and value systems.
3. Cultural myopia is the corporation's failure to understand host-country cultural differences that require different approaches to marketing and management.

Bibliography

Bailey, P., Parisotto, A. and Renshaw, G. (1993), *Multinationals and Employment: The Global Economy of the 1990s*, ILO.

Bartlett, C.A. and Ghoshal, S. (1989), *Managing Across Borders: The Transnational Solution*, Harvard University Press.

Bartlett, C.A. and Ghoshal, S. (1992), *Managing Across Borders: The Transnational Solution*, Century Business.

Cowling, A. and Chloe, M. (1990), *Managing Human Resources*, Edward Arnold.

The Economist, (June 24th 1995), 'A Survey of Multinationals'.

Guest, D.E. (1989), 'Human Resource Management: Its Implications for Industrial Relations', in Storey, J. (1989) *New Perspectives on Human Resource Management*, Routledge.

Hamel, G. and Prahalad, C.K. (1989), *Competing For The Future*, Harvard University Press.

Johnson, G. (1987), *Strategic Change and the Management Process*, Blackwell.

Johnson, G. and Scholes, K. (1988), *Exploring Corporate Strategy*, Prentice Hall.

Kobrin, S.J. (1994), 'Geocentric Mindset and Multinational Strategy', *Journal of International Business Studies*, Vol. 2, No. 5, pp. 11-24.

Miller, P. (1983), 'Strategic Industrial Relations and Human Resource Management - Distinction, Definition and Recognition', *Journal of Management Studies*, Vol. 2, No. 4, pp. 46-47.

Mintzberg, H. (1987), 'Crafting Strategy', *Harvard Business Review*, July-August.

Porter, M.E. (1980), *Competitive Strategy*, New York, Free Press.

Porter, M.E. (1985), *Competitive Advantage*, New York, Free Press.

Porter, M.E. (1990), *The Competitive Advantage of Nations*, New York, Free Press.

Rosenzweig, P.M. and Nohira (1994), 'Influences on Human Resource Management Practices in Multinational Corporations', *Journal of International Business Studies*, Vol. 2, No. 5, pp.31-42.